SCOTTISH SATIRICAL VERSE

EDWIN MORGAN

SCOTTISH SATIRICAL VERSE

an anthology

CARCANET NEW PRESS
Manchester

Acknowledgements are due to the following in respect of copyright material: Constable & Co. Ltd. for 'Dockens afore his Peers' by Charles Murray from *A Sough o' War*; Mrs Katherine Elliott-Binns for 'The Puddock' by J. M. Caie; Mrs Valda Grieve and Martin Brian & O'Keeffe Ltd. for 'Crowdieknowe', 'An Apprentice Angel', 'Glasgow 1960', and extracts from *A Drunk Man Looks at the Thistle* and *To Circumjack Cencrastus*, from *Complete Poems*, also to Granada Publishing Ltd. for 'Prayer for a Second Flood' from *A Lap of Honour*, all by Hugh MacDiarmid; the Trustees of the National Library of Scotland for the poems by William Soutar; George Bruce and Edinburgh University Press for 'Transplant'; Robert Garioch and M. Macdonald for the poems; Norman MacCaig and Hogarth Press Ltd. for 'Street Preacher' from *Measures*, 'Milne's Bar' from *The White Bird*, and 'Wild Oats' from *A Man in my Position*; William MacLellan for the poems of Douglas Young; Mrs Hazel Smith and John Calder Ltd. for the poems by Sydney Goodsir Smith from *Collected Poems*; Tom Scott for his poems; Maurice Lindsay and Robert Hale Ltd. for 'The Vacant Chair' and 'One Day at Shieldaig' from *Selected Poems 1942-1972*; Edwin Morgan and Penguin Books Ltd. for 'The Flowers of Scotland' from *Penguin Modern Poets 15*, Carcanet Press Ltd. for 'School's Out' and 'Letters of Mr Lonelyhearts' from *The New Divan* and *From Glasgow to Saturn* respectively, and Ian McKelvie for 'Instamatic Translunar Space March 1972' from *Instamatic Poems*; Alexander Scott and Akros Publications for the poems from *Selected Poems 1943-1974*; George Mackay Brown and Hogarth Press Ltd. for 'Ikey on the People of Hellya' from *The Year of the Whale*; Alastair Mackie for 'Beethoven's Chuntie', and Akros Publications for 'In Absentia' and 'Scots Pegasus' from *Clytach*; William Price Turner for 'Wig Block', 'Colour Supplement', and 'A Few Novelties from our Extensive Range', and Barrie & Jenkins Ltd. for 'Fable from Life' and 'Hard Times' from *The Moral Rocking-Horse*; Iain Crichton Smith for his poem; Tom Buchan and Barrie & Rockliff Ltd. for 'Scotland the Wee' and 'Weekend Naturalist' from *Dolphins at Cochin*, also to Poni Press for 'Letter to a Partisan' from *Poems 1969-1972*; Duncan Glen and Akros Publications for 'Progress' and 'Dresst to Kill' from *In Appearances*; Alan Jackson and Fulcrum Press for 'Wifie', 'And so it goes on', and 'The Worstest Beast' from *The Grim Wayfarer*, and the author for the other poems; Donald Campbell and Reprographia for 'Vietnam on my Mind' from *Rhymes 'n Reasons*; Tom Leonard and E. & T. O'Brien Ltd. for 'The Voyeur' from *Poems*.

SBN 85635 183 0 – hardcover SBN 85635 220 9 – paperback

First published 1980 by CARCANET NEW PRESS LIMITED
330 Corn Exchange, Manchester M4 3BG

The publisher acknowledges the financial assistance of the Scottish Arts Council.
Printed in England by Billings, Guildford.

CONTENTS

INTRODUCTION

The satiric mode has been very persistent in Scottish poetry. Satire of one kind or another has marked the work of all the leading poets, from Henryson and Dunbar and Lyndsay to Fergusson, Burns, and MacDiarmid, and it is still a thriving mode today. This is an unusual state of affairs, and one can only speculate on the reasons for it. National generalizations ('the prickly Scot') are always rather suspect, yet there must be something about the conditions of life in Scotland which has given rise to so much satire, especially as there is no shortage of it in Gaelic poetry either (not represented in the present anthology). A combination of geographical, political, and religious factors can be seen at work. In a country where life tended to be harder, and people poorer, than in England, uppishness and pretentiousness were ready targets for mockery, and the well-known and not always very amiable Scottish 'reductive idiom' makes its appearance, lying in wait to bring down every climbing hypocrisy and puncture every vain aspiration. Burns's 'To a Louse' is a modest, good-humoured example of this sometimes fierce spirit; in the same author's 'Holy Willie's Prayer' more stops are pulled out, though the reductionism is subtly internalized within the character himself; in Dunbar's 'Fenyeit Freir' the attack is ruthless and relentless, despite the fact that the continental alchemist, charlatan or not, did risk life and limb in a scientific experiment; in MacDiarmid's 'Glasgow 1960' it is a relief to see the reductive spirit being itself given its comeuppance, while at the same time amusement is extracted from the operation.

How far does all this bespeak some worry about the national psyche, the national identity? The gentry in Burns's 'The Twa Dogs' are mocked for truckling to international culture, for enjoying the guitars and bullfighting of Spain. The dour Borderers of MacDiarmid's 'Crowdieknowe' have an approved contempt for the angels of the Last Trump, who appear like frivolous and tinselly Frenchmen. The anonymous poet on 'Ane anser to ane Inglis railar' regards all the English, nearer home, as sons of Beelzebub. On the other hand, there is no lack of Scottish self-criticism. Whether this would include the Lowland gibe against work-shy Highlanders in the anonymous 'How the first Hielandman was maid' is an arguable point, but there is no denying the national self-mockery in Hogg's 'Sir Morgan O'Doherty', Lord

Neaves's 'Let us all be Unhappy on Sunday', Alastair Mackie's 'Scots Pegasus', Tom Buchan's 'Scotland the Wee', or Alan Jackson's 'Knox'; to which could be added the more local love-hate relations shown in Alexander Scott's 'Heart of Stone' and George Mackay Brown's 'Ikey on the People of Hellya'. Many of these and other poems posit two deep self-inflicted wounds —Calvinism, and the Union. In some poets the two are connected, in some not. Satire attaches readily to both, but in conditions which may make it easier to say what one is against than what one is for. The charmless accidents and grim phases of Scottish history have induced a much fragmented national consciousness, extremely unsure of its ideals, deeply aware of a strict moral and religious inheritance yet divided as to whether strength can be drawn from its apparent joylessness or whether any vacuum left by its being demolished would be better than falling into the traps of replacement ideologies. A vacuum can be a merry place, and the Scottish gift for satire—perhaps it is a curse, disguised by the Little People as a gift—has filled it with an extraordinary variety of raillery, from the shameless—

And why shouldna poor folk mowe, mowe, mowe,
  And why shouldna poor folk mowe:
The great folk hae siller, and houses and lands,
  Poor bodies hae naething but mowe.

(Burns, 'When princes and prelates')

to the refined—

It's strange that God should fash to frame
  The yearth and lift sae hie,
An' clean forget to explain the same
  To a gentleman like me.

(Stevenson, 'The Counterblast Ironical')

Stevenson's gentleman, like a sort of Holy Willie turned inside out, cannot understand why his natural superiority to the common herd has not been rewarded by God with a clear explanation of the scheme of things, and tries to blackmail his unresponsive creator: no explanation, no worship. The gentleman is mocked, but so is a Scottish desire for logic and dogma which may be busy building splendid watertight mental prison-houses, vacuums themselves of a new kind. Burns's poem, on the theme 'make love not war', claims that the history of Europe would have been better for all concerned if Europe's rulers had spent more time in bed than on the battlefield, but its social as distinct from its political point—that poor folk, unlike 'princes and prelates', have in fact no other pleasure to look forward to—is allowed to disappear in a benign conclusion, with a toast to the king and queen and many happy copulations. The poem withdraws its own sting: 'But truce with commotions and new-fangled notions'. Here, the vacuum returns, echoing with laughter.

But can Scottish poets really be so different from such English satirists as Dryden and Pope, who start from cultural and social positives—values it is up to them to defend—and who know what they want as well as what they do not want? Surely Henryson's 'The Fox and the Wolf' attacks abuses of the sacrament of penance, not to discredit his Church but to cleanse and uphold it? Surely the extract from MacDiarmid's *To Circumjack Cencrastus* derides Unionists, and their reiteration of the blessings the Union has brought Scotland, in order to recommend and further the cause of Scottish independence? Surely Fergusson's 'Hame Content' and Donald Campbell's 'Vietnam on my Mind' share, in their very different ways, a conservative vision of the native place and experience? One could give a yes to these questions, and still feel that such examples do not most typically express the Scottish spirit of satire. (Needless to say, this is not an adverse comment on their poetic value.) Perhaps we can get nearer to that spirit in other poems: what about Burns's 'Holy Willie's Prayer', Dunbar's 'Tretis of the Tua Mariit Wemen and the Wedo', Fergusson's 'To the Principal and Professors of the University of St Andrews'? Holy Willie's unctuous self-centredness and religious self-assurance are drawn with enormous skill, and editors have shown how closely knowledgeable the poem shows Burns to have been in the theology of election and reprobation; so as a study in ludicrously deluded conviction of grace, and of some of the dangers inherent in Scottish Calvinist ideology, Willie's prayer should present few problems. Yet the very masterfulness of the exercise causes problems to appear. Northrop Frye in his *Anatomy of Criticism* (Third Essay: Theory of Myth: Irony and Satire), after admitting that satire needs 'at least an implicit moral standard' (though it may be no more than implicit), instances what he regards as an inescapable dubiousness attaching to poems like 'Holy Willie's Prayer':

> Any really devout person would surely welcome a satirist who cauterized hypocrisy and superstition as an ally of true religion. Yet once a hypocrite who sounds exactly like a

> good man is sufficiently blackened, the good man also may begin to seem a little dingier than he was. Those who would agree even with the theoretical parts of *Holy Willie's Prayer* in Burns look rather like Holy Willies themselves.

Satirist as underminer-in-chief is by no means an unlikely picture, but I am not sure that the ambiguity of that particular poem is as Frye sees it: indeed the opposite may be the case. Any intense identification, in a dramatic monologue, and no matter how satirical the motive-force may be, tends to produce cumulatively a sort of grotesque sympathy. Holy Willie, scrabbling about in his irritation and spite, his boasts and confessions, his fleshly lusts and petulant comminations, his concern for gear as well as grace, is an appalling figure but a very human one, even granting the specialized limitations of the religious system which produced him. After all, who cares about Gavin Hamilton—that estimable Laodicean?

Dunbar's 'Tretis' is doubtless a satire on women, and editors refer us to traditions of medieval anti-feminist writing as well as to the conventions of courtly love which the comedy of contrasts in the poem delightedly and coarsely undercuts. But most readers sense positives as well as negatives. Where do they come from? On the stylistic level, they go with the racy, vigorous deployment of the long alliterative line; on the level of character, they are part and parcel of the buoyancy and gusto of the widow, who may be not much better than a somewhat superior harlot but who has such a takingly ironic self-awareness that she is almost (not quite) as hard to resist as Chaucer's Wife of Bath.

> Quhen that I go to the kirk, cled in cair weid,
> As foxe in a lambis fleise fenye I my cheir;
> Than lay I furght my bright buke one breid one my kne,
> With mony lusty letter ellumynit with gold;
> And drawis my clok forthwart our my face quhit,
> That I may spy, unaspyit, a space me beside:
> Full oft I blenk by my buke, and blynis of devotioun,
> To se quhat berne is best brand or bredest in schulderis,
> Or forgeit is maist forcely to furnyse a bancat
> In Venus chalmer, valyeandly, withoutin vane ruse:
> And, as the new mone all pale, oppressit with change,
> Kythis quhilis her cleir face through cluddis of sable,
> So keik I through my clokis, and castis kynd lukis
> To knychtis, and to clerkis, and cortly personis.

In such a passage, it is the play of irony which is significant, rather than any potential condemnation of the laxity of church officers or the bad habits of congregations; the widow belongs to a believing age, when churches were much more a part of life than they are now, and were widely used not only for assignations but for the transaction of a range of worldly business – all of which might have been, but is not in fact, the object of attack in the poem. We are concerned less with her vices than with her survival, with its alarming, piquant mixture of flamboyance and calculation. The satire is not deflected, but slightly dislodged, like a geological fault.

In 'To the Principal and Professors', Fergusson offers in the first place the automatic Scottish reaction to Dr Johnson's naughty dictionary definition of *oats* as 'a grain which, in England, is generally given to horses, but in Scotland supports the people', and attacks the University of St Andrews for giving such a rascal an expensive and exotic dinner. Why not make him go through the hoop of things Scottish – haggis, sheep's head, brose, and certainly oatcakes – and see how he comes out of that? With much skill Fergusson makes food which might in fact be very tasty seem as gross and unmanageable as Johnson would find it. With the Doctor revolted and routed, he can then come round full circle to the theme of Scottish poverty – and admit it.

> Ah! willawins, for Scotland now,
> Whan she maun stap ilk birky's mow
> Wi' eistacks, grown as 'tware in pet
> In foreign land, or green-house het,
> When cog o' brose an' cutty spoon
> Is a' our cottar childer's boon,
> Wha thro' the week, till Sunday's speal,
> Toil for pease-clods an' gude lang kail.

It is a poem where emotion struggles with emotion, and where the eventual overall effect is more complex than the simple instigating-point. There is little danger here of the satirized character becoming sympathetic; Johnson's predicament is visualized like an incident in an early slapstick film comedy. But the fact that Fergusson returns to the attack in another poem, 'To Dr Samuel Johnson: Food for a new Edition of his Dictionary', which is written in English and parodies Johnson's latinate and ponderous style, might raise the reflection that repeated satire of the same thing suggests some underlying attraction, and therefore some tension of aims in the poet.

It may well be that Fergusson had divided feelings about this famous Englishman's interest in and exploitation of the English language, and unlike Burns he is a poet who if he had lived might have gone on to write good poetry in English as well as in Scots, as the best of his English verse clearly shows. Yet that famous Englishman was equally a symbolic target of alienness, to be attacked on sight. There would seem to be a similar tension at work in Burns's attitude to Calvinism, as in Dunbar's attitude to women. Burns, however deist or humanist his beliefs became, had biblical and Christian teaching in his bones and was insider as well as outsider in every religious satire he wrote. Dunbar shows considerable interest in and knowledge of women's position in Scottish society, whether as wives forced into bitterly regretted marriages or as widows who suddenly found a new freedom and power. Although the two wives in his poem are hard-hearted viragos who badmouth their husbands like demented macaws, it is given to one of them to make the serious social point:

> Apone sic materis I mus, at mydnyght, full oft,
> And murnys so in my mynd I murdris my selfin;
> Than ly I walkand for wa, and walteris about,
> Wariand oft my wekit kyn, that me away cast
> To sic a craudone but curage, that knyt my cler bewte,
> And ther so mony kene knyghtis this kenrik within.

Foreign observers in early Scotland commented on the freedom of behaviour and expression of the women, and the Australian poet A. D. Hope has even suggested, without real proof but in an argument of some interest, that there were secret societies of women in medieval Scotland, and that Dunbar's poem, not anti-feminist but pro-feminist, shows this, with the almost 'faery' meeting of the three women, dressed in green, 'under the hill' as in folklore.* Whether or not one believes this, Dunbar's 'Tretis' is certainly something more than a simple satire on women or on courtly love; something more than a satire, in fact; a ritual, a celebration?

It has always been the central paradox of satire that the better

---

**A Midsummer Eve's Dream*, Australian National University Press, Canberra, 1971.

it is the less unambiguous is the trajectory of attack. The crude parable of *Animal Farm* is soon understood, and yields diminishing returns. On the other hand, criticism never exhausts *Gulliver's Travels* and *A Tale of a Tub*, or *Volpone* and *The Alchemist*, or *Tartuffe* and *Le Misanthrope*. But what if the problem is less intellectual, and inheres more in the bizarre nature of the whole world a satire presents? Satire needs a good going fiction, but where does fantasy take over, and what gives Scottish satire its marked fondness for the grotesque?

The intention of the fantasy in a nonsense-poem like the anonymous 'King Berdok' is at least clear, if we read the poem as a satire on medieval romances; since the romances themselves deploy strange and marvellous happenings, the satire must be even stranger, with a hero who lives naked in a cockle-shell, playing a harp and languishing after a one-eyed three-year-old called the cuckoo of Maryland. We recognise it as a literary satire by its ironic tags, 'as myne auctor sayis' or 'Boece said, of poyettis that wes flour'. But it is also clear enough that the anonymous poet delighted in the fantasy for its own sake, and draws humour from it unconnected with satirical intent. The same is true of W. Price Turner's 'A Few Novelties from our Extensive Range' and Tom Buchan's 'Letter from a Partisan'. Dunbar's 'Remonstrance to the King', once he has stepped on to the roller-coaster of his catalogues, is going that way, though still held in a fairly purposeful grip. And for a similar reason, the pathetic inventory of worldly possessions in the anonymous 'Wowing of Jok and Jynny' seems to be moving towards a world of comic unreality, because of the method of plodding, spotlighted delineation of so many wretched and miscellaneous objects, like the vacuous conveyor-belt reward of a TV panel game.

Fantasy, catalogues, and a far more grotesque pullulation of images characterize the extreme and peculiarly Scottish kind of satire called the flyting. If brief, directed wit applied to a defined object of attack, as in Douglas Young's 'On a North British Devolutionary', is at one end of the satiric spectrum, the wild, scabrous, open-ended fantasy of Alexander Montgomerie's 'Flyting between Montgomerie and Polwart' is at the other. The flyting, as a contest in virtuosity of vituperation between rival poets, has some antecedents or analogues in other poetic traditions, including especially Gaelic tradition, and in part at least it may be regarded as a ritualized, aestheticized survival of the belief in bardic power, anciently shown in superstitious conviction that an enemy could be 'rhymed to death'. Something of this dark power remains in the Scottish flytings, and greatly adds to their interest, even although the two poets concerned are friends not enemies, as we are either told or are entitled to assume. The flytings are comic entertainment, yet the fact that the abuse has been ritualized has not removed, but rather heightened, the unease, the sense of nightmare, which the performance produces in us. 'The Flyting of Dunbar and Kennedie' is as outrageous as any lexicographer could wish, but we know that Dunbar makes respectful reference elsewhere to Walter Kennedy as a fellow-poet; each is using the other as a sounding-board for an explosion of the imagination and a satirical exploration of the language. In a flyting between James V and Sir David Lyndsay, of which only Lyndsay's part survives, the poet does his best, but his heart is not in it—'Now schir, fairweill, because I can nocht flyte'—which suggests that flyting is best done between equals. Indeed, an address to the reader which prefaces Montgomerie's flyting with Polwart makes the point that the joy of flyting comes from 'generous emulation' between writers who (like Montgomerie and Polwart) have neither envy nor malice to motivate them. Whether this generous emulation stretched across the Highland line is a question interestingly raised by the extant fragment of a flyting between Montgomerie and a Gaelic poet, where Montgomerie uses a macaronic mixture of Scots and dog-Gaelic to bring his satire home. In his flyting with Polwart, in the extract included here, the eerie Halloween setting, the riding of the elves, fairies and demons, the discovery and cursing of the monstrous child by the weird sisters, its christening and resonant dedication to the service of Satan through the medium of Hecate as a grisly sort of Virgin Mary surrogate, and finally its grotesque, ludicrous fondling and fostering by the witches as hags and baby vie with one another in blood-curdling yells and screams—all this drives the satire out into a poetry of nightmare and black comedy too, where the release of the imagination is astonishing. That the Queen of the Witches, Nikniven, may have been a real witch, burned in Scotland in the sixteenth century when Montgomerie was a young man*, serves to

---

**See* A. Hanham, ' "The Scottish Hecate": A Wild Witch Chase', *Scottish Studies*, 13, i, 1969.

underline the power the poem has of probing and uncovering sensitive areas of historical and folk experience. A sense of the supernatural lingered long in Scotland, and was made use of by serious writers like Scott, Hogg, and Stevenson. And Bram Stoker, it may be recalled, wrote *Dracula* when he was living on the coast of Buchan. When satire enters the realm of 'northern Gothic', hideous historical truth and persistently surfacing legend seem to combine to produce a distinctive charge.

The aim of satirists to correct public abuses and lash the vices of the time has always been accepted as at least the appearance, and often the reality, of what they are doing, and plenty of Scottish examples will be found in this collection. But satire has also its secret and unacknowledged wellsprings, deep in the imagination, and in comedy, and in language, and these too are illustrated here. It is hoped that the reader will gain pleasure from both approaches.

* * * * *

The texts of poems drawn from such a lengthy period as that from medieval to contemporary times can hardly be chosen on any single set of principles, but in general the older texts have been interfered with as little as possible, except occasionally where varieties of spelling seemed unnecessarily distracting for the general reader; e.g. in the opening poem, the several variants 'gowly', 'gowlly', and 'guly' have been regularized to the more familiar 'gully' (= knife). The letters i/j and u/v have been normalized in accordance with usual practice. Eighteenth-century printing habits in punctuation and capitalization seemed to be worth preserving for their flavour. Any anthologist of the earlier poetry owes a great debt to the Scottish Text Society, even if the readings in their volumes have not always been followed, especially where volumes were edited a long time ago. I would like to acknowledge the invaluable help of Mr Alexander Scott during initial discussions of the scope of the anthology. I must also thank Professor and Mrs Sydney Checkland, Dr John Carr, Mr Keith Brace, Mr Kemble Williams, and Mrs Amy Stewart Fraser for various sorts of assistance, and Miss Ingrid Swanson for her cheerful typing of outlandish texts.

ANON.

How the first Hielandman was maid

God and Sanct Petir was gangand be the way
Heich up in Argyll quhair thair gait lay.
Sanct Petir said to God in a sport word,
'Can ye nocht mak a Hielandman of this hors turd?'
God turnd owre the hors turd with his pykit staff
And up start a Hielandman blak as ony draff.
Quod God to the Hielandman, 'Quhair wilt thou now?'
'I will doun in the Lawland, Lord, and thair steill a cow.'
'And thou steill a cow, carle, thair thay will hang thee.'
'Quhattrack, Lord, of that? for anis mon I die.'
God than he leuch and owre the dyk lap
And out of his scheith his gully outgatt.
Sanct Petir socht this gully fast up and doun,
Yit could not find it in all that braid roun.
'Now,' quod God, 'heir a marvell! How can this be
That I sould want my gully and we heir bot thre!'
'Humff!' quod the Hielandman and turned him about
And at his plaid nuk the gully fell out.
'Fy!' quod Sanct Petir, 'thou wilt nevir do weill,
And thou bot new maid sa sone gais to steill.'
'Umff,' quod the Hielandman and swere be yon kirk
'Sa lang as I may geir gett to steill, will I nevir wirk.'

The Wowing of Jok and Jynny

Robeyn's Jok come to wow our Jynny,
On our feist-evin quhen we wer fow;
Scho brankit fast, and maid hir bony,
And said, 'Jok, come ye for to wow?'
Scho birneist hir baith breist and brow,
And maid hir cleir as ony clok;
Than spak hir dame, and said, 'I trow
Ye come to wow our Jynny, Jok.'

Jok said, 'Forsuth I yern full fane,
To luk my heid, and sit doun by yow.'

Than spak hir modir, and said agane,
'My bairne hes tocher-gud annuch to ge yow.'
'Te he,' quod Jynny, 'keik, keik, I se yow;
Muder, yone man makis yow a mok.'
'I schro the, lyar! full leis me yow,
I come to wow your Jynny,' quoth Jok.

'My berne,' scho sayis, 'hes of hir awin,
Ane guss, ane gryce, ane cok, ane hen,
Ane calf, ane hog, ane fute-braid sawin,
Ane kirn, ane pin, that ye weill ken,
Ane pig, ane pot, ane raip thair ben,
Ane fork, ane flaik, ane reill, ane rok,
Dischis and dublaris nyne or ten:
Come ye to wow our Jynny, Jok?

Ane blanket, and ane wecht also,
Ane schule, ane scheit, and ane lang flail,
Ane ark, ane almry, and laidillis two,
Ane milk-syth, with ane swyne-taill,
Ane rowsty quhittill to scheir the kaill,
Ane quheill, ane mell the beir to knok,
Ane coig, ane caird wantand ane naill:
Come ye to wow our Jynny, Jok?

Ane furme, ane furlet, ane pott, ane pek,
Ane tub, ane barrow, with ane quheilband,
Ane turf, ane troch, and ane meil-sek,
Ane spurtill braid, and ane elwand.'
Jok tuk Jynny be the hand,
And cryd ane feist, and slew ane cok,
And maid a brydell up alland;
'Now haif I gottin your Jynny,' quoth Jok.

'Now, dame, I haif your bairne mareit;
Suppoiss ye mak it nevir sa tuche,
I lat yow wit schoss nocht miskareit,
It is weill kend I haif annuch:
Ane crukit gloyd fell our ane huch,
Ane spaid, ane speit, ane spur, ane sok,
Withouttin oxin I haif a pluche;
To gang to gidder, Jynny and Jok.

I haif ane helter, and eik ane hek.
Ane coird, ane creill, and als ane cradill,
Fyve fidder of raggis to stuff ane jak,
Ane auld pannell of ane laid sadill,
Ane pepper-polk maid of a padill,
Ane spounge, ane spindill wantand ane nok,
Two lusty lippis to lik ane laiddill;
To gang to gidder, Jynny and Jok.

Ane brechame, and twa brochis fyne,
Weill buklit with a brydill renye,
Ane sark maid of the Lynkome twyne,
Ane gay grene cloke that will nocht stenye;
And yit for mister I will nocht fenye,
Fyive hundreth fleis now in a flok.
Call ye nocht that ane joly menye,
To go to giddir, Jynny and Jok?

Ane trene truncheour, ane ramehorne spone,
Twa buttis of barkit blasnit ledder,
All graith that ganis to hobbill schone,
Ane thrawcruk to twyne ane tedder,
Ane brydeill, ane girth, and ane swyne bledder,
Ane maskene-fat, ane fetterit lok,
Ane scheip weill keipit fra ill wedder;
To gang to giddir, Jynny and Jok.

Tak thair for my parte of the feist;
It is weill knawin I am weill bodin;
Ye may nocht say my parte is leist.'
The wyfe said, 'Speid, the kaill ar soddin,
And als the laverok is fust and loddin;
Quhen ye haif done tak hame the brok.'
The rost wes tuche, sa wer thay bodin;
Syne gaid to giddir bayth Jynny and Jok.

The Bewteis of the Fute-ball

Brissit brawnis and brokin banis,
Stryf, discord, and waistie wanis,
Cruikit in eild, syne halt withall –
Thir are the bewteis of the fute-ball.

The Wyf of Auchtermuchty

In Auchtermuchty thair dwelt ane man,
Ane husband as I hard it tauld,
Quha weill could tippill out a can,
And nathir luvit hungir nor cauld,
Quhill anis it fell upoun a day
He yokkit his pluch upoun the plane:
Gif it be trew as I hard say,
The day was fowll for wind and rane.

He lowsit the pluche at the landis end,
And draif his oxin hame at e'en;
Quhen he come in he lukit bend
And saw the wyf baith dry and clene
And sittand at ane fyre, beikand bauld,
With ane fat soup, as I hard say:
The man being verry weit and cauld,
Betwene thay twa it was na play.

Quoth he, quhair is my horssis corne?
My ox hes nathir hay nor stray.
Dame, ye mon to the pluch to morne,
I salbe hussy, gif I may.
Husband, quoth scho, content am I
To tak the pluche my day about,
Sa ye will rowll baith calvis and ky
And all the hous baith in and out.

Bot sen that ye will husyeskep ken,
First ye sall sift and syne sall kned,
And ay as ye gang but and ben
Luk that the bairnis dryt not the bed.
Yeis lay ane soft wisp to the kill,
We haif ane deir ferme on our heid;
And ay as ye gang furth and in,
Keip weill the gaslingis fra the gled.

The wyf was up richt lait at e'en,
I pray god gif hir evill to fair,
Scho kyrnd the kyrne and skumd it clene,

And left the gudman bot the bledoch bair.
Than in the mornyng up scho gatt
And on hir hairt laid hir disjune,
Scho put alsmekle in hir lap
As micht haif serd thame baith at nune.

Sayis, Jok, will thou be maistir of wark,
And thou sall hald and I sall kaa,
Ise promeis the ane gud new sark
Athir of round claith or of smaa.
Scho lowsit oxin aucht or nyne
And hynt ane gadstaff in hir hand,
And the gudman rais eftir syne
And saw the wyf had done command.

And kaa'd the gaislingis furth to feid,
Thair was bot sevinsum of thame all,
And by thair cumis the gredy gled
And likkit up fyve, left him bot twa.
Than out he ran in all his mane,
How sone he hard the gaislingis cry,
Bot than or he come in agane
The calvis brak lowse and soukit the ky.

The calvis and ky being met in the lone,
The man ran with ane rung to red;
Than by thair cumis ane ill willy cow
And brodit his buttok quhill that it bled.
Than hame he ran to ane rok of tow
And he satt doun to say the spynning;
I trow he lowtit owre neir the low:
Quoth he, this wark hes ill begynning.

Than to the kyrn that he did stoure,
And jumlit at it quhill he swatt;
Quhen he had jumlit a full lang houre
The sorrow crap of butter he gatt.
Albeit na butter he could gett,
Yit he wes cummerit with the kyrne,
And syne he het the milk owre hett
And sorrow spark of it wald yyrne.

Than ben thair come ane gredy sow,
I trow he cund hir littill thank,
And in scho schot hir mekle mow
And ay scho winkit and scho drank.
He cleikit up ane crukit club
And thocht to hitt the sow ane rout;
The twa gaislingis the gled had left,
That straik dang baith thair harnis out.

He gat his foot upon the spyre,
To have gotten the flesch doune to the pat,
He fell backward into the fyre,
And brack his head on the keming stock:
Yit he gat the mekle pat upon the fyre,
And gat twa cannes and ran to the spout,
Er he came it, quhat thoucht ye of that?
The fyre brunt aw the pat arss out.

Than he beur kendling to the kill,
Bot scho start all up in ane low;
Quhatevir he hard, quhatevir he saw,
That day he had na will to mow.
Than he yeid to tak up the bairnis,
Thocht to haif fund thame fair and clene:
The first that he gat in his armis
Was all bedirtin to the ene.

The first that he gat in his armis
It was all dirt up to the ene:
The diuill cutt of thair handis, quoth he,
That fild yow all sa fow this strene.
He trailit the fowll scheitis doun the gait,
Thocht to haif wesht thame on ane stane;
The burne wes rissin grit of spait,
Away fra him the scheitis hes tane.

Than up he gat on ane know heid,
On hir to cry, on hir to schout;
Scho hard him and scho hard him not
Bot stoutly steird the stottis about.
Scho draif the day unto the nicht,

Scho lowsit the pluch and syne come hame,
Scho fand all wrang that sould bene richt:
I trow the man thocht richt grit schame.

Quoth he, my office I forsaik
For all the dayis of my lyf,
For I wald put ane hows to wraik
Had I bene twenty dayis gudwyf.
Quoth scho, weill mot ye bruke your place
For trewlie I will nevir excep it;
Quoth he, feind fall the lyaris face
Bot yit ye may be blyth to get it.

Than up scho gat ane mekle rung
And the gudman maid to the dur.
Quoth he, dame I sall hald my tung
For and we fecht I'll gett the woir;
Quoth he, quhen I forsuk my pluche
I trow I bot forsuk my seill
And I will to my pluch agane,
For I and this hows will nevir do weill.

Ane anser to ane Inglis railar praising his awin genalogy

Ye, Inglische hursone, sumtyme will avant
Your progeny from Brutus to haif tane,
And sumtyme from ane angell or ane sanct,
As Angelus and Anglus bayth war ane.

Angellis in erth yit hard I few or nane,
Except the feyndis with Lucifer that fell.
Avant you, villane, of that lord allane,
Tak thy progeny from Pluto, prince of Hell.

Becaus ye use in hoillis to hyd your sell,
Anglus is cum from Angulus in deid.
Above all uderis Brutus bure the bell
Quha slew his fader, houping to succeid.

Than chus you ane of thais, I rek not ader:
Tak Beelzebub or Brutus to your fader.

King Berdok

Sym of Lyntoun, be the ramis horn,
Quhen Phebus rang in sing of Capricorn,
And the mone wes past the gussis cro,
Thair fell in France ane jeperdie forlo,
Be the grit king of Babilon, Berdok,
That dwelt in symmer in till ane bowkaill stok;
And into winter, quhen the frostis ar fell,
He dwelt for cauld in till a cokkil schell:
Kingis usit nocht to weir clayis in tha dayis,
Bot yeid naikit, as myne auctor sayis;
Weill coud he play in clarschocht and on lute,
And bend ane aiprim bow, and nipschot schute;
He wes ane stalwart man of hairt and hand;
He wowit the golk sevin yeir, of Maryland,
Mayiola, and scho wes bot yeiris thre,
Ane bony bird, and had bot ane e;
Nevirtheless king Berdok luvit hir weill,
For hir foirfute wes langar than hir heill.
The king Berdok he fure owre se and land,
To reveiss Mayok the golk of Maryland,
And nane with him bot ane bow and ane bowtt;
Syne hapnit him to cum amang the nowtt,
And as this Berdok about him coud espy;
He saw Mayok milkand hir muderis ky,
And in ane creill upoun his bak hir kest;
Quhen he come hame it wes ane howlat nest,
Full of skait birdis, and than this Berdok grett,
And ran agane Mayok for to gett.
The king of Fary hir fadir than blew out,
And socht Berdok all the land about,
And Berdok fled in till a killogy;
Thair wes no grace bot gett him or ellis die;
Thair wes the kingis of Pechtis and Portingaill,
The king of Naippillis and Navern alhaill,
With bowis and brandis with segis thay umbeset him,
Sum bad tak, sum slay, sum bad byd quhill thay get him;
Thay stellit gunis to the killogy laich,
And proppit gunis with bulettis of raw daich:
Than Jupiter prayit to god Saturn,

In liknes of ane tod he wald him turn;
Bot sone the gracious god Mercurius
Turnit Berdok in till ane braikane buss;
And quhen thay saw the buss waig to and fra,
Thay trowd it wes ane gaist, and thay to ga:
Thir fell kingis thus Berdok wald haif slane,
All this for lufe, luveris sufferis pane,
Boece said, of poyettis that wes flour,
Thocht lufe be sweit, oft syiss it is full sour.

ROBERT HENRYSON

The Fox and the Wolf

Leif we this wedow glaid, I yow assure,
Of Chantecleir mair blyith than I can tell,
And speik we of the subtell aventure
And destenie that to this foxe befell,
Quhilk durst na mair with waitting intermell,
Als lang as leme or licht wes of the day,
Bot, bydand nicht, full styll lurkand he lay,

Quhill that Thetes the Goddes of the flude
Phebus had callit to the harbery,
And Hesperous put up his cluddie hude,
Schawand his lustie visage in the sky.
Than Lowrence luikit up, quhair he couth ly,
And kest his hand upon his ee on hicht,
Merie and glade that cummit wes the nicht.

Out of the wod unto ane hill he went,
Quhair he micht se the twinkling sternis cleir,
And all the planetis of the firmament,
Thair cours, and eik thair moving in the spheir,
Sum retrograde, and sum stationeir,
And of the zodiak, in quhat degre
Thay wer ilk ane, as Lowrence leirnit me.

Than Saturne auld wes enterit in Capricorne,
And Juppiter movit in Sagittarie,
And Mars up in the Rammis heid wes borne,
And Phebus in the Lyoun furth can carie;
Venus the Crab, the Mone wes in Aquarie;
Mercurius, the God of Eloquence,
Into the Virgyn maid his residence.

But astrolab, quadrant, or almanak,
Teichit of nature be instructioun,
The moving of the hevin this tod can tak,
Quhat influence and constellatioun
Wes lyke to fall upon the eirth adoun.

And to him self he said, withoutin mair,
'Weill worth my father, that send me to the lair.

'My destenie, and eik my weird I ken,
My aventure is cleirlie to me kend;
With mischeif myngit is my mortall men,
My misleving the soner bot gif I mend:
It is reward of sin ane schamefull end.
Thairfoir I will ga seik sum Confessour,
And schryiff me clene of my sinnis to this hour.

'Allace' (quod he), 'rich waryit ar we thevis,
Our lyifis set ilk nicht in aventure;
Our cursit craft full mony man mischevis;
For ever we steill, and ever ar lyke pure:
In dreid and schame our dayis we indure;
Syne widdinek, and crakraip callit als,
And till our hyre hangit up be the hals.'

Accusand thus his cankerit conscience,
In to ane craig he kest about his ee;
So saw he cummand ane lyttill than frome hence,
Ane worthie Doctour in Divinitie,
Freir Wolf Waitskaith, in science wonder sle,
To preich and pray new cummit fra the closter
With beidis in hand, sayand his pater noster.

Seand this wolf, this wylie tratour tod
On kneis fell, with hude in to his nek:
'Welcome, my gostlie father under God'
(Quod he), with mony binge and mony bek.
'Ha' (quod the wolf), 'Schir Tod, for quhat effek
Mak ye sic feir? Ryse up, put on your hude.'
'Father' (quod he), 'I haif grit cause to dude.

'Ye ar mirrour, lanterne, and sicker way,
Suld gyde sic sempill folk as me to grace.
Your bair feit, and your russet coull of gray,
Your lene cheik, your paill pietious face,
Schawis to me your perfite halines.
For weill wer him, that anis in his lyve
Had hap to yow his sinnis for to schryve.'

'Na, selie Lowrence' (quod the wolf), and leuch:
'It plesis me that ye ar penitent.'
'Of reif and stouth, Schir, I can tell aneuch,
That causis me full sair for to repent.
Bot, father, byde still heir upon the bent,
I you beseik, and heir me to declair
My conscience, that prikkis me sa sair.

'Weill' (quod the wolf), 'sit doun upon thy kne.'
And he doun bairheid sat full humilly,
And syne began with Benedicitie.
Quhen I this saw, I drew ane lytill by,
For it effeiris nouther to heir, nor spy,
Nor to reveill thing said under that seill:
Unto the tod this gait the wolf couth kneill.

'Art thow contrite, and sorie in thy spreit
For thy trespas?' 'Na, Schir, I can not duid:
Me think that hennis ar sa honie sweit,
And lambes flesche that new ar lettin bluid;
For to repent my mynd can not concluid,
Bot off this thing, that I haif slane sa few.'
'Weill' (quod the wolf), 'in faith, thow art ane schrew.

'Sen thow can not forthink thy wickitnes,
Will thow forbeir in tyme to cum and mend?'
'And I forbeir, how sall I leif, allace,
Haifand nane uther craft me to defend?
Neid causis me to steill quhair evir I wend.
I eschame to thig, I can not wirk, ye wait,
Yit wald I fane pretend to gentill stait.'

'Weill' (quod the wolf), 'thow wantis pointis twa,
Belangand to perfyte confessioun.
To the thrid part of penitence let us ga:
Will thou tak pane for thy transgressioun?'
'Na, Schir, considder my complexioun,
Selie and waik, and off my nature tender;
Lo, will ye se, I am baith lene and sklender.

'Yit, nevertheles, I wald, swa it wer licht,
Schort, and not grevand to my tendernes,

Tak part of pane, fulfill it gif I micht,
To set my selie saull in way of grace.'
'Thou sall' (quod he), 'forbeir flesch untill pasche,
To tame this corps, that cursit carioun;
And heir I reik the full remissioun.'

'I grant thairto, swa ye will giff me leif
To eit puddingis, or laip ane lyttill blude,
Or heid, or feit, or paynches let me preif,
In cace I fall no flesch unto my fude.'
'For grit mister I gif the leif to dude
Twyse in the oulk, for neid may haif na law.'
'God yeild yow, Schir, for that text weill I knaw.'

Quhen this wes said, the wolf his wayis went.
The foxe on fuit he fure unto the flude –
To fang him fisch haillelie wes his intent.
Bot quhen he saw the watter, and wallis woude,
Astonist all still in to ane staire he stude,
And said, 'better that I had biddin at hame,
Nor bene ane fischar in the Devillis name.

'Now mai I scraip my meit out of the sand,
And I haif nouther boittis nor net bait.'
As he wes thus for falt of meit murnand,
Lukand about his leving for to lait,
Under ane tre he saw ane trip of gait;
Than wes he blyith, and in ane heuch him hid,
And fra the gait he stall ane lytill kid.

Syne over the heuch unto the see he hyis,
And tuke the kid be the hornis twane,
And in the watter outher twyis or thryis
He dowkit him, and till him can he sayne:
'Ga doun, Schir Kid, cum up Schir Salmond agane!'
Quhill he wes deid; syne to the land him drewch,
And of that new maid salmond eit anewch.

Thus fynelie fillit with young tender meit,
Unto ane derne for dreid he him addrest,
Under ane busk, quhair that the sone can beit,

To beik his breist and bellie he thocht best.
And rekleslie he said, quhair he did rest,
Straikand his wame aganis the sonis heit,
'Upon this wame set wer ane bolt full meit.'

Quhen this wes said, the keipar of the gait,
Cairfull in hart his kid wes stollen away,
On everilk syde full warlie couth he wait,
Quhill at the last he saw quhair Lowrence lay.
Ane bow he bent, ane flane with fedderis gray
He haillit to the heid, and, or he steird,
The foxe he prikkit fast unto the eird.

'Now' (quod the foxe), 'allace and wellaway!
Gorrit I am, and may na forther gane.
Me think na man may speik ane word in play,
Bot now on dayis in ernist it is tane.'
He harlit him, and out he drew his flane;
And for his kid, and uther violence,
He tuke his skyn, and maid ane recompence.

MORALITAS.

This suddand deith, and unprovysit end
Of this fals tod, without provision,
Exempill is exhortand folk to amend,
For dreid of sic ane lyke confusioun;
For mony now hes gude professioun,
Yit not repentis, nor for thair sinnis greit,
Because thay think thair lustie lyfe sa sweit.

Sum bene also throw consuetude and ryte,
Vincust with carnall sensualitie;
Suppose thay be as for the tym contryte,
Can not forbeir, nor fra thair sinnis fle;
Use drawis nature swa in propertie
Of beist and man, that neidlingis thay man do,
As thay of lang tyme hes bene hantit to.

Be war, gude folke, and feir this suddane schoit,
Quhilk smytis sair withoutin resistence.
Attend wyislie, and in your hartis be noit,

Aganis deith may na man mak defence.
Ceis of your sin, remord your conscience,
Obey unto your God and ye sall wend,
Efter your deith, to blis withouttin end.

WILLIAM DUNBAR

Remonstrance to the King

Schir, ye have mony servitouris
And officiaris of dyvers curis;
Kirkmen, courtmen, and craftismen fyne;
Doctouris in jure, and medicyne;
Divinouris, rethoris, and philosophouris,
Astrologis, artistis, and oratouris;
Men of armes, and vailyeand knychtis,
And mony uther gudlie wichtis;
Musicianis, menstralis, and mirrie singaris:
Chevalouris, cawandaris, and flingaris;
Cunyouris, carvouris, and carpentaris,
Beildaris of barkis and ballingaris;
Masounis lyand upon the land,
And schipwrichtis hewand upone the strand;
Glasing wrichtis, goldsmythis, and lapidaris,
Pryntouris, payntouris, and potingaris;
And all of thair craft cunning,
And all at anis lawboring;
Quhilk pleisand ar and honorable,
And to your hienes profitable,
And richt convenient for to be
With your hie regale majestie;
Deserving of your grace most ding
Bayth thank, rewarde, and cherissing.
And thocht that I, amang the laif,
Unworthy be ane place to have,
Or in thair nummer to be tald,
Als lang in mynd my wark sall hald,
Als haill in everie circumstance,
In forme, in mater, and substance,
But wering, or consumptioun,
Roust, canker, or corruptioun,
As ony of thair werkis all,
Suppois that my rewarde be small.
Bot ye sa gracious ar and meik,
That on your hienes followis eik
Ane uthir sort, more miserabill,

Thocht thai be nocht sa profitable:
Fenyeouris, fleichouris, and flatteraris;
Cryaris, craikaris, and clatteraris;
Soukaris, groukaris, gledaris, gunnaris;
Monsouris of France, gud clarat-cunnaris;
Innopportoun askaris of Yrland kynd;
And meit revaris, lyk out of mynd;
Scaffaris, and scamleris in the nuke,
And hall huntaris of draik and duik;
Thrimlaris and thristaris, as thay war woid,
Kokenis, and kennis na man of gude;
Schulderaris, and schowaris, that hes no schame,
And to no cunning that can clame;
And can non uthir craft nor curis
Bot to mak thrang, Schir, in your duris,
And rusche in quhair thay counsale heir,
And will at na man nurtir leyr:
In quintiscence, eik, ingynouris joly,
That far can multiplie in folie;
Fantastik fulis, bayth fals and gredy,
Off toung untrew, and hand evill deidie:
Few dar, of all this last additioun,
Cum in tolbuyth without remissioun.
   And thocht this nobill cunning sort,
Quhom of befoir I did report,
Rewardit be, it war bot ressoun,
Thairat suld no man mak enchessoun:
Bot quhen the uther fulis nyce,
That feistit at Cokelbeis gryce,
Ar all rewardit, and nocht I,
Than on this fals world I cry, Fy!
My hart neir bristis than for teyne,
Quhilk may nocht suffer nor sustene
So grit abusioun for to se,
Daylie in court befoir myn e!
   And yit more panence wald I have,
Had I rewarde amang the laif,
It wald me sumthing satisfie,
And les of my malancolie,
And gar me mony falt ouerse,
That now is brayd befoir myn e:

My mind so fer is set to flyt,
That of nocht ellis I can endyt;
For owther man my hart to breik,
Or with my pen I man me wreik;
And sen the tane most nedis be,
In to malancolie to de,
Or lat the vennim ische all out,
Be war, anone, for it will spout,
Gif that the tryackill cum nocht tyt
To swage the swalme of my dispyt!

The Fenyeit Freir of Tungland

As yung Awrora, with cristall haile,
In orient schew hir visage paile,
A swevyng swyth did me assaile,
   Off sonis of Sathanis seid;
Me thocht a Turk of Tartary
Come throw the boundis of Barbary,
And lay forloppin in Lumbardy
   Full lang in waithman weid.
Fra baptasing for to eschew,
Thair a religious man he slew,
And cled him in his abeit new,
   For he cowth wryte and reid.
Quhen kend was his dissimulance,
And all his cursit govirnance,
For feir he fled and come in France,
   With littill of Lumbard leid.
To be a leiche he fenyt him thair,
Quhilk mony a man micht rew evirmair,
For he left nowthir seik nor sair
   Unslane, or he hyne yeid.
Vane organis he full clenely carvit,
Quhen of his straik so mony starvit,
Dreid he had gottin that he desarvit,
   He fled away gud speid.

In Scotland than the narrest way
He come, his cunnyng till assay;

To sum man thair it was no play
   The preving of his sciens.
On pottingry he wrocht grit pyne,
He murdreist mony in medecyne;
The jow was of a grit engyne,
   And generit was of gyans.
In leichecraft he was homecyd;
He wald haif, for a nicht to byd,
A haiknay and the hurt manis hyd,
   So meikle he was of myance.
His irnis was rude as ony rawchtir,
Quhair he leit blude it was no lawchtir,
Full mony instrument for slawchtir
   Was in his gardevyance.

He cowth gif cure for laxatyve,
To gar a wicht hors want his lyve,
Quha evir assay wald, man or wyve,
   Thair hippis yeid hiddy giddy.
His practikis nevir war put to preif
But suddane deid, or grit mischeif;
He had purgatioun to mak a theif
   To dee withowt a widdy.
Unto no mes pressit this prelat,
For sound of sacring bell nor skellat;
As blaksmyth bruikit was his pallatt
   For battering at the study.
Thocht he come hame a new maid channoun,
He had dispensit with matynnis cannoun,
On him come nowther stole nor fannoun
   For smowking of the smydy.

Me thocht seir fassonis he assailyeit,
To mak the quintessance, and failyet;
And quhen he saw that nocht availyeit,
   A fedrem on he tuke,
And schupe in Turky for to fle;
And quhen that he did mont on he,
All fowill ferleit quhat he sowld be,
   That evir did on him luke.
Sum held he had bene Dedalus,

Sum the Menatair marvelus,
Sum Martis blaksmyth Vulcanus,
And sum Saturnus kuke.
And evir the cuschettis at him tuggit,
The rukis him rent, the ravynis him druggit,
The hudit crawis his hair furth ruggit,
The hevin he micht not bruke.

The myttane, and Sanct Martynis fowle,
Wend he had bene the hornit howle,
Thay set aupone him with a yowle,
And gaif him dynt for dynt.
The golk, the gormaw, and the gled,
Beft him with buffettis quhill he bled;
The sparhalk to the spring him sped,
Als fers as fyre of flynt.
The tarsall gaif him tug for tug,
A stanchell hang in ilka lug,
The pyot furth his pennis did rug,
The stork straik ay but stynt.
The bissart, bissy but rebuik,
Scho was so cleverus of hir cluik,
His bawis he micht not langer bruik,
Scho held thame at ane hint.

Thik was the clud of kayis and crawis,
Of marleyonis, mittanis, and of mawis,
That bikkrit at his berd with blawis
In battell him abowt.
Thay nybbillit him with noyis and cry,
The rerd of thame rais to the sky,
And evir he cryit on Fortoun, Fy!
His lyfe was in to dowt.
The ja him skrippit with a skryke,
And skornit him as it was lyk;
The egill strong at him did stryke,
And rawcht him mony a rowt.
For feir uncunnandly he cawkit,
Quhill all his pennis war drownd and drawkit,
He maid a hundreth nolt all hawkit
Beneth him with a spowt.

He schewre his feddreme that was schene,
And slippit owt of it full clene,
And in a myre, up to the ene,
  Amang the glar did glyd.
The fowlis all at the fedrem dang,
As at a monster thame amang,
Quhill all the pennis of it owsprang
  In till the air full wyde.
And he lay at the plunge evirmair,
So lang as any ravin did rair;
The crawis him socht with cryis of cair
  In every schaw besyde.
Had he reveild bene to the ruikis,
Thay had him revin all with thair cluikis:
Thre dayis in dub amang the dukis
  He did with dirt him hyde.
The air was dirkit with the fowlis,
That come with yawmeris and with yowlis,
With skryking, skrymming, and with scowlis,
  To tak him in the tyde.
I walknit with the noyis and schowte,
So hiddowis beir was me abowte;
Sensyne I curs that cankerit rowte,
  Quhair evir I go or ryde.

To the Merchantis of Edinburgh

Quhy will ye, merchantis of renoun,
Lat Edinburgh, your nobill toun,
For laik of reformatioun
The commone proffeitt tyine and fame?
  Think ye not schame,
That onie uther regioun
Sall with dishonour hurt your name!

May nane pas throw your principall gaittis
For stink of haddockis and of scattis,
For cryis of carlingis and debaittis,
For fensum flyttingis of defame:
  Think ye not schame,

Befoir strangeris of all estaittis
That sic dishonour hurt your name!

Your stinkand Scull, that standis dirk,
Haldis the lycht fra your parroche kirk;
Your foirstairis makis your housis mirk,
Lyk na cuntray bot heir at hame:
  Think ye not schame,
Sa litill polesie to wirk
In hurt and sklander of your name!

At your hie Croce, quhar gold and silk
Sould be, thair is bot crudis and milk;
And at your Trone bot cokill and wilk,
Pansches, pudingis of Jok and Jame:
  Think ye not schame,
Sen as the world sayis that ilk
In hurt and sclander of your name!

Your commone menstrallis hes no tone
Bot 'Now the day dawis,' and 'Into Joun';
Cunningar men man serve Sanct Cloun,
And nevir to uther craftis clame:
  Think ye not schame,
To hald sic mowaris on the moyne,
In hurt and sclander of your name!

Tailyouris, soutteris, and craftis vyll,
The fairest of your streitis dois fyll;
And merchandis at the Stinkand Styll
Ar hamperit in ane hony came:
  Think ye not schame,
That ye have nether witt nor wyll
To win yourselff ane bettir name!

Your burgh of beggeris is ane nest,
To schout thai swentyouris will not rest;
All honest folk they do molest,
Sa piteuslie thai cry and rame:
  Think ye not schame,
That for the poore hes nothing drest,
In hurt and sclander of your name!

Your proffeit daylie dois incres,
Your godlie workis les and les;
Through streittis nane may mak progres
For cry of cruikit, blind and lame:
Think ye not schame,
That ye sic substance dois posses,
And will nocht win ane bettir name!

Sen for the Court and the Sessioun,
The great repair of this regioun
Is in your burgh, thairfoir be boun
To mend all faultis that ar to blame,
And eschew schame;
Gif thai pas to ane uther toun
Ye will decay, and your great name!

Thairfoir strangeris and leigis treit,
Tak not ouer meikle for thair meit,
And gar your merchandis be discreit,
That na extortiounes be, proclame
All fraud and schame:
Keip ordour, and poore nighbouris beit,
That ye may gett ane bettir name!

Singular proffeit so dois yow blind,
The common proffeit gois behind:
I pray that Lord remeid to fynd,
That deit into Jerusalem,
And gar yow schame!
That sum tyme ressoun may yow bind,
For to [ ] yow guid name.

The Tretis of the Tua Mariit Wemen and the Wedo

Apon the Midsummer evin, mirriest of nichtis,
I muvit furth allane, neir as midnicht wes past,
Besyd ane gudlie grein garth, full of gay flouris,
Hegeit, of ane huge hicht, with hawthorne treis;
Quhairon ane bird, on ane bransche, so birst out hir notis
That never ane blythfullar bird was on the beuche harde:

Quhat throw the sugarat sound of hir sang glaid,
And throw the savour sanative of the sueit flouris,
I drew in derne to the dyk to dirkin efter mirthis;
The dew donkit the daill and dynnit the feulis.
   I hard, under ane holyn hevinlie grein hewit,
Ane hie speiche, at my hand, with hautand wourdis;
With that in haist to the hege so hard I inthrang
That I was heildit with hawthorne and with heynd leveis:
Throw pykis of the plet thorne I presandlie luikit,
Gif ony persoun wald approche within that plesand garding.
   I saw thre gay ladeis sit in ane grene arbeir,
All grathit in to garlandis of fresche gudlie flouris;
So glitterit as the gold wer thair glorius gilt tressis,
Quhill all the gressis did gleme of the glaid hewis;
Kemmit was thair cleir hair, and curiouslie sched
Attour thair schulderis doun schyre, schyning full bricht;
With curches, cassin thair abone, of kirsp cleir and thin:
Thair mantillis grein war as the gress that grew in May
      sessoun,
Fetrit with thair quhyt fingaris about thair fair sydis:
Off ferliful fyne favour war thair faceis meik,
All full of flurist fairheid, as flouris in June;
Quhyt, seimlie, and soft, as the sweit lillies
New upspred upon spray, as new spynist rose;
Arrayit ryallie about with mony rich vardour,
That nature full nobillie annamalit with flouris
Off alkin hewis under hevin, that ony heynd knew,
Fragrant, all full of fresche odour fynest of smell.
Ane cumlie tabil coverit wes befoir tha cleir ladeis,
With ryalle cowpis apon rawis full of ryche wynis.
And of thir fair wlonkes, tua weddit war with lordis,
Ane wes ane wedow, I wis, wantoun of laitis.
And, as thai talk at the tabill of many taill sindry,
Thay wauchtit at the wicht wyne and waris out wourdis;
And syne thai spak more spedelie, and sparit no matiris.

   Bewrie, said the Wedo, ye woddit wemen ying,
Quhat mirth ye fand in maryage, sen ye war menis wyffis;
Reveill gif ye rewit that rakles conditioun,
Or gif that ever ye luffit leyd upone lyf mair
Nor thame that ye your fayth hes festinit for ever;

Or gif ye think, had ye chois, that ye wald cheis better.
Think ye it nocht ane blist band that bindis so fast,
That none undo it a deill may bot the deith ane?

Than spak ane lusty belyf with lustie effeiris:
It, that ye call the blist band that bindis so fast,
Is bair of blis, and bailfull, and greit barrat wirkis.
Ye speir, had I fre chois, gif I wald cheis better?
Chenyeis ay ar to eschew; and changeis ar sueit:
Sic cursit chance till eschew, had I my chois anis,
Out of the chenyeis of ane churle I chaip suld for evir.
God gif matrimony were made to mell for ane yeir!
It war bot merrens to be mair, bot gif our myndis pleisit:
It is agane the law of luf, of kynd, and of nature,
Togiddir hairtis to strene, that stryveis with uther:
Birdis hes ane better law na bernis be meikill,
That ilk yeir, with new joy, joyis ane maik,
And fangis thame ane fresche feyr, unfulyeit, and constant,
And lattis thair fulyeit feiris flie quhair thai pleis.
Cryst gif sic ane consuetude war in this kith haldin!
Than weill war us wemen that evir we war fre;
We suld have feiris as fresche to fang quhen us likit,
And gif all larbaris thair leveis, quhen thai lak curage.
My self suld be full semlie in silkis arrayit,
Gymp, jolie, and gent, richt joyus, and gentill.
I suld at fairis be found new faceis to se;
At playis, and at preichingis, and pilgrimages greit,
To schaw my renone, royaly, quhair preis was of folk,
To manifest my makdome to multitude of pepill,
And blaw my bewtie on breid, quhair bernis war mony;
That I micht cheis, and be chosin, and change quhen me
lykit.
Than suld I waill ane full weill, our all the wyd realme,
That suld my womanheid weild the lang winter nicht;
And when I gottin had ane grome, ganest of uther,
Yaip, and ying, in the yok ane yeir for to draw;
Fra I had preveit his pitht the first plesand moneth,
Than suld I cast me to keik in kirk, and in markat,
And all the cuntre about, kyngis court, and uther,
Quhair I ane galland micht get aganis the nixt yeir,
For to perfurneis furth the werk quhen failyeit the tother;

A forky fure, ay furthwart, and forsy in draucht,
Nother febill, nor fant, nor fulyeit in labour,
But als fresche of his forme as flouris in May;
For all the fruit suld I fang, thocht he the flour burgeoun.

I have ane wallidrag, ane worme, ane auld wobat carle,
A waistit wolroun, na worth bot wourdis to clatter;
Ane bumbart, ane drone bee, ane bag full of flewme,
Ane skabbit skarth, ane scorpioun, ane scutarde behind;
To see him scart his awin skyn grit scunner I think.
Quhen kissis me that carybald, than kyndillis all my sorow;
As birs of ane brym bair, his berd is als stif,
Bot soft and soupill as the silk is his sary lume;
He may weill to the syn assent, bot sakles is his deidis.
With goreis his tua grym ene ar gladderrit all about,
And gorgeit lyk twa gutaris that war with glar stoppit;
Bot quhen that glowrand gaist grippis me about,
Than think I hiddowus Mahowne hes me in armes;
Thair ma na sanyne me save fra that auld Sathane;
For, thocht I croce me all cleine, fra the croun doun,
He wil my corse all beclip, and clap me to his breist.
Quhen schaiffyne is that ald schalk with a scharp rasour,
He schowis one me his schevill mouth and schedis my lippis,
And with his hard hurcheone skyn sa heklis he my chekis,
That as a glemand gleyd glowis my chaftis;
I schrenk for the scharp stound, bot schout dar I nought,
For schore of that auld schrew, schame him betide!
The luf blenkis of that bogill, fra his blerde ene,
As Belzebub had on me blent, abasit my spreit;
And quhen the smy one me smyrkis with his smake smolet,
He fepillis like a farcy aver that flyrit one a gillot.
    Quhen that the sound of his saw sinkis in my eris,
Than ay renewis my noy, or he be neir cumand:
Quhen I heir nemmyt his name, than mak I nyne crocis,
To keip me fra the cummerans of that carll mangit,
That full of eldnyng is and anger and all evill thewis.
I dar nought luke to my luf for that lene gib,
He is sa full of jelusy and engyne fals,
Ever ymagynyng in mynd materis of evill,
Compasand and castand casis a thousand
How he sall tak me, with a trawe, at trist of ane othir:

I dar nought keik to the knaip that the cop fillis,
For eldnyng of that ald schrew that ever one evill thynkis;
For he is waistit and worne fra Venus werkis,
And may nought beit worth a bene in bed of my mystirs.
He trowis that young folk I yerne, yeild for he gane is,
Bot I may yuke all this yer, or his yerd help.
Ay quhen that caribald carll wald clyme one my wambe,
Than am I dangerus and daine and dour of my will;
Yit leit I never that larbar my leggis ga betueene,
To fyle my flesche, na fumyll me, without a fee gret;
And thoght his pene purly me payis in bed,
His purse pays richely in recompense efter:
For, or he clym on my corse, that carybald forlane,
I have conditioun of a curche of kersp allther fynest,
A goun of engranyt claith, right gaily furrit,
A ring with a ryall stane, or other riche jowell,
Or rest of his rousty raid, thoght he were rede wod:
For all the buddis of Johne Blunt, quhen he abone clymis,
Me think the baid deir aboucht, sa bawch ar his werkis;
And thus I sell him solace, thoght I it sour think:
Fra sic a syre, God yow saif, my sueit sisteris deir!
Quhen that the semely had said her sentence to end,
Than all thai leuch apon loft with latis full mery,
And raucht the cop round about full of riche wynis,
And ralyeit lang, or thai wald rest, with ryatus speche.

The wedo to the tothir wlonk warpit ther wordis:
Now, fair sister, fallis yow but fenyeing to tell,
Sen man ferst with matrimony yow menskit in kirk,
How haif ye farne be your faith? confese us the treuth:
That band of blise, or to ban, quhilk yow best thinkis?
Or how ye like lif to leid in to leill spousage?
And syne my self ye exeme one the samyn wise,
And I sall say furth the south, dissymyland no word.

The plesand said, I protest, the treuth gif I schaw,
That of your toungis ye be traist. The tothir twa grantit;
With that sprang up hir spreit be a span hechar.
To speik, quoth scho, I sall nought spar; ther is no spy neir:
I sall a ragment reveil fra rute of my hert,
A roust that is sa rankild quhill risis my stomok;

Now sall the byle all out brist, that beild has so lang;
For it to beir one my brist wes berdin our hevy:
I sall the venome devoid with a vent large,
And me assuage of the swalme, that suellit wes gret.
My husband wes a hur maister, the hugeast in erd,
Tharfor I hait him with my hert, sa help me our Lord!
He is a young man ryght yaip, bot nought in youth flouris,
For he is fadit full far and feblit of strenth:
He wes as flurising fresche within this few yeris,
Bot he is falyeid full far and fulyeid in labour;
He has bene lychour so lang quhill lost is his natur,
His lume is waxit larbar, and lyis in to swonne:
Wes never sugeorne werse na one that snaill tyrit,
For efter vii oulkis rest, it will nought rap anys;
He has bene waistit apone wemen, or he me wif chesit,
And in adultre, in my tyme, I haif him tane oft:
And yit he is als brankand with bonet one syde,
And blenkand to the brichtest that in the burgh duellis,
Alse curtly of his clething and kemmyng of his hair,
As he that is mare valyeand in Venus chalmer;
He semys to be sumthing worth, that syphyr in bour,
He lukis as he wald luffit be, thocht he be litill of valour;
He dois as dotit dog that damys on al bussis,
And liftis his leg apone loft, thoght he nought list pische;
He has a luke wihout lust and lif without curage;
He has a forme without force and fessoun but vertu,
And fair wordis but effect, all fruster of dedis;
He is for ladyis in luf a right lusty schadow,
Bot in to derne, at the deid, he salbe drup fundin;
He ralis, and makis repet with ryatus wordis,
Ay rusing him of his radis and rageing in chalmer;
Bot God wait quhat I think quhen he so thra spekis,
And how it settis him so syde to sege of sic materis.
Bot gif him self, of sum evin, myght ane say amang thaim,
Bot he nought ane is, bot nane of naturis possessoris.
Scho that has ane auld man nought all is begylit;
He is at Venus werkis na war na he semys:
I wend I josit a gem, and I haif geit gottin;
He had the glemyng of gold, and wes bot glase fundin.
Thought men be ferse, wele I fynd, fra falye ther curage,
Thar is bot eldnyng or anger ther hertis within.

Ye speik of berdis one bewch: of blise may thai sing,
That, one Sanct Valentynis day, ar vacandis ilk yer;
Hed I that plesand prevelege to part quhen me likit,
To change, and ay to cheise agane, than, chastite, adew!
Than suld I haif a fresch feir to fang in myn armes:
To hald a freke, quhill he faynt, may foly be calit.
Apone sic materis I mus, at mydnyght, full oft,
And murnys so in my mynd I murdris my selfin;
Than ly I walkand for wa, and walteris about,
Wariand oft my wekit kyn, that me away cast
To sic a craudoune but curage, that knyt my cler bewte,
And ther so mony kene knyghtis this kenrik within:
Than think I on a semelyar, the suth for to tell,
Na is our syre be sic sevin; with that I sych oft:
Than he ful tenderly dois turne to me his tume person,
And with a yoldin yerd dois yolk me in armys,
And sais, 'My soverane sueit thing, quhy sleip ye no betir?
Me think ther haldis yow a hete, as ye sum harme alyt.'
Quoth I, 'My hony, hald abak, and handill me nought sair;
A hache is happinit hastely at my hert rut.'
With that I seme for to swoune, thought I na swerf tak;
And thus beswik I that swane with my sueit wordis:
I cast on him a crabit e, quhen cleir day is cummyn,
And lettis it is a luf blenk, quhen he about glemys,
I turne it in a tender luke, that I in tene warit,
And him behaldis hamely with hertly smyling.
I wald a tender peronall, that myght na put thole,
That hatit men with hard geir for hurting of flesch,
Had my gud man to hir gest; for I dar God suer,
Scho suld not stert for his straik a stray breid of erd.
And syne, I wald that ilk band, that ye so blist call,
Had bund him so to that bryght, quhill his bak werkit;
And I wer in a beid broght with berne that me likit,
I trow that bird of my blis suld a bourd want.

Onone, quhen this amyable had endit hir speche,
Loudly lauchand the laif allowit hir mekle:
Thir gay Wiffis maid game amang the grene leiffis;
Thai drank and did away dule under derne bewis;
Thai swapit of the sueit wyne, thai swanquhit of hewis,
Bot all the pertlyar in plane thai put out ther vocis.

Than said the Weido, I wis ther is no way othir;
Now tydis me for to talk; my taill it is nixt:
God my spreit now inspir and my speche quykkin,
And send me sentence to say, substantious and noble;
Sa that my preching may pers your perverst hertis,
And make yow mekar to men in maneris and conditiounis.
I schaw yow, sisteris in schrift, I wes a schrew evir,
Bot I wes schene in my schrowd, and schew me innocent;
And thought I dour wes, and dane, dispitous, and bald,
I wes dissymblit suttelly in a sanctis liknes:
I semyt sober, and sueit, and sempill without fraud,
Bot I couth sexty dissaif that suttillar wer haldin.
Unto my lesson ye lyth, and leir at me wit,
Gif you nought list be forleit with losingeris untrew:
Be constant in your governance, and counterfeit gud maneris,
Thought ye be kene, inconstant, and cruell of mynd;
Thought ye as tygris be terne, be tretable in luf,
And be as turtoris in your talk, thought ye haif talis brukill;
Be dragonis baith and dowis ay in double forme,
And quhen it nedis yow, onone, note baith ther strenthis;
Be amyable with humble face, as angellis apperand,
And with a terrebill tail be stangand as edderis;
Be of your luke like innocentis, thoght ye haif evill myndis;
Be courtly ay in clething and costly arrayit,
That hurtis yow nought worth a hen; yowr husband pays for all.
Twa husbandis haif I had, thai held me baith deir,
Thought I dispytit thaim agane, thai spyit it na thing.
Ane wes ane hair hogeart, that hostit out flewme;
I hatit him like a hund, thought I it hid preve:
With kissing and with clapping I gert the carll fone;
Weil couth I claw his cruke bak, and kemm his cowit noddill,
And with a bukky in my cheik bo on him behind,
And with a bek gang about and bler his ald e,
And with a kynd contynance kys his crynd chekis;
In to my mynd makand mokis at that mad fader,
Trowand me with trew lufe to treit him so fair.
This cought I do without dule and na dises tak,
Bot ay be mery in my mynd and myrth full of cher.

I had a lufsummar leid my lust for to slokyn,
That couth be secrete and sure and ay saif my honour,
And sew bot at certayne tymes and in sicir placis;
Ay when the ald did me anger, with akword wordis,
Apon the galland for to goif it gladit me agane.
I had sic wit that for wo weipit I litill,
Bot leit the sueit ay the sour to gud sesone bring.
Quhen that the chuf wald me chid, with girnand chaftis,
I wald him chuk, cheik, and chyn, and cheris him so mekill,
That his cheif chymys I had chevist to my sone,
Suppos the churll wes gane chaist, or the child wes gottin:
As wis woman ay I wrought and not as wod fule,
For mar with wylis I wan na wichtnes of handis.

Syne maryit I a marchand, myghti of gudis:
He was a man of myd eld and of mene statur;
Bot we na fallowis wer in frendschip or blud,
In fredome, na furth bering, na fairnes of persoune,
Quhilk ay the fule did foryhet, for febilnes of knawlege,
Bot I sa oft thoght him on, quhill angrit his hert,
And quhilum I put furth my voce and Pedder him callit:
I wald ryght tuichandly talk be I wes tuyse maryit,
For endit wes my innocence with my ald husband:
I wes apperand to be pert within perfit eild;
Sa sais the curat of our kirk, that knew me full ying:
He is our famous to be fals, that fair worthy prelot;
I salbe laith to lat him le, quhill I may luke furth.
I gert the buthman obey, ther wes no bute ellis;
He maid me ryght hie reverens, fra he my rycht knew:
For, thocht I say it my self, the severance wes mekle
Betuix his bastard blude and my birth noble.
That page wes never of sic price for to presome anys
Unto my persone to be peir, had pete nought grantit.
Bot mercy in to womanheid is a mekle vertu,
For never bot in a gentill hert is generit ony ruth.
I held ay grene in to his mynd that I of grace tuk him,
And for he couth ken him self I curtasly him lerit:
He durst not sit anys my summondis, for, or the secund
charge,
He wes ay redy for to ryn, so rad he wes for blame.
Bot ay my will wes the war of womanly natur;

The mair he loutit for my luf, the les of him I rakit;
And eik, this is a ferly thing, or I him faith gaif,
I had sic favour to that freke, and feid syne for ever:
Quhen I the cure had all clene and him ourcummyn haill,
I crew abone that craudone, as cok that wer victour;
Quhen I him saw subject and sett at myn bydding,
Than I him lichtlyit as a lowne and lathit his maneris.
Than woxe I sa unmerciable to martir him I thought,
For as a best I broddit him to all boyis laubour:
I wald haif ridden him to Rome with raip in his heid,
Wer not ruffill of my renoune and rumour of pepill.
And yit hatrent I hid within my hert all;
Bot quhilis it hepit so huge, quhill it behud out:
Yit tuk I nevir the wosp clene out of my wyde throte,
Quhill I oucht wantit of my will or quhat I wald desir.
Bot quhen I severit had that syre of substance in erd,
And gottin his biggingis to my barne, and hie burrow landis,
Than with a stew stert out the stoppell of my hals,
That he all stunyst throu the stound, as of a stele wappin.
Than wald I, efter lang, first sa fane haif bene wrokin,
That I to flyte wes als fers as a fell dragoun.
I had for flattering of that fule fenyeit so lang,
Mi evidentis of heritagis or thai wer all selit,
My breist, that wes gret beild, bowdyn wes sa huge,
That neir my baret out brist or the band makin.
Bot quhen my billis and my bauchles wes all braid selit,
I wald na langar beir on bridill, bot braid up my heid;
Thar myght na molet mak me moy, na hald my mouth in:
I gert the renyeis rak and rif into sondir;
I maid that wif carll to werk all womenis werkis,
And laid all manly materis and mensk in this eird.
Than said I to my cumaris in counsall about,
'Se how I cabeld yone cout with a kene brydill!
The cappill, that the crelis kest in the caf mydding,
Sa curtasly the cart drawis, and kennis na plungeing,
He is nought skeich, na yit sker, na scippis nought one syd:'
And thus the scorne and the scaith scapit he nothir.
He wes no glaidsum gest for a gay lady,
Tharfor I gat him a game that ganyt him bettir;
He wes a gret goldit man and of gudis riche;
I leit him be my lumbart to lous me all misteris,

And he wes fane for to fang fra me that fair office,
And thoght my favoris to fynd through his feill giftis.
He grathit me in a gay silk and gudly arrayis,
In gownis of engranyt claith and gret goldin chenyeis,
In ringis ryally set with riche ruby stonis,
Quhill hely raise my renoune amang the rude peple.
Bot I full craftely did keip thai courtly wedis,
Quhill eftir dede of that drupe, that doth nought in chalmir:
Thought he of all my clathis maid cost and expense,
Ane othir sall the worschip haif, that weildis me eftir;
And thoght I likit him bot litill, yit for luf of otheris,
I wald me prunya plesandly in precius wedis,
That luffaris myght apone me luke and ying lusty gallandis,
That I held more in daynte and derer be ful mekill
Ne him that dressit me so dink: full dotit wes his heyd.
Quhen he wes heryit out of hand to hie up my honoris,
And payntit me as pako, proudest of fedderis,
I him miskennyt, be Crist, and cukkald him maid;
I him forleit as a lad and lathlyit him mekle:
I thoght my self a papingay and him a plukit herle;
All thus enforsit he his fa and fortifyit in strenth,
And maid a stalwart staff to strik him selfe doune.
   Bot of ane bowrd in to bed I sall yow breif yit:
Quhen ha ane hail year was hanyt, and him behuffit rage,
And I wes laith to be loppin with sic a lob avoir,
Alse lang as he wes on loft, I lukit on him never,
Na leit never enter in my thoght that he my thing persit,
Bot ay in mynd ane other man ymagynit that I haid;
Or ellis had I never mery bene at that myrthles raid.
Quhen I that grome geldit had of gudis and of natur,
Me thought him gracelese one to goif, sa me God help:
Quhen he had warit all one me his welth and his substance,
Me thoght his wit was all went away with the laif;
And so I did him despise, I spittit quhen I saw
That super spendit evill spreit, spulyeit of all vertu.
For, weill ye wait, wiffis, that he that wantis riches
And valyeandnes in Venus play, is ful vile haldin:
Full fruster is his fresch array and fairnes of persoune,
All is bot frutlese his effeir and falyeis at the upwith.

  I buskit up my barnis like baronis sonnis,
And maid bot fulis of the fry of his first wif.
I banyst fra my boundis his brethir ilkane;
His frendis as my fais I held at feid evir;
Be this, ye belief may, I luffit nought him self,
For never I likit a leid that langit till his blude:
And yit thir wisemen, thai wait that all wiffis evill
Ar kend with ther conditionis and knawin with the samin.
  Deid is now that dyvour and dollin in erd:
With him deit all my dule and my drery thoghtis;
Now done is my dolly nyght, my day is upsprungin,
Adew dolour, adew! my daynte now begynis:
Now am I a wedow, I wise and weill am at ese;
I weip as I were woful, but wel is me for ever;
I busk as I wer bailfull, bot blith is my hert;
My mouth it makis murnyng, and my mynd lauchis;
My clokis thai ar caerfull in colour of sabill,
Bot courtly and ryght curyus my corse is ther undir:
I drup with a ded luke in my dule habit,
As with manis daill [I] had done for dayis of my lif.
  Quhen that I go to the kirk, cled in cair weid,
As foxe in a lambis fleise fenye I my cheir;
Than lay I furght my bright buke one breid one my kne,
With mony lusty letter ellummynit with gold;
And drawis my clok forthwart our my face quhit,
That I may spy, unaspyit, a space me beside:
Full oft I blenk by my buke, and blynis of devotioun,
To se quhat berne is best brand or bredest in schulderis,
Or forgeit is maist forcely to furnyse a bancat
In Venus chalmer, valyeandly, withoutin vane ruse:
And, as the new mone all pale, oppressit with change,
Kythis quhilis her cleir face through cluddis of sable,
So keik I through my clokis, and castis kynd lukis
To knychtis, and to cleirkis, and cortly personis.
  Quhen frendis of my husbandis behaldis me one fer,
I haif a watter spunge for wa, within my wyde clokis,
Than wring I it full wylely and wetis my chekis,
With that watteris myn ene and welteris doune teris.
Than say thai all, that sittis about, 'Se ye nought, allace!
Yone lustlese led so lelely scho luffit hir husband:
Yone is a pete to enprent in a princis hert,

That sic a perle of plesance suld yone pane dre!'
I sane me as I war ane sanct, and semys ane angell;
At langage of lichory I leit as I war crabit:
I sich, without sair hert or seiknes in body;
According to my sable weid I mon haif sad maneris,
Or thai will se all the suth; for certis, we wemen
We set us all fra the syght to syle men of treuth:
We dule for na evill deid, sa it be derne haldin.
    Wise wemen has wayis and wonderfull gydingis
With gret engyne to bejaip ther jolyus husbandis;
And quyetly, with sic craft, convoyis our materis
That, under Crist, no creatur kennis of our doingis.
Bot folk a cury may miscuke, that knawledge wantis,
And has na colouris for to cover thair awne kindly fautis;
As dois thir damysellis, for derne dotit lufe,
That dogonis haldis in dainte and delis with thaim so lang,
Quhill all the cuntre knaw ther kyndnes and faith:
Faith has a fair name, bot falsheid faris bettir:
Fy one hir that can nought feyne her fame for to saif!
Yit am I wise in sic werk and wes all my tyme;
Thoght I want wit in warldlynes, I wylis haif in luf,
As ony happy woman has that is of hie blude:
Hutit be the halok las a hunder yeir of eild!
    I have ane secrete servand, rycht sobir of his toung,
That me supportis of sic nedis, quhen I a syne mak:
Thoght he be sympill to the sicht, he has a tong sickir;
Full mony semelyar sege wer service dois mak:
Thought I haif cair, under cloke, the cleir day quhill nyght,
Yit haif I solace, under serk, quhill the sone ryse.
    Yit am I haldin a haly wif our all the haill schyre,
I am sa peteouse to the pur, quhen ther is personis mony.
In passing of pilgrymage I pride me full mekle,
Mair for the prese of peple na ony perdoun wynyng.
    Bot yit me think the best bourd, quhen baronis and
        knychtis,
And othir bachilleris, blith blumyng in youth,
And all my luffaris lele, my lugeing persewis,
And fyllis me wyne wantonly with weilfair and joy:
Sum rownis; and sum ralyeis: and sum redis ballatis;
Sum raiffis furght rudly with riatus speche;
Sum plenis, and sum prayis; sum prasis mi bewte,

Sum kissis me; sum clappis me; sum kyndnes me proferis;
Sum kerffis to me curtasli; sum me the cop giffis;
Sum stalwardly steppis ben, with a stout curage,
And a stif standand thing staiffis in my neiff;
And mony blenkis ben our, that but full fer sittis,
That mai, for the thik thrang, nought thrif as thai wald.
Bot, with my fair calling, I comfort thaim all:
For he that sittis me nixt, I nip on his finger;
I serf him on the tothir syde on the samin fasson;
And he that behind me sittis, I hard on him lene;
And him befor, with my fut fast on his I stramp;
And to the bernis far but sueit blenkis I cast:
To every man in speciall speke I sum wordis
So wisly and so womanly, quhill warmys ther hertis.
   That is no liffand leid so law of degre
That sall me luf unluffit, I am so loik hertit;
And gif his lust so be lent into my lyre quhit,
That he be lost or with me lig, his lif sall nocht danger.
I am so mercifull in mynd, and menys all wichtis,
My sely saull salbe saif, quhen Sabot all jugis.
Ladyis leir thir lessonis and be no lassis fundin:
This is the legeand of my lif, thought Latyne it be nane.

   Quhen endit had her ornat speche, this eloquent wedow,
Lowd thai lewch all the laif, and loffit hir mekle,
And said thai suld exampill tak of her soverane teaching,
And wirk efter hir wordis, that woman wes so prudent.
Than culit thai thair mouthis with confortable drinkis,
And carpit full cummerlik with cop going round.

   Thus draif thai our that deir nyght with danceis full noble,
Quhill that the day did up daw, and dew donkit flouris;
The morow myld wes and meik, the mavis did sing,
And all remuffit the myst, and the meid smellit;
Silver schouris doune schuke as the schene cristall,
And berdis schoutit in schaw with thair schill notis;
The goldin glitterand gleme so gladit ther hertis;
Thai maid a glorious gle amang the grene bewis.
The soft sowch of the swyr and soune of the stremys,
The sueit savour of the sward and singing of foulis,

Myght confort ony creatur of the kyn of Adam,
And kindill agane his curage, thocht it wer cald sloknyt.
Than rais thir ryall roisis, in ther riche wedis,
And rakit hame to ther rest through the rise blumys;
And I all prevely past to a plesand arber,
And with my pen did report thair pastance most mery.

Ye auditoris most honorable, that eris has gevin
Oneto this uncouth aventur, quhilk airly me happinnit:
Of thir thre wantoun wiffis, that I haif writtin heir,
Quhilk wald ye waill to your wif, gif ye suld wed one?

SIR DAVID LYNDSAY

from *Ane Satyre of the Thrie Estaitis*
(i) An interlude with the Pardoner

PARDONER

Bona dies, Bona dies.
Devoit peopill, gude day I say yow.
Now tarie ane lytill quhyll I pray yow,
Till I be with yow knawin:
Wait ye weill how I am namit?
Ane nobill man and undefamit
Gif all the suith war schawin.
I am sir Robert Rome-raker,
Ane perfite publike pardoner,
Admittit be the Paip.
Sirs I sall schaw yow for my wage
My pardons and my privilage,
Quhilk ye sall se and graip.
I give to the devill with gude intent,
This unsell wickit New-testament,
With them that it translaitit:
Sen layik men knew the veritie,
Pardoners gets no charitie,
Without that thay debait it
Among the wives with wrinks and wyles,
As all my marrowis men begyles
With our fair fals flattrie:
Yea all the crafts I ken perqueir,
As I was teichit be ane Freir,
Callit Hypocrisie.
Bot now allace, our greit abusioun
Is cleirlie knawin till our confusioun,
That we may sair repent:
Of all credence now I am quyte,
For ilk man halds me at dispyte,
That reids the New-test'ment.
Duill fell the braine that hes it wrocht,
Sa fall them that the Buik hame brocht:
Als I pray to the Rude
That Martin Luther that fals loun,
Black Bullinger and Melancthoun,

Had bene smorde in their cude.
Be him that buir the crowne of thorne,
I wald Sanct Paull had never bene borne,
And als I wald his buiks
War never red into the kirk,
Bot amangs freirs into the mirk,
Or riven amang ruiks.

Heir sall he lay doun his geir upon ane buird and say.

My patent pardouns ye may se,
Cum fra the Cane of Tartarie,
Weill seald with oster-schellis.
Thocht ye have na contritioun,
Ye sall have full remissioun,
With help of buiks and bellis.
Heir is ane relict lang and braid,
Of Fine Macoull the richt chaft blaid,
With teith and al togidder:
Of Collings cow heir is ane horne,
For eating of Makconnals corne,
Was slaine into Baquhidder.
Heir is ane coird baith great and lang,
Quhilk hangit Johnye Armistrang,
Of gude hemp soft and sound:
Gude halie peopill I stand for'd,
Quha ever beis hangit with this cord,
Neids never to be dround.
The culum of Sanct Brydis kow,
The gruntill of Sanct Antonis sow,
Quhilk buir his haly bell:
Quha ever he be heiris this bell clinck
Gif me ane ducat for till drink,
He sall never gang to hell,
Without he be of Baliell borne.
Maisters trow ye that this be scorne?
Cum win this pardoun, cum.
Quha luifis thair wyfis nocht with thair hart,
I have power them for till part.
Me think yow deif and dum.
Hes naine of yow curst wickit wyfis,

That halds yow into sturt and stryfis?
Cum tak my dispensatioun:
Of that cummer I sall mak yow quyte,
Howbeit your selfis be in the wyte,
And mak ane fals narratioun.
Cum win the pardoun, now let se,
For meill, for malt or for monie,
For cok, hen, guse or gryse.
Of relicts heir I have ane hunder.
Quhy cum ye nocht? This is ane wonder.
I trow ye be nocht wyse.

from *Ane Satyre of the Thrie Estaitis*

(ii) Ecclesiastics on trial

COUNSALL

Begin first at the Spritualitie,
And tak of them examinatioun,
Gif they can use their divyne dewetie.
And als I mak yow supplicatioun,
All thay that hes thair offices misusit,
Of them mak haistie deprivatioun,
Sa that the peopill be na mair abusit.

CORRECTIOUN

Ye ar ane Prince of Spritualitie.
How have ye usit your office now let se.

SPRITUALITIE

My Lords quhen was thair ony Prelats wont
Of thair office till ony King mak count?
Bot of my office gif ye wald have the feill,
I let yow wit I have it usit weill.
For I tak in my count twyse in the yeir,
Wanting nocht of my teind ane boll of beir.
I gat gude payment of my temporall lands,
My buttock-maill, my coattis and my offrands,
With all that dois perteine my benefice.
Consider now my Lord gif I be wyse.
I dar nocht marie contrair the common law:
Ane thing thair is my Lord that ye may knaw:

Howbeit I dar nocht plainlie spouse ane wyf,
Yit concubeins I have had four or fyfe,
And to my sons I have givin rich rewairds,
And all my dochters maryit upon lairds.
I let yow wit my Lord I am na fuill,
For quhy I ryde upon ane amland muill.
Thair is na temporall lord in all this land
That maks sic cheir I let yow understand.
And als my Lord I gif with gude intentioun
To divers temporall lords ane yeirlie pensioun,
To that intent that thay with all thair hart
In richt and wrang sal plainlie tak my part.
Now have I tauld yow sir on my best ways
How that I have exercit my office.

CORRECTIOUN
I weind your office had bene for til preich,
And Gods law to the peopill teich.
Quhairfoir weir ye that mytour ye me tell?

SPRITUALITIE
I wat nocht man be him that herryit hel.

CORRECTIOUN
That dois betakin that ye with gude intent
Sould teich and preich the Auld and New Test'ment.

SPRITUALITIE
I have ane freir to preiche into my place:
Of my office ye heare na mair quhill Pasche.

CHASTITIE
My Lords this Abbot and this Priores
Thay scorne thair gods: this is my reason quhy.
Thay beare an habite of feinyeit halines,
And in thair deid thay do the contrary:
For to live chaist thay vow solemnitly,
Bot fra that thay be sikker of thair bowis,
That live in huirdome and in harlotry.
Examine them sir, how thay observe thair vowis.

CORRECTIOUN
Sir Scribe ye sall at Chastities requeist
Pas and exame yon thrie in gudlie haist.

SCRIBE
Father Abbot this counsall bids me speir,
How ye have usit your Abbay thay wald heir.
And als thir Kings hes givin to me commissioun,
Of your office for to mak inquisitioun.

ABBOT
Tuiching my office I say to yow plainlie,
My monks and I, we leif richt easelie.
Thair is na monks from Carrick to Carraill
That fairs better and drinks mair helsum aill.
My Prior is ane man of great devotioun:
Thairfoir daylie he gets ane double portioun.

SCRIBE
My Lords how have ye keipit your thrie vows?

ABBOT
Indeid richt weill till I gat hame my bows.
In my Abbay quhen I was sure professour,
Then did I leife as did my predecessour.
My paramours is baith als fat and fair
As ony wench into the toun of Air.
I send my sons to Pareis to the scullis:
I traist in God that thay salbe na fuillis.
And all my douchters I have weill providit.
Now judge ye gif my office be weill gydit.

SCRIBE
Maister Person schaw us gif ye can preich.

PERSON
Thocht I preich not I can play at the caiche.
I wait thair is nocht ane amang yow all,
Mair ferilie can play at the fut-ball.
And for the carts, the tabilis and the dyse,
Above all persouns I may beir the pryse.

Our round bonats we mak them now four nuickit,
Of richt fyne stuiff gif yow list cum and luik it.
Of my office I have declarit to the.
Speir quhat ye pleis, ye get na mair of me.

SCRIBE

Quhat say ye now my Ladie Priores?
How have ye usit your office can ye ges?
Quhat was the caus ye refusit harbrie
To this young lustie Ladie Chastitie?

PRIORES

I wald have harborit hir with gude intent,
Bot my complexioun thairto wald not assent:
I do my office efter auld use and wount:
To your Parliament I will mak na mair count.

ALEXANDER MONTGOMERIE

from *The Flyting between Montgomerie and Polwart*

THE SECOND INVECTIVE

Vyld venymous vipper, wanthreivinest of thingis,
Half ane elph, half ane aip, of nature denyit,
Thow flyttis and thow freittis, thow fartis and thow flingis;
Bot this bargane, unbeist, deir sall thow by it.
'The kuif is weill wairit that twa home bringis,'
This proverb, peild pellet, to the is applyit:
Sprung speidder of spyt, thow spewis furth springis;
Wanschaippin wowbat, of the weirdis invyit,
I can schaw how, quhair, and quhat begate the,
  Quhilk wes nather man nor wyf,
  Nor humane creature on lyf;
  Fals stinkand steirar up of stryf,
    Hurkland howlat, have at the!

Into the hinderend of harvest, on ane alhallow evin,
Quhen our goode nichtbouris ryddis, if I reid richt,
Sum buklit on ane bunwyd, and sum on ane bene,
Ay trippand in trowpis fra the twie-licht,
Sum saidlit ane scho aip all grathit into grene,
Sum hobling on hempstaikis, hovand on hicht,
The King of Pharie, with the court of the Elph Quene,
With mony alrege incubus, ryddand that nicht.
Thair ane elph, and ane aip, ane unsell begate,
  In ane peitpot, by Powmathorne;
  That brachart in ane buss wes borne;
  They fand ane monstour on the morne,
    War facit nor ane cat.

The wird sisteris wandering, as they wer wont than,
Saw revinis ruge at this rat be ane rone-ruite.
They musit at this mandrak mismaid lyk ane man;
Ane beist bund with ane bunwyd in ane auld bute.
How this ghaist haid bene gottin, to ges they begane,
Swir sweillit in ane swyneskin and smeirit our with sute.
The bellie that it buir they bitterlie ban.
Of that mismaid mowdywart, mischeif they mute.

That cankerit camscheocht, uncristnit, they curs;
And baid that it suld nevir be but
The glengoir, gravell, and the gut,
And all the plaigis that evir wes put
In Pandorus poysonit purs.

'The coche, the connoche, the collik, and the cauld,
The coirdis, the colt evill, the claspis, and the cleikis,
The hunger, the hart evill, the hoist, mot the hauld;
The boche, and the barbillis, and the Cannogait breikis,
The ringbane, the bainespavin, on thy sprung spauld,
The feirsie, the falling evill, that fellis mony freikis,
Ourgane with angilberreis, as thow growis auld,
The choikis, the charbunkill, with wormis in thy cheikis,
The snuf, the snoir, the scheippisch, the schanker,
With the bleids and bellithraw,
The bytting battis, the baneschaw,
The mischeif on thy melt and maw,
The scabbis, and the canker.

'The frenesie, the fluikis, the fykis, and the felt,
The feveris, the totteris, with the spenyie fleis,
The doyt, and the dysmell, indifferentlie delt,
The pelodie, the palsie, the poikis lyk peis,
The sneising, the snytting, with swaming to swelt,
The wandevill, the wildfyre, the womeit, the weis,
The mair, the migram, the mureill, the melt,
The warbillis, the wood-worme, that doggis of deis,
The phtiseik, the twithyaik, the tittis, and the tirrillis,
The panefull poplasie, the pest,
The rottin roup, the auld rest,
With paines and parlasie opprest,
And nippit with the nirrilis.

'The bruik, the byllis, with blisteris and blainis,
Baith beld and bleirit, brokin bakit, staneblind,
Wirriand on wind flaiffis, and windie wainis,
The hoikis in the choikis, hakkit heillis ay behind,
The swyne poikis, the poistrume, and pisching with pane,
Hydropasie, herschaw, and hyves, sall the bind.
The skunnering cattaris and hartskaid remanis,

Baith kruikit and crampit, and chitterrit to the chin,
The stayne and the sturdie, the stane and the sturdie,
Lipper lispane of the lidder ill,
Of dubbis and dreggis to drink thy fill;
No wyf will wische the wors with hir will,
For thow art not wurdie.

'The messillis, the muillis, the mallange mak the mantane,
The fumyng, the flewme, the foothing, the flame,
The gelling, the gulsocht, the gall-hauld, the gauntane,
The stane worme, the ringworme, not slaiking of swame,
The wirsome, the wraittis, not wormis be thow wantane,
The pluirasie, the pluckevill, ay dwynand in ane dwame,
Hoikis hoillis in thy heillis, with the fyre of St Antane,
The louslie phirasie, the tarrie uncame,
Ay ryvand of ane reif of venymeous water,
The lymphat, lunscheocht, lithargie,
The aikand aixis extasie,
Desyrand daylie for to die,
Bot nevir the better.

'Wo worth,' quod the weirdis, 'the wichtis that the wrocht!
Threid bair be thair thrift as thow art wanthrevin!
Als hard be thair hansell that helpis the to ocht!
The rottin rim of thy womb with ruikis salbe revin;
All boundis quhair thow byddis to baill salbe brocht;
Thy gall and thy gwissorne to the glaidis salbe gevin;
Ay schort be thy sollace; with schame be thou socht:
In hell mot thow hawnt, and hyd the from heavin;
And ay as thow growis auld, so eik in thy anger,
To live with lymmeris and outlawis,
With hurcheonis, aittand hipis and hawis;
Bot quhen thow cumes quhair the cok crawis,
Tarie no langer.

'Botht schame and sorrow on hir snowt that sufferis the to sowk,
Or scho that cairis for thy creidill, cauld be hir cast,
Or bringis onie bedding for thy blae bowk,
Or lowsis af thy ludyeotis so long as they lest,
Or offerris the ony thing all the lang oulk,
Or first refreschis the with fuide, albeit thow suld fast,

Or quhen thy duddis ar bedirtin, that givis thame ane dowk;
Als gromes, quhair thow grainis, at thy gruntill be agast;
Als freamit be thy fortoune, as foule is thy forme.
First, sevin yeir, be thow dum and deif,
And eftir that, a commoun theif:
Thow art markit for a meischeif,
Foul unworthie worme!

'Untrowit be thy tounge, yit tratling all tymes.
Ay fals be thy fingeris, bot laith to confess.
All cuntreis quhair thow cumes accuse the of crymes.
Ay the langer that thow live thy luk be the less.
Yit still be thow reivand, bot rude of thy rymes.
All ill be thow usand, and ay in excess.
Ilk moone be thow mad, fra past be the prymes;
Syne plaigit with povertie, thy pryde to oppres.
With wolfis and wildcattis thy weird be to wander;
Draiglit throw dirtie dubbis and dykis;
Taigilt and towsilt with toun tykis.
Say, lowsie lowne, quhat evir thow lykis;
Thy tounge is no sclander.'

Fra the weird sisteris saw the schaip of that schit,
'Littill luk be thy lot,' quod they, 'quhair thow lyis.'
'Thy fowmart face,' quod the first, 'to flyt salbe fit.'
'Nikniven,' quod the nixt, 'sall nureische the thryse;
To ryde post in Elphin none abiller nor it.'
'To dryve doggis furth to dryt,' the third did devyse:
'All they dayis sall thow be of thy bodie bot a bit.
As suche as thow seames, als scharp be thy syse.'
Then dewlie they deimit, quhat deid it suld die.
The first said, 'suirlie of a schot';
The nixt said, 'in a rynnand knot';
The thrid, 'be thrawing of the throt,
Lyk a tyk on a trie.'

Then wilfullie voitit the weirdis in ane voce,
The deid of that daiblet, and then they withdrew;
To let it ly thair allone, they thocht littill lose,
In ane den be ane dyksyde, or the day dew.
Thair a cleir cumpany cum eftir close,

Nickniven with hir nymphis, in nomber anew,
With chairmes from Cathnes and Chanrie of Ross,
Quhais cunning consistis in casting a clew;
Sein that same thing they said to thameself:
'This maikles monstour is meit for us,
And for our craft commodious;
Ane uglie aip and incubus,
And gottin of elf.'

Thir venerabill virginis quhome ye wald call wiches,
In tyme of thair triumph, they tirlt me that taid;
Sum bakward on broidsuis, and sum on blak bicheis,
Sum, in steid of ane staig, over ane stark munk straid.
From the heavinis to the hellis, sum hobbillis, sum hichis;
With thair mowthis to the moone, sick murgeonis they maid.
Sum, be force, and effect, the four windis fichis,
And nyne tymes, wirdersones, about the thorne raid,
And glowrand to the ground grivouslie gaipis,
By craft conjurand feyndis by force,
Furth of ane carne, bysyde ane croce,
Thir ladyis lichtit fra thair hors,
And band thame with raipis.

Syne bairfute and bair ledgit, to bapteis that barne,
To ane well went they west, by ane wood syde;
They saw the schit all beschyttin and soipit in charne.
On ane thre headit Hecate in haist thair they cryit:
'As we have fund in this feild this fundlin forfarne,
First, his faith he forsaikis, in the feynd to confyde,
Be vertew of thir wordis and of this raw yarne,
And thryse thre and threttie knottis on ane blew threed,
And of deid menis memberis, weill schewit in ane schoe,
Quhilk we have band from top and tae,
Evin of ane hundreth men and mae:
Now grant us, devillis, ere we gae
Our dewtie to doe.

'Be the moving of the mone, mapamone, and the Kingis Ell,
Be Phlegitoun, the Sevin Starnis, and the Chairlwane,
Be the hicht of the heavin, and lawnes of hell,
Be all the brether of Belliallis buird in ane band,

Be the pollis, the planeittis, and singis all tuell,
Be the michtis of the moone – lat mirknes remane –
Be the elementis all that our craft can compell,
Be the floodis infernall, and fureis of pane,
Be all the ghaistis of our gang, that dwellis thair doun,
    In signe of Stikis, that stinking strand,
    And Pluto, that our court command,
    Resave this harlot of our hand,
        In name of Mahoun.

'That this worme, in our wark, sick wonder can wirk;
And, throw poysoun of this poyd, our practic prevaill
To cut of our cummer to cum to the kirk,
For the half of our help I hauld heir is haill.
Let nevir this undoche of evill doing irk,
All boundis quhair it bydis may brocht be to baill.
Of bliss let it be als bair as the birk,
That tittest that taidrell may tell ane ill taill:
Let no wo in this warld to this wrache be wantit.'
    Be they haid said, the fyre flauch flew,
    Bothe thunder, weit, and windis blew,
    Quhair be the cuning cummeris knew
        Thair asking wes grantit.

Quhen the cummeris that crab with Pluto contractit,
They promeist, as parentis, syne, for thair awin pairt,
Ane mother of mischeif, an they micht mak it,
Ane imp of all ill most meit for thair airt.
Nikniven, as nurische, to teich it, gart tak it,
To saill the see in a sive, bot compas or cairt;
And milk of ane harin tedder, that wyfis suld be wrakit,
And the kow give ane choppin wes wont give a quart;
That bairnis suld bane baith bloode and banis,
    Quhen they have neither milk nor meill;
    Compellit be hunger for to steill,
    Then sall they give him to the deill,
        Ofter nor anes.

Fra the dames devoitlie haid done thair devoir,
In having that hurchoun, they haistit thame hame,
Of that mater to mak amangis thame na moir,

Saifing, nixt, that the nunes that nirlend suld name.
Thay cowit ther the kytrell, the face of it bair,
And nippit it so done neir, that to sie it wes schame;
Syne callit it peild pollart, they peild it so sair.
'Quhair we clip' quod the cummeris, 'it cummeris na kame,
For we have heght to Mahoun for hansell his hair.'
They maid it lyk a scrapit swyne,
And ay as they pold it, they gart it quhryn,
And schuif, as we may sie syne,
The face of it bair.

Be ane eftir midnicht, thair office they endit;
For then it wes na tyme for trumpouris to tairie.
Sum bakward on biches and broodsouis bendit,
That cruikit crokadeill they quyt with thame they carie.
Unto the cocatrice in ane creill they send it;
Quhair sevin yeiris it sowkit, sweillit, singit and sarie,
The kin of it be the cry, incontinent kend it,
Feching fude for to feid it, from the feild of Pharie.
Ilk elph of thame all brocht ane almous-hous oster,
Bot it wes no dayntie dische,
Ane foul phlegmatik fowsum fiche:
Insteid of sauthe, on it they piche.
Sic fude feid sick a foster!

And first fra the father, syne sindrie haid fed it,
Mony munkis and marmaidynis come with the mother.
'Black boiche on thair bouk,' quod thay, 'that first breid it!'
Ay offerring that undoche fra ane to ane uther:
Quhair that serpent had sowkit, sair wes to sched it.
Bot belvye it began to bukill the brother.
In the bark of ane bowrtrie, quyllumis they bed it.
Thair taillis with the tounge of it, they lyk and ruther;
Sum fartand, sum flyrand, thair phisnomeis thei flyp;
Sum schevilland thair chaftis, and slavere chekis;
Sum luiking lyce in the croun of it keikis;
Sum in thair oxteris it cleikis,
Lyk a bagpype.

With mudgeounes, and murgeonis, and mowing the bane,
They leit it, they lift it, they loif it, they lak it,

They graip it, they grip it; it greitis, they grane;
They bind it, they baw it, they bed it, they brat it.
It skitterit, it squeillit; they skirlit ilk ane,
Quhill the ky in the cuntrie startillit and chaisit,
Quhilkis rairing ran rid wood, rowtand in a rane.
The wild deir in thair den the din hes displasit.
The cry wes sa uglie, of aipis, elfis, and owlis,
That geis and geislingis cryis and craikis;
In dubbis dowkit duikis and draikis;
All folkis, for feir, the feildis forsaikis;
And the toun tykis yowlis.

Sick ane mirthles music thes menstrallis did mak,
That cattell keist capriellis behind with thair heillis;
Bot littill tent to thair time the toune leit thame tak,
Bot rameist ran reid-wood, and raveld the reillis.
Fra the cummeris thame knew, they come with a crak,
To conjure the undoche, with clewis and creillis;
All the boundis thairabout grew bleknit and blak:
For the din of that daiblet raisit the deillis.
To conjure with a clap, fra caves they came far,
And for godbarne gift they gave,
To teich that theif to steill and rave,
Bot ay the langer that it live,
The warld be the war.

WILLIAM DRUMMOND

A Character of the Anti-Covenanter, or Malignant

Would yee know these royall knaves
Of free Men would turne us slaves;
Who our Union doe defame
With Rebellions Wicked Name?
Read these Verses, and yee'il spring them,
Then on Gibbetes straight cause hing them.
They complaine of sinne and follye,
In these tymes so passing hollye,
They their substance will not give,
Libertines that we maye live;
Hold that people too too wanton,
Under an old king dare canton,
They neglecte our circular Tables,
Scorne our actes and lawes as fables,
Of our battales talke but meeklye,
With sermones foure content them weeklye,
Sweare King Charles is neither Papist,
Armenian, Lutherian, Atheist;
But that in his Chamber-Prayers,
Which are pour'd 'midst Sighs and Tears,
To avert God's fearful Wrath,
Threatning us with Blood and Death,
Persuade they would the Multitude,
This King too holy is and good.
They avouch we'll weep and groan
When Hundred Kings we serve for one,
That each Shire but Blood affords
To serve the Ambition of young Lords,
Whose Debts ere now had been redoubled,
If the State had not been troubled.
Slow they are our Oath to swear,
Slower for it Arms to bear;
They do Concord love and Peace,
Would our Enemies embrace,
Turn Men Proselytes by the Word,
Not by Musket, Pike, and Sword.
They Swear that for Religion's Sake

We may not massacre, burn, sack;
That the Beginning of these Pleas
Sprang from the ill-sped ABC's;
For Servants that it is not well
Against their Masters to Rebel;
That that Devotion is but slight
Doth force men first to swear, then fight;
That our Confession is indeed
Not the *Apostolick CREED*,
Which of Negations we contrive,
Which *Turk* and *Jew* may both subscrive;
That Monies should Men's Daughters marry,
They on frantick War miscarry,
Whilst dear the Souldiers they pay,
At last who will snatch all away,
And as Times turn worse and worse,
Catechise us by the Purse;
That Debts are paid with bold stern Looks,
That Merchants pray on their Compt-books;
That Justice, dumb and sullen, frowns
To see in Croslets hang'd her Gowns;
That Preachers ordinary Theme
Is 'gainst Monarchy to declaim;
That since Leagues we began to swear,
Vices did ne're so black appear;
Oppression, Blood-shed, ne're more rife,
Foul Jars between the Man and Wife;
Religion so contemn'd was never,
Whilst all are raging in a Fever.
They tell by Devils and some sad Chance
That that detestable League of *France*,
Which cost so many Thousand Lives,
And Two Kings by Religious Knives,
Is amongst us, though few descry;
Though they speak Truth, yet say they Lye.
Hee that sayes that night is night,
That halting folk walk not upright,
That the owles into the spring
Doe not nightingalles outsing;
That the seas wee can not plough,
Plant strawberryes in the raine-bow;

That waking men doe not sound sleep,
That the fox keepes not the sheep;
That alls not gold doth gold appeare,
Believe him not although hee sweere.
To such syrenes stope your eare,
Their societyes forbeare.
Tossed you may be like a wave,
Veritye may you deceave;
True fools they may make of you;
Hate them worse than Turke or Jew.
Were it not a dangerous Thing,
Should yee againe obey the king,
Lordes losse should souveraigntie,
Souldiours haste backe to Germanie,
Justice should in your Townes remaine,
Poore Men possesse their own againe,
Brought out of Hell that word of plunder
More terrible than divell and Thunder,
Should with the Covenant flye away,
And charitye amongst us stay?
When yee find those lying fellowes,
Take and flowere with them the Gallowes;
On otheres yee maye too laye hold,
In purse or chestes if they have Gold.
Who wise or rich are in the Nation,
Malignants are by protestation.
Peace and plentie should us nurish,
True religion with us flourish.

On Pime

When Pime last night descended into Hell,
Ere hee his coupes of Lethe did carouse,
What place is this (said hee) I pray mee tell?
To whom a Divell: This is the lower howse.

ALLAN RAMSAY

Lucky Spence's Last Advice

Three Times the Carline grain'd and rifted,
Then frae the Cod her Pow she lifted,
In bawdy Policy well gifted,
When she now faun,
That Death na langer wad be shifted,
She thus began:

My loving Lasses, I maun leave ye,
But dinna wi' ye'r Greeting grieve me,
Nor wi' your Draunts and Droning deave me,
But bring's a Gill;
For Faith, my Bairns, ye may believe me,
'Tis 'gainst my Will.

O black Ey'd *Bess* and mim Mou'd *Meg*,
O'er good to work or yet to beg;
Lay Sunkots up for a sair Leg,
For whan ye fail,
Ye'r Face will not be worth a Feg,
Nor yet ye'r Tail.

Whan e'er ye meet a Fool that's fow,
That ye're a Maiden gar him trow,
Seem nice, but stick to him like Glew;
And whan set down,
Drive at the Jango till he spew,
Syne he'll sleep soun.

Whan he's asleep, then dive and catch
His ready Cash, his Rings or Watch;
And gin he likes to light his Match
At your Spunk-box,
Ne'er stand to let the fumbling Wretch
E'en take the Pox.

Cleek a' ye can be Hook or Crook,
Ryp ilky Poutch frae Nook to Nook;

Be sure to truff his Pocket-book,
Saxty Pounds *Scots*
Is nae deaf Nits: In little Bouk
Lie great Bank-Notes.

To get a Mends of whinging Fools,
That's frighted for Repenting-Stools,
Wha often, whan their Metal cools,
Turn sweer to pay,
Gar the Kirk-Boxie hale the Dools
Anither Day.

But dawt Red Coats, and let them scoup,
Free for the Fou of cutty Stoup;
To gee them up, ye need na hope
E'er to do well:
They'll rive ye'r Brats and kick your Doup,
And play the Deel.

There's ae sair Cross attends the Craft,
That curst Correction-house, where aft
Vild Hangy's Taz ye'r Riggings saft
Makes black and blae,
Enough to pit a Body daft;
But what'll ye say?

Nane gathers Gear withouten Care,
Ilk Pleasure has of Pain a Skare;
Suppose then they should tirl ye bare,
And gar ye fike,
E'en learn to thole; 'tis very fair
Ye're Nibour like.

Forby, my Looves, count upo' Losses,
Ye'r Milk-white Teeth and Cheeks like Roses,
Whan Jet-black Hair and Brigs of Noses,
Faw down wi' Dads
To keep your Hearts up 'neath sic Crosses,
Set up for Bawds.

Wi' well crish'd Loofs I hae been canty,
Whan e'r the Lads wad fain ha'e faun t'ye;

To try the auld Game *Taunty Raunty*,
Like Coosers keen,
They took Advice of me your Aunty,
If ye were clean.

Then up I took my Siller Ca'
And whistl'd benn whiles ane, whiles twa;
Roun'd in his Lug, That there was a
Poor Country *Kate*,
As halesom as the Well of *Spaw*,
But unka blate.

Sae whan e'er Company came in,
And were upo' a merry Pin,
I slade away wi' little Din,
And muckle Mense,
Left Conscience Judge, it was a' ane
To Lucky *Spence*.

My Bennison come on good Doers,
Who spend their Cash on Bawds and Whores;
May they ne'er want the Wale of Cures
For a sair Snout:
Foul fa' the Quacks wha that Fire smoors,
And puts nae out.

My Malison light ilka Day
On them that drink, and dinna pay,
But tak a Snack and rin away;
May't be their Hap
Never to want a *Gonorrhoea*,
Or rotten Clap.

Lass gi'e us in anither Gill,
A Mutchken, Jo, let's tak our Fill;
Let Death syne registrate his Bill
Whan I want Sense,
I'll slip away with better Will,
Quo' Lucky *Spence*.

ROBERT FERGUSSON

Braid Claith

Ye wha are fain to hae your name
Wrote in the bonny book of fame,
Let merit nae pretension claim
To laurel'd wreath,
But hap ye weel, baith back and wame,
In gude Braid Claith.

He that some ells o' this may fa,
An' slae-black hat on pow like snaw,
Bids bauld to bear the gree awa',
Wi' a' this graith,
Whan bienly clad wi' shell fu' braw
O' gude Braid Claith.

Waesuck for him wha has na fek o't!
For he's a gowk they're sure to geck at,
A chiel that ne'er will be respekit
While he draws breath,
Till his four quarters are bedeckit
Wi' gude Braid Claith.

On Sabbath-days the barber spark,
Whan he has done wi' scrapin wark,
Wi' siller broachie in his sark,
Gangs trigly, faith!
Or to the Meadow, or the Park,
In gude Braid Claith.

Weel might ye trow, to see them there,
That they to shave your haffits bare,
Or curl an' sleek a pickle hair,
Wou'd be right laith,
Whan pacing wi' a gawsy air
In gude Braid Claith.

If ony mettl'd stirrah green
For favour frae a lady's ein,

He maunna care for being seen
Before he sheath
His body in a scabbard clean
O' gude Braid Claith.

For, gin he come wi' coat thread-bare,
A feg for him she winna care,
But crook her bonny mou' fu' sair,
And scald him baith.
Wooers shou'd ay their travel spare
Without Braid Claith.

Braid Claith lends fock an unco heese,
Makes mony kail-worms butter-flies,
Gies mony a doctor his degrees
For little skaith:
In short, you may be what you please
Wi' gude Braid Claith.

For thof ye had as wise a snout on
As *Shakespear* or Sir *Isaac Newton*,
Your judgement fouk wou'd hae a doubt on,
I'll tak my aith,
Till they cou'd see ye wi' a suit on
O' gude Braid Claith.

To the Tron-Kirk Bell

Wanwordy, crazy, dinsome thing,
As e'er was fram'd to jow or ring,
What gar'd them sic in steeple hing
They ken themsel',
But weel wat I they coudna bring
War sounds frae hell.

What de'il are ye? that I shud ban,
Your neither kin to pat nor pan;
Not *uly pig*, nor *master-cann*
But weel may gie
Mair pleasure to the ear o' man
Than stroak o' thee.

Fleece merchants may look bald, I trow,
Sin a' Auld Reikie's childer now
Maun stap their lugs wi' teats o' woo,
Thy sound to bang,
And keep it frae gawn thro' and thro'
Wi' jarrin twang.

Your noisy tongue, there's nae abideint,
Like scaulding wife's, there is nae guideint:
Whan I'm 'bout ony bus'ness eident,
It's sair to thole;
To deave me, than, ye tak a pride in't
Wi' senseless knoll.

O! war I provost o' the town,
I swear by a' the pow'rs aboon,
I'd bring ye wi' a reesle down;
Nor shud you think
(Sae sair I'd crack and clour your crown)
Again to clink.

For whan I've toom'd the muckle cap,
An' fain wud fa' owr in a nap,
Troth I cud doze as sound's a tap,
Wer't na for thee,
That gies the tither weary chap
To waukin me.

I dreamt ae night I saw Auld Nick;
Quo he, 'this bell o' mine's a trick,
'A wylie piece o' politic,
'A cunnin snare
'To trap fock in a cloven stick,
''Ere they're aware.

'As lang's my dautit bell hings there,
'A' body at the kirk will skair;
'Quo they, gif he that preaches there
'Like it can wound,
'We douna care a single hair
'For joyfu' sound.'

If magistrates wi' me wud 'gree,
For ay *tongue-tackit* shud you be,
Nor fleg wi' *antimelody*
                    Sic honest fock,
Whase lugs were never made to dree
                    Thy doolfu' shock.

But far frae thee the *bailies* dwell,
Or they wud scunner at your knell,
Gie the *foul thief* his riven bell,
                    And than, I trow,
The by-word hads, 'the de'il himsel'
                    'Has got his due.'

Hame Content

TO ALL WHOM IT MAY CONCERN

Some fock, like *Bees*, fu glegly rin
To bykes bang'd fu' o' strife and din,
And thieve and huddle crumb by crumb,
Till they have scrapt the dautit *Plumb*,
Then craw fell crously o' their wark,
Tell o'er their turners *mark* by *mark*,
Yet darna think to lowse the pose,
To aid their neighbours ails and woes.
    Gif *Gowd* can fetter thus the heart,
And gar us act sae base a part,
Shall *Man*, a niggard near-gawn elf!
Rin to the tether's end for pelf;
Learn ilka cunzied scoundrel's trick,
Whan a's done sell his saul to *Nick*:
I trow they've coft the purchase dear,
That gang sic lengths for warldly gear.
    Now whan the *Dog-day* heats begin
To birsel and to peel the skin,
May I lie streekit at my ease,
Beneath the caller shady trees,
(Far frae the din o' Borrowstown,)
Whar water plays the haughs bedown,

To jouk the simmer's rigor there,
And breath a while the caller air
'Mang herds, an' honest cottar fock,
That till the farm and feed the flock;
Careless o' mair, wha never fash
To lade their *kist* wi' useless *cash*,
But thank the *gods* for what they've sent
O' health eneugh, and blyth content,
An' *pith*, that helps them to stravaig
Our ilka cleugh and ilka craig,
Unkend to a' the weary granes
That aft arise frae gentler banes,
On easy-chair that pamper'd lie,
Wi' banefu' viands gustit high,
And turn and fald their weary clay,
To rax and gaunt the live-lang day.
    Ye sages, tell, was man e'er made
To dree this hatefu' sluggard trade?
Steekit frae Nature's beauties a'
That daily on his presence ca';
At hame to girn, and whinge, and pine
For fav'rite dishes, fav'rite wine:
Come then, shake off thir sluggish ties,
And wi' the bird o' dawning rise;
On ilka bauk the clouds hae spread
Wi' blobs o' dew a pearly bed;
Frae falds nae mair the owsen rout,
But to the fatt'ning clever lout,
Whare they may feed at heart's content,
Unyokit frae their winter's stent.
    Unyoke then, man, an' binna sweer
To ding a hole in ill-haind gear;
O think that *eild*, wi' wyly fitt,
Is wearing nearer bit by bit;
Gin yence he claws you wi' his paw,
What's siller for? Fiend haet awa,
But *gowden* playfair, that may please
The second *Sharger* till he dies.
    Some daft chiel reads, and takes advice;
The chaise is yokit in a trice;
Awa drives he like huntit de'il,

And scarce tholes *time* to cool his wheel,
Till he's Lord kens how far awa,
At Italy, or Well o' Spaw,
Or to Montpelier's safter air;
For far aff *fowls* hae *feathers* fair.
There rest him weel; for eith can we
Spare mony glakit gouks like he;
They'll tell whare *Tibur's* waters rise;
What *sea* receives the drumly prize,
That never wi' their feet hae mett
The *marches* o' their ain estate.
The *Arno* and the *Tibur* lang
Hae run fell clear in Roman sang;
But, save the reverence of schools!
They're baith but lifeless dowy pools.
Dought they compare wi' bonny Tweed,
As clear as ony lammer-bead?
Or are their shores mair sweet and gay
Than Fortha's haughs or banks o' Tay?
Tho' there the herds can jink the show'rs
'Mang thriving vines an' myrtle bow'rs,
And blaw the reed to kittle strains,
While echo's tongue commends their pains,
Like ours, they canna warm the heart
Wi' simple, saft, bewitching art.
On Leader haughs an' Yarrow braes,
Arcadian herds wad tyne their lays,
To hear the mair melodious sounds
That live on our *poetic* grounds.
Come, *Fancy*, come, and let us tread
The simmer's flow'ry velvet bed,
And a' your *springs* delightfu' lowse
On *Tweeda*'s banks or *Cowdenknows*,
That, ta'en wi' thy inchanting sang,
Our Scottish lads may round ye thrang,
Sae pleas'd, they'll never fash again
To court you on Italian plain;
Soon will they guess ye only wear
The simple garb o' *Nature* here;
Mair comely far, an' fair to sight
Whan in her easy cleething dight,

Than in disguise ye was before
On Tibur's, or on Arno's shore.
   O *Bangour*! now the hills and dales
Nae mair gi'e back thy tender tales!
The birks on Yarrow now deplore
Thy mournfu' muse has left the shore:
Near what bright burn or chrystal spring
Did you your winsome whistle hing?
The muse shall there, wi' *wat'ry* eie,
Gi'e the dunk swaird a tear for thee;
And Yarrow's genius, dowy dame!
Shall there forget her blude-stain'd stream,
On thy sad grave to seek repose,
Wha mourn'd her fate, condol'd her woes.

To the Principal and Professors of the University of St Andrews, on their superb treat to Dr Samuel Johnson

St Andrews town may look right gawsy,
Nae grass will grow upon her cawsey,
Nor wa'-flow'rs of a yellow dye,
Glour dowy o'er her *Ruins* high,
Sin *Samy's* head weel pang'd wi' lear
Has seen the *Alma Mater* there:
Regents, my winsome billy boys!
'Bout him you've made an unco noise;
Nae doubt for him your bells wad clink,
To find him upon Eden's brink,
An' a' things nicely set in order,
Wad kep him on the Fifan border:
I'se warrant now frae France an' Spain,
Baith *Cooks* and *Scullions* mony ane
Wad gar the pats an' kettles tingle
Around the college kitchen ingle,
To fleg frae a' your craigs the roup,
Wi' reeking het and crieshy soup;
And *snails* and *puddocks* mony hunder
Wad beeking lie the hearth-stane under,
Wi' roast and boild, an' a' kin kind,
To heat the body, cool the mind.

But hear me lads! gin I'd been there,
How I wad trimm'd the bill o' fare!
For ne'er sic surly wight as he
Had met wi' sic respect frae me,
Mind ye what *Sam*, the lying loun!
Has in his Dictionar laid down?
That Aits in England are a feast
To cow an' horse, an' sican beast,
While in Scots ground this growth was common
To gust the gab o' *Man* an' *Woman.*
Tak tent, ye *Regents*! then, an' hear
My list o' gudely hamel gear,
Sic as ha'e often rax'd the wyme
O' blyther fallows mony time;
Mair hardy, souple, steive an' swank,
Than ever stood on *Samy's* shank.
Imprimis, then, a haggis fat,
Weel tottl'd in a seything pat,
Wi' *spice* and *ingans* weel ca'd thro',
Had help'd to gust the stirrah's mow,
And plac'd itsel in truncher clean
Before the gilpy's glowrin een.
Secundo, then a gude sheep's head
Whase hide was singit, never flead,
And four black trotters cled wi' girsle,
Bedown his throat had learn'd to hirsle.
What think ye neist, o' gude fat brose
To clag his ribs? a dainty dose!
And white and bloody puddins routh,
To gar the Doctor skirl, O Drouth!
Whan he cou'd never houp to merit
A cordial o' reaming claret,
But thraw his nose, and brize and pegh
O'er the contents o' sma' ale quegh:
Then let his wisdom girn an' snarl
O'er a weel-tostit girdle farl,
An' learn, that maugre o' his wame,
Ill bairns are ay best heard at hame.
Drummond, lang syne, o' Hawthornden,
The wyliest an' best o' men,
Has gi'en you dishes ane or mae,

That wad ha' gard his grinders play,
Not to *roast beef*, old England's life,
But to the auld *east nook of Fife*,
Whare Creilian crafts cou'd weel ha'e gi'en
Scate-rumples to ha'e clear'd his een;
Then neist, whan *Samy's* heart was faintin,
He'd lang'd for scate to mak him wanton.
Ah! willawins, for Scotland now,
Whan she maun stap ilk birky's mow
Wi' eistacks, grown as 'tware in pet
In foreign land, or green-house het,
When cog o' brose an' cutty spoon
Is a' our cottar childer's boon,
Wha thro' the week, till Sunday's speal,
Toil for pease-clods an' gude lang kail.
Devall then, Sirs, and never send
For daintiths to regale a friend,
Or, like a torch at baith ends burning,
Your house'll soon grow mirk and mourning.
What's this I hear some cynic say?
Robin, ye loun! it's nae fair play;
Is there nae ither subject rife
To clap your thumb upon but Fife?
Gi'e o'er, young man, you'll meet your corning,
Than caption war, or charge o' horning;
Some canker'd surly sour-mow'd carline
Bred near the abbey o' Dumfarline,
Your shoulders yet may gi'e a lounder,
An' be of verse the mal-confounder.
Come on ye blades! but 'ere ye tulzie,
Or hack our flesh wi' sword or gulzie,
Ne'er shaw your teeth, nor look like stink,
Nor o'er an empty bicker blink:
What weets the wizen an' the wyme,
Will mend your prose and heal my rhyme.

ROBERT BURNS

The Twa Dogs

'Twas in that place o' *Scotland*'s isle,
That bears the name o' auld king *Coil*,
Upon a bonie day in June,
When wearing thro' the afternoon,
Twa Dogs, that were na thrang at hame,
Forgather'd ance upon a time.

The first I'll name, they ca'd him *Caesar*,
Was keepet for his Honor's pleasure;
His hair, his size, his mouth, his lugs,
Show'd he was nane o' Scotland's dogs;
But whalpet some place far abroad,
Whar sailors gang to fish for Cod.

His locked, letter'd braw brass-collar,
Show'd him the *gentleman* an' *scholar;*
But tho' he was o' high degree,
The fient a pride na pride had he,
But wad hae spent an hour caressan,
Ev'n wi' a Tinkler-gipsey's *messan*:
At *Kirk* or *Market*, *Mill* or *Smiddie*,
Nae tawtied *tyke*, tho' e'er sae duddie,
But he wad stan't, as glad to see him,
An' stroan't on stanes an' hillocks wi' him.

The tither was a *ploughman's collie*,
A rhyming, ranting, raving billie,
Wha for his friend an' comrade had him,
And in his freaks had *Luath* ca'd him;
After some dog in *Highlan Sang*,
Was made lang syne, lord knows how lang.

He was a gash an' faithfu' *tyke*,
As ever lap a sheugh, or dyke!
His honest, sonsie, baws'nt *face*,
Ay gat him friends in ilka place;
His *breast* was white, his towzie *back*,

Weel clad wi' coat o' glossy black;
His gawsie tail, wi' upward curl,
Hung owre his hurdies wi' a swirl.

Nae doubt but they were fain o' ither,
An' unco pack an' thick the gither;
Wi' social *nose* whyles snuff'd an' snowcket;
Whyles mice an' modewurks they howcket;
Whyles scour'd awa in lang excursion,
An' worry'd ither in *diversion*;
Till tir'd at last wi' mony a farce,
They set them down upon their arse:
An' there began a lang digression
About the *lords o' the creation.*

CAESAR

I've aften wonder'd, honest *Luath,*
What sort o' life poor dogs like you have;
An' when the *gentry*'s life I saw,
What way *poor bodies* liv'd ava.

Our *Laird* gets in his racked rents,
His coals, his kane, an' a' his stents;
He rises when he likes himsel;
His flunkies answer at the bell;
He ca's his coach; he ca's his horse;
He draws a bonie, silken purse
As lang's my *tail,* whare thro' the steeks,
The yellow, letter'd *Geordie* keeks.

Frae morn to een it's nought but toiling,
At baking, roasting, frying, boiling:
An' tho' the gentry first are steghan,
Yet ev'n the *ha' folk* fill their peghan
Wi' sauce, ragouts, an' sic like trashtrie,
That's little short o' downright wastrie.
Our *Whipper-in,* wee, blastiet wonner,
Poor, worthless elf, it eats a dinner,
Better than ony *Tenant-man*
His Honor has in a' the lan':
An' what poor *Cot-folk* pit their painch in,
I own it's past my comprehension. –

LUATH

Trowth, *Caesar*, whyles they're fash'd eneugh;
A *Cotter* howckan in a sheugh,
Wi' dirty stanes biggan a dyke,
Bairan a quarry, an' sic like,
Himsel, a wife, he thus sustains,
A smytrie o' wee, duddie weans,
An' nought but his han'-daurk, to keep
Them right an' tight in *thack an' raep.*

An' when they meet wi' sair disasters,
Like loss o' health, or want o' masters,
Ye maist wad think, a wee touch langer,
An' they maun starve o' cauld an' hunger:
But how it comes, I never kent yet,
They're maistly wonderfu' contented;
An' buirdly chiels, an' clever hizzies,
Are bred in sic a way as this is.

CAESAR

But then, to see how ye're negleket,
How huff'd, an cuff'd, an disrespeket!
Lord man, our gentry care as little
For *delvers, ditchers,* an' sic cattle;
They gang as saucy by poor folk,
As I wad by a stinkan brock.

I've notic'd, on our Laird's *court-day*,
An' mony a time my heart's been wae,
Poor *tenant-bodies*, scant o' cash,
How they maun thole a *factor's* snash;
He'll *stamp* an' threaten, curse an' swear,
He'll *apprehend* them, *poind* their gear,
While they maun stand, wi' aspect humble,
An' hear it a', an' fear an' tremble!

I see how folk live that hae riches,
But surely poor-folk maun be *wretches*!

LUATH

They're no sae wretched 's ane wad think;
Tho' constantly on poortith's brink,

They're sae accustom'd wi' the sight,
The view o't gies them little fright.

Then chance an' fortune are sae guided,
They're ay in less or mair provided;
An' tho' fatigu'd wi' close employment,
A blink o' rest's a sweet enjoyment.

The dearest comfort o' their lives,
Their grushie weans, an' faithfu' wives;
The *prattling things* are just their pride,
That sweetens a' their fire-side.

An' whyles, twalpennie-worth o' *nappy*
Can mak the bodies unco happy;
They lay aside their private cares,
To mind the Kirk an' State affairs;
They'll talk o' *patronage* an' *priests,*
Wi' kindling fury i' their breasts,
Or tell what new taxation's comin,
An' ferlie at the folk in *Lon'on.*

As bleak-fac'd Hallowmass returns,
They get the jovial, rantan *Kirns,*
When *rural life,* of ev'ry station,
Unite in common recreation;
Love blinks, Wit slaps, an' social Mirth
Forgets there's *care* upo' the earth.

That *merry day* the year begins,
They bar the door on frosty win's;
The nappy reeks wi' mantling ream,
An' sheds a heart-inspiring steam;
The luntan pipe, an' sneeshin mill,
Are handed round wi' right guid will;
The cantie, auld folks, crackan crouse,
The young anes rantan thro' the house –
My heart has been sae fain to see them,
That I for joy hae *barket* wi' them.

Still it's owre true that ye hae said,
Sic game is now owre aften play'd;

There's mony a creditable *stock*
O' decent, honest, fawsont folk,
Are riven out baith root an' branch,
Some rascal's pridefu' greed to quench,
Wha thinks to knit himsel the faster
In favor wi' some *gentle Master,*
Wha, aiblins, thrang a parliamentin,
For *Britain's guid* his saul indentin –

CAESAR

Haith lad, ye little ken about it;
For Britain's guid! guid faith! I doubt it.
Say rather, gaun as *Premiers* lead him,
An' saying *aye* or *no*'s they bid him:
At Operas an' Plays parading,
Mortgaging, gambling, masquerading:
Or maybe, in a frolic daft,
To *Hague* or *Calais* takes a waft,
To make a *tour* an' take a whirl,
To learn *bon ton* an' see the worl'.

There, at *Vienna* or *Versailles,*
He rives his father's auld entails;
Or by *Madrid* he takes the rout,
To thrum *guittarres* an' fecht wi' *nowt*;
Or down *Italian Vista* startles,
Whore-hunting amang groves o' myrtles:
Then bowses drumlie *German-water,*
To make himsel look fair an' fatter,
An' purge the bitter ga's an' cankers,
O' curst Venetian bores an' chancres.
For Britain's guid! for her destruction!
Wi' dissipation, feud an' faction!

LUATH

Hech man! dear sirs! is that the gate,
They waste sae mony a braw estate!
Are we sae foughten an' harass'd
For gear to gang that gate at last!

O would they stay aback frae courts,
An' please themsels wi' countra sports,

It wad for ev'ry ane be better,
The *Laird*, the *Tenant*, an' the *Cotter*!
For thae frank, rantan, ramblan billies,
Fient haet o' them 's illhearted fellows;
Except for breakin o' their timmer,
Or speakin lightly o' their *Limmer*;
Or shootin of a hare or moorcock,
The ne'er-a-bit they're ill to poor folk.

But will ye tell me, master *Caesar*,
Sure *great folk's* life's a life o' pleasure?
Nae cauld nor hunger e'er can steer them,
The vera thought o't need na fear them.

CAESAR
Lord man, were ye but whyles where I am,
The *gentles* ye wad ne'er envy them!

It's true, they needna starve or sweat,
Thro' Winter's cauld, or Summer's heat;
They've nae sair-wark to craze their banes,
An' fill *auld-age* wi' grips an' granes:
But *human-bodies* are sic fools,
For a' their Colledges an' Schools,
That when nae *real* ills perplex them,
They *mak* enow themsels to vex them;
An' ay the less they hae to sturt them,
In like proportion, less will hurt them.

A country fellow at the pleugh,
His *acre's* till'd, he's right eneugh;
A country girl at her wheel,
Her *dizzen's* done, she's unco weel;
But Gentlemen, an' Ladies warst,
Wi' ev'n down *want o' wark* they're curst.
They loiter, lounging, lank an' lazy;
Tho' deil-haet ails them, yet uneasy;
Their days, insipid, dull an' tasteless,
Their nights, unquiet, lang an' restless.

An' ev'n their sports, their balls an' races,
Their galloping thro' public places,

There's sic parade, sic pomp an' art,
The joy can scarcely reach the heart.

The *Men* cast out in *party-matches*,
Then sowther a' in deep debauches.
Ae night, they're mad wi' drink an' whoring,
Niest day their life is past enduring.

The *Ladies* arm-in-arm in clusters,
As great an' gracious a' as sisters;
But hear their *absent thoughts* o' ither,
They're a' run-deils an' jads the gither.
Whyles, owre the wee bit cup an' platie,
They sip the *scandal-potion* pretty;
Or lee-lang nights, wi' crabbet leuks,
Pore owre the devil's *pictur'd beuks*;
Stake on a chance a farmer's stackyard,
An' cheat like ony *unhang'd blackguard.*

There's some exceptions, man an' woman;
But this is Gentry's life in common.

By this, the sun was out o' sight,
An' darker gloamin brought the night:
The *bum-clock* humm'd wi' lazy drone,
The kye stood rowtan i' the loan;
When up they gat, an' shook their lugs,
Rejoic'd they were na *men* but *dogs;*
An' each took off his several way,
Resolv'd to meet some ither day.

Holy Willie's Prayer

And send the Godly in a pet to pray – *Pope.*

ARGUMENT

Holy Willie was a rather oldish batchelor Elder in the parish of Mauchline, and much and justly famed for that polemical chattering which ends in tippling Orthodoxy, and for that Spiritualized Bawdry which refines to Liquorish Devotion. In a Sessional process with a gentleman in Mauchline, a Mr Gavin Hamilton, Holy

Willie, and his priest, father Auld, after full hearing in the Presbytry of Ayr, came off but second best; owing partly to the oratorical powers of Mr Robt. Aiken, Mr Hamilton's Counsel; but chiefly to Mr Hamilton's being one of the most irreproachable and truly respectable characters in the country. On losing his Process, the Muse overheard him at his devotions as follows –

O thou that in the heavens does dwell!
Wha, as it pleases best thysel,
Sends ane to heaven and ten to hell,
A' for thy glory!
And no for ony gude or ill
They've done before thee. –

I bless and praise thy matchless might,
When thousands thou has left in night,
That I am here before thy sight,
For gifts and grace,
A burning and a shining light
To a' this place. –

What was I, or my generation,
That I should get such exaltation?
I, wha deserv'd most just damnation,
For broken laws
Sax thousand years ere my creation,
Thro' Adam's cause!

When from my mother's womb I fell,
Thou might hae plunged me deep in hell,
To gnash my gooms, and weep, and wail,
In burning lakes,
Where damned devils roar and yell
Chain'd to their stakes. –

Yet I am here, a chosen sample,
To shew thy grace is great and ample:
I'm here, a pillar o' thy temple
Strong as a rock,
A guide, a ruler and example
To a' thy flock. –

But yet – O Lord – confess I must –
At times I'm fash'd wi' fleshly lust;
And sometimes too, in warldly trust
Vile Self gets in;
But thou remembers we are dust,
Defil'd wi' sin. –

O Lord – yestreen – thou kens – wi' Meg –
Thy pardon I sincerely beg!
O may't ne'er be a living plague,
To my dishonor!
And I'll ne'er lift a lawless leg
Again upon her. –

Besides, I farther maun avow,
Wi' Leezie's lass, three times – I trow –
But Lord, that Friday I was fou
When I cam near her;
Or else, thou kens, thy servant true
Wad never steer her. –

Maybe thou lets this fleshly thorn
Buffet thy servant e'en and morn,
Lest he o'er proud and high should turn,
That he's sae gifted;
If sae, thy hand maun e'en be borne
Untill thou lift it. –

Lord bless thy Chosen in this place,
For here thou has a chosen race;
But God, confound their stubborn face,
And blast their name,
Wha bring thy rulers to disgrace
And open shame. –

Lord mind Gaun Hamilton's deserts!
He drinks, and swears, and plays at cartes,
Yet has sae mony taking arts
Wi' Great and Sma',
Frae God's ain priest the people's hearts
He steals awa. –

And when we chasten'd him therefore,
Thou kens how he bred sic a splore,
And set the warld in a roar
O' laughin at us:
Curse thou his basket and his store,
Kail and potatoes. –

Lord hear my earnest cry and prayer
Against the Presbytry of Ayr!
Thy strong right hand, Lord, make it bare
Upon their heads!
Lord visit them, and dinna spare,
For their misdeeds!

O Lord my God, that glib-tongu'd Aiken!
My very heart and flesh are quaking
To think how I sat, sweating, shaking,
And pass'd wi' dread,
While Auld wi' hingin lip gaed sneaking
And hid his head!

Lord, in thy day o' vengeance try him!
Lord visit him that did employ him!
And pass not in thy mercy by them,
Nor hear their prayer;
But for thy people's sake destroy them,
And dinna spare!

But Lord, remember me and mine
Wi' mercies temporal and divine!
That I for grace and gear may shine,
Excell'd by nane!
And a' the glory shall be thine!
Amen! Amen!

Address to the Deil

O Prince, O chief of many throned pow'rs,
That led th' embattl'd Seraphim to war –
Milton.

O thou, whatever title suit thee!
Auld Hornie, Satan, Nick, or Clootie,
Wha in yon cavern grim an' sooty
Clos'd under hatches,
Spairges about the brunstane cootie,
To scaud poor wretches!

Hear me, *auld Hangie,* for a wee,
An' let poor, *damned bodies* bee;
I'm sure sma' pleasure it can gie,
Ev'n to a *deil,*
To skelp an' scaud poor dogs like me,
An' hear us squeel!

Great is thy pow'r, an' great thy fame;
Far ken'd, an' noted is thy name;
An' tho' yon *lowan heugh's* thy hame,
Thou travels far;
An' faith! thou's neither lag nor lame,
Nor blate nor scaur.

Whyles, rangin like a roaring lion,
For prey, a' holes an' corners tryin;
Whyles, on the strong-wing'd Tempest flyin,
Tirlain the *kirks*;
Whyles, in the human bosom pryin,
Unseen thou lurks.

I've heard my rev'rend *Graunie* say,
In lanely glens ye like to stray;
Or where auld, ruin'd castles, gray,
Nod to the moon,
Ye fright the nightly wand'rer's way,
Wi' eldritch croon.

When twilight did my *Graunie* summon,
To say her pray'rs, douse, honest woman,
Aft 'yont the dyke she's heard you bumman,
Wi' eerie drone;
Or, rustling, thro' the boortries coman,
Wi' heavy groan.

Ae dreary, windy, winter night,
The stars shot down wi' sklentan light,
Wi' you, *mysel,* I gat a fright
Ayont the lough;
Ye, like a *rash-buss,* stood in sight,
Wi' waving sugh:

The cudgel in my nieve did shake,
Each bristl'd hair stood like a stake,
When wi' an eldritch, stoor *quaick, quaick,*
Amang the springs,
Awa ye squatter'd like a *drake,*
On whistling wings.

Let *Warlocks* grim, an' wither'd *Hags,*
Tell, how wi' you, on ragweed nags,
They skim the muirs an' dizzy crags,
Wi' wicked speed;
And in kirk-yards renew their leagues,
Owre howcket dead.

Thence, countra wives, wi' toil an' pain,
May plunge an' plunge the *kirn* in vain;
For Och! the yellow treasure's taen,
By witching skill;
An' dawtit, twal-pint *Hawkie*'s gane
As yell's the Bill.

Thence, mystic knots mak great abuse,
On *Young-Guidmen,* fond, keen an' croose;
When the best *warklum* i' the house,
By cantraip wit,
Is instant made no worth a louse,
Just at the bit.

When thowes dissolve the snawy hoord,
An' float the jinglan icy boord,
Then, *Water-kelpies* haunt the foord,
By your direction,
An' nighted Trav'llers are allur'd
To their destruction.

An' aft your moss-traversing *Spunkies*
Decoy the wight that late an' drunk is:
The bleezan, curst, mischievous monkies
Delude his eyes,
Till in some miry slough he sunk is,
Ne'er mair to rise.

When *Masons'* mystic word an' *grip*,
In storms an' tempests raise you up,
Some cock, or cat, your rage maun stop,
Or, strange to tell!
The *youngest Brother* ye wad whip
Aff straught to *Hell*.

Lang syne in *Eden*'s bonie yard,
When youthfu' lovers first were pair'd,
An' all the Soul of Love they shar'd,
The raptur'd hour,
Sweet on the fragrant, flow'ry swaird,
In shady bow'r:

Then you, ye auld, snick-drawing dog!
Ye cam to Paradise incog,
An' play'd on man a cursed brogue,
(Black be your fa'!)
An' gied the infant warld a shog,
'Maist ruin'd a'.

D'ye mind that day, when in a bizz,
Wi' reeket duds, an' reestet gizz,
Ye did present your smoutie phiz
'Mang better folk,
An' sklented on the *man of Uz*
Your spitefu' joke?

An' how ye gat him i' your thrall,
An' brak him out o' house an' hal',
While scabs an' botches did him gall,
Wi' bitter claw,
An' lows'd his ill-tongu'd, wicked *Scawl*
Was warst ava?

But a' your doings to rehearse,
Your wily snares an' fechtin fierce,
Sin' that day *Michael* did you pierce,
Down to this time,
Wad ding a' *Lallan* tongue, or *Erse,*
In Prose or Rhyme.

An' now, auld *Cloots,* I ken ye're thinkan,
A certain *Bardie*'s rantin, drinkin,
Some luckless hour will send him linkan,
To your black pit;
But faith! he'll turn a corner jinkan,
An' cheat you yet.

But fare you weel, auld *Nickie-ben*!
O wad ye tak a thought an' men'!
Ye aiblins might – I dinna ken –
Still hae a *stake* –
I'm wae to think upo' yon den,
Ev'n for your sake.

To a Louse, on seeing one on a Lady's Bonnet at Church

Ha! whare ye gaun, ye crowlan ferlie!
Your impudence protects you sairly:
I canna say but ye strunt rarely,
Owre *gawze* and *lace;*
Tho' faith, I fear ye dine but sparely,
On sic a place.

Ye ugly, creepan, blastet wonner,
Detested, shunn'd, by saunt an' sinner,
How daur ye set your fit upon her,
Sae fine a *Lady*!
Gae somewhere else and seek your dinner,
On some poor body.

Swith, in some beggar's haffet squattle;
There ye may creep, and sprawl, and sprattle,
Wi' ither kindred, jumping cattle,
In shoals and nations;
Whare *horn* nor *bane* ne'er daur unsettle
Your thick plantations.

Now haud you there, ye're out o' sight,
Below the fatt'rels, snug and tight,
Na faith ye yet! ye'll no be right,
Till ye've got on it,
The vera tapmost, towrin height
O' *Miss's bonnet.*

My sooth! right bauld ye set your nose out,
As plump an' gray as onie grozet:
O for some rank, mercurial rozet,
Or fell, red smeddum,
I'd give you sic a hearty dose o't,
Wad dress your droddum!

I wad na been surpriz'd to spy
You on an auld wife's *flainen toy*;
Or aiblins some bit duddie boy,
On's *wylecoat*;
But Miss's fine *Lunardi,* fye!
How daur ye do 't?

O *Jenny* dinna toss your head,
An' set your beauties a ' abread!
Ye little ken what cursed speed
The blastie's makin!
Thae *winks* and *finger-ends,* I dread,
Are notice takin!

O wad some Pow'r the giftie gie us
To see oursels as others see us!
It wad frae monie a blunder free us
An' foolish notion:
What airs in dress an' gait wad lea'e us,
And ev'n Devotion!

Address of Beelzebub

To the Rt Honble *John, Earl of Breadalbane,* President of the Rt Honble the *Highland Society,* which met, on the 23d of May last, at the Shakespeare, Covent Garden, to concert ways and means to frustrate the designs of *five hundred Highlanders* who, as the Society were informed by Mr McKenzie of Applecross, were so audacious as to attempt an escape from theire lawful lords and masters whose property they are emigrating from the lands of Mr McDonald of Glengary to the wilds of *Canada,* in search of that fantastic thing – *Liberty* –

Long life, My lord, an' health be yours,
Unskaith'd by hunger'd *Highlan Boors*!
Lord grant, nae duddie, desp'rate beggar,
Wi' durk, claymore, or rusty trigger,
May twin auld *Scotland* o' a *life*,
She likes – as *butchers* like a *knife*!

Faith, you and Applecross were right
To keep the Highlan hounds in sight!
I doubt na! they wad bid nae better
Than let them ance out owre the water;
Then up amang thae lakes an' seas
They'll mak what rules an' laws they please.

Some daring Hancocke, or a Frankline,
May set their *Highlan* bluid a ranklin;
Some Washington again may head them,
Or some *Montgomery,* fearless, lead them;
Till, God knows what may be effected,
When by such *heads* an' *hearts* directed:
Poor, dunghill sons of dirt an' mire,
May to *Patrician rights aspire*;
Nae sage North, now, nor sager Sackville,
To watch an' premier owre the pack vile!
An' whare will ye get Howes an' Clintons
To bring them to a right repentance,
To cowe the rebel generation,
An' save the honor o' the *Nation*?

They! an' be damned! what right hae they
To Meat, or Sleep, or light o' day,
Far less to riches, pow'r, or freedom,
But what your lordship *please to gie them*?

But, hear me, my lord! Glengary, hear!
Your *hand's owre light on them,* I fear:
Your *factors, greives, trustees* an' *bailies*,
I canna say but they do gailies;
They lay aside a' tender mercies
An' tirl the *hallions* to the *birsies;*
Yet, while they're only poin'd, and herriet,
They'll keep their stubborn Highlan spirit.
But smash them! crush them a' to spails!
An' rot the *dyvors* i' the *jails*!
The young dogs, swinge them to the labour,
Let *wark* an' *hunger* mak them sober!
The *hizzies,* if they're oughtlins fausont,
Let them in *Drury Lane* be lesson'd!
An' if the wives, an' dirty brats,
Come thiggan at your doors an' yets,
Flaffan wi' duds, an' grey wi' beese,
Frightan awa your deucks an' geese;
Get out a *horse-whip,* or a *jowler,*
The langest thong, the fiercest growler,
An' gar the tatter'd gipseys pack
Wi' a' their bastarts on their back!

Go on, my lord! I lang to meet you
An' in my *house at hame* to greet you;
Wi' *common lords* ye shanna mingle,
The benmost newk, beside the ingle
At my right hand, assign'd your seat
'Tween *Herod*'s hip, an' *Polycrate;*
Or, if ye on your station tarrow,
Between *Almagro* and *Pizarro;*
A seat, I'm sure ye're weel deservin't;
An' till ye come – your humble servant

Beelzebub.

Hell 1st June Anno Mundi 5790

'When princes and prelates . . .'

Tune: *The Campbells are Coming*

When princes and prelates and het-headed zealots
All Europe hae set in a lowe,
The poor man lies down, nor envies a crown,
And comforts himself with a mowe. –

CHORUS –

And why shouldna poor folk mowe, mowe, mowe,
And why shouldna poor folk mowe:
The great folk hae siller, and houses and lands,
Poor bodies hae naething but mowe. –

2

When Brunswick's great Prince cam a cruising to France,
Republican billies to cowe,
Bauld Brunswic's great Prince wad hae shawn better sense,
At hame with his Princess to mowe.–

And why should na &c.

3

Out over the Rhine proud Prussia wad shine,
To spend his best blood he did vow;
But Frederic had better ne'er forded the water,
But spent as he docht in a mowe. –

And why &c.

4

By sea and by shore! the Emperor swore,
In Paris he'd kick up a row;
But Paris sae ready just leugh at the laddie
And bade him gae tak him a mowe. –

And why &c.

5

Auld Kate laid her claws on poor Stanislaus,
And Poland has bent like a bow:
May the deil in her arse ram a huge prick o' brass!
And damn her in hell with a mowe!

And why &c.

6

But truce with commotions and new-fangled notions,
A bumper I trust you'll allow:
Here's George our gude king and Charlotte his queen
And lang may they tak a gude mowe!

JAMES HOGG

The Village of Balmaquhapple

D'ye ken the big village of Balmaquhapple,
The great muckle village of Balmaquhapple?
'Tis steep'd in iniquity up to the thrapple,
An' what's to become o' poor Balmaquhapple?
Fling a' aff your bannets, an' kneel for your life, fo'ks,
And pray to St Andrew, the god o' the Fife fo'ks;
Gar a' the hills yout wi' sheer vociferation,
And thus you may cry on sic needfu' occasion:

'O, blessed St Andrew, if e'er ye could pity fo'k,
Men fo'k or women fo'k, country or city fo'k,
Come for this aince wi' the auld thief to grapple,
An' save the great village of Balmaquhapple
Frae drinking an' leeing, an' flyting an' swearing,
An' sins that ye wad be affrontit at hearing,
An' cheating an' stealing; O, grant them redemption,
All save an' except the few after to mention:

'There's Johnny the elder, wha hopes ne'er to need ye
Sae pawkie, sae holy, sae gruff, an' sae greedy;
Wha prays every hour as the wayfarer passes,
But aye at a hole where he watches the lasses;
He's cheated a thousand, an' e'en to this day yet,
Can cheat a young lass, or they're leears that say it;
Then gie him his gate; he's sae slee an' sae civil,
Perhaps in the end he may wheedle the devil.

'There's Cappie the cobbler, an' Tammie the tinman,
An Dickie the brewer, an' Peter the skinman,
An' Geordie our deacon, for want of a better,
An' Bess, wha delights in the sins that beset her.
O, worthy St Andrew, we canna compel ye,
But ye ken as weel as a body can tell ye,
If these gang to heaven, we'll a' be sae shockit,
Your garret o' blue will but thinly be stockit.

'But for a' the rest, for the women's sake, save them,
Their bodies at least, an' their sauls, if they have them;
But it puzzles Jock Lesly, an' sma' it avails,
If they dwell in their stamocks, their heads, or their tails.
An' save, without word of confession auricular,
The clerk's bonny daughters, an' Bell in particular;
For ye ken that their beauty's the pride an' the staple
Of the great wicked village of Balmaquhapple!'

The Lass o' Carlisle

I'll sing ye a wee bit sang,
A sang i' the aulden style,
It is of a bonny young lass
Wha lived in merry Carlisle.
An' O but this lass was bonny,
An' O but this lass was braw,
An' she had gowd in her coffers,
An' that was best of a'.
Sing hey, hickerty dickerty,
Hickerty dickerty dear;
The lass that has gowd an' beauty
Has naething on earth to fear!

This lassie had plenty o' wooers,
As beauty an' wealth should hae;
This lassie she took her a man,
An' then she could get nae mae.
This lassie had plenty o' weans,
That keepit her hands astir;
And then she dee'd and was buried,
An' there was an end of her.
Sing hey, hickerty dickerty,
Hickerty dickerty dan,
The best thing in life is to make
The maist o't that we can!

Sir Morgan O'Doherty's Farewell to Scotland

Farewell, farewell, beggarly Scotland,
Cold and beggarly poor countrie!
If ever I cross thy border again,
The muckle deil must carry me.
There's but one tree in a' the land,
And that's the bonnie gallows tree:
The very nowte look to the south,
And wish that they had wings to flee.

Farewell, farewell, beggarly Scotland,
Brose and bannocks, crowdy and kale!
Welcome, welcome, jolly old England,
Laughing lasses and foaming ale!
'Twas when I came to merry Carlisle,
That out I laughed loud laughters three;
And if I cross the Sark again
The muckle deil maun carry me.

Farewell, farewell, beggarly Scotland,
Kiltit kimmers, wi' carroty hair,
Pipers, who beg that your honours would buy
A bawbee's worth of their famished air!
I'd rather keep Cadwaller's goats,
And feast upon toasted cheese and leeks,
Than go back again to the beggarly North,
To herd 'mang loons with bottomless breeks.

SIR WALTER SCOTT

Proud Maisie

Proud Maisie is in the wood,
   Walking so early;
Sweet Robin sits on the bush.
   Singing so rarely.

'Tell me, thou bonny bird,
   When shall I marry me?'
'When six braw gentlemen
   Kirkward shall carry ye.'

'Who makes the bridal bed,
   Birdie, say truly?'
'The grey-headed sexton
   That delves the grave duly.

'The glow-worm o'er grave and stone
   Shall light thee steady.
The owl from the steeple sing,
   "Welcome, proud lady." '

ALLAN CUNNINGHAM

The Wee, Wee German Lairdie

Wha the deil hae we got for a King,
But a wee, wee German lairdie!
An' when we gade to bring him hame,
He was delving in his kail-yardie
Sheughing kail an' dibbling leeks,
Scarce of hose and scant o' breeks,
Up his beggar duds he cleeks,
The wee, wee German lairdie.

An' he's clapt down in our gudeman's chair,
The wee, wee German lairdie;
O' stinking weeds he's brought the seeds,
An' sawed them in our yardie.
He's pu'd the rose o' English clowns,
An' brak the harp o' Irish lowns,
But the thristle tap will jag his thumbs,
The wee, wee German lairdie.

Come up amang the Highland hills,
Thou wee, wee German lairdie;
An' see how Charlie's lang kail thrive,
He dibblit in his yardie.
An' if a stock ye daur to pu',
Or haud the yoking of a pleugh,
We'll break yere sceptre o'er yere mou',
Thou wee bit German lairdie.

Our hills are steep, our glens are deep,
Nor fitting for a yardie;
An' our norlan' thristles winna pu',
Thou wee, wee German lairdie!
An' we've the trenching blades o' weir,
Wad twine ye o' yere German gear;
An' pass ye 'neath the claymore's shear,
Thou feckless German lairdie!

ALEXANDER RODGER

Sawney now the King's come

Air: *Carle an' the King come.*
Written in 1822

Sawney, now the king's come,
Sawney, now the king's come,
Kneel, and kiss his gracious bum,
Sawney, now the king's come.

In Holyroodhouse lodge him snug,
And butter weel his sacred lug,
Wi' stuff wad gar a Frenchman *ugg*,
Sawney, now the king's come.
Sawney, &c.

Tell him he is great and good,
And come o' Scottish royal blood –
To your hunkers – lick his fud –
Sawney, now the king's come.
Sawney, &c.

Tell him he can do nae wrang,
That he's mighty, heigh, and strang,
That you and yours to him belang,
Sawney, now the king's come.
Sawney, &c.

Swear he's sober, chaste, and wise,
Praise his portly shape and size,
Roose his whiskers to the skies,
Sawney, now the king's come.
Sawney, &c.

Mak' your lick-fud bailie core
Fa' down behint him – not before,
His great posteriors to adore,
Sawney, now the king's come.
Sawney, &c.

Mak' your tribe in good black claith,
Extol, till they rin short o' breath,
The great "Defender o' the Faith,"
Sawney, now the king's come.
    Sawney, &c.

Mak' your Peers o' high degree,
Crouching low on bended knee,
Greet him wi' a 'Wha wants me?'
Sawney, now the king's come.
    Sawney, &c.

Mak' his glorious kinship dine
On good sheep-heads and haggis fine,
Hotchpotch, too, Scotch collops syne,
Sawney, now the king's come.
    Sawney, &c.

And if there's in St. James' Square
Ony *thing* that's fat and fair,
Treat him nightly wi' sic ware,
Sawney, now the king's come.
    Sawney, &c.

Shaw him a' your biggings braw,
Your castle, college, brigs, an' a',
Your jail, an' royal forty-twa,
Sawney, now the king's come.
    Sawney, &c.

An' when he rides Auld Reekie through,
To bless you wi' a kingly view,
Charm him wi' your 'Gardyloo,'
Sawney, now the king's come.
    Sawney, &c.

Shaving Banks

OR, MATTHEW'S CALL TO THE WORTHLESS, TO COME AND BE SHAVED O' THEIR SILLER

Being the substance of a speech delivered by Matthew, (not the Evangelist), at a Public Meeting held in the –, on the – day of –, 1818, on the utility of 'Shaving Banks.'

Ho! ye worthless, thriftless trash;
Worthless, because ye haena cash –
Thriftless, because ye try to dash
Like your superiors;
Come hither, till I lay the lash
To your posteriors.

Sae lost are ye to a' reflection –
To wisdom, prudence, circumspection –
That naething but some smart correction
I see will do;
And naething else than pure affection
Mak's me fa' to.

And now, ye thochtless, wairdless sinners,
O' tippling weavers, cotton-spinners,
Smiths, nailers, founders, braziers, tinners,
What right hae ye
To sit down to your flesh-meat dinners –
Your toast and tea?

What right hae ye to sit an' drink
Till ance your e'en begin to blink,
Keeping your families on the brink
O' yawning ruin?
Stop, sirs! – I charge ye, stop an' think
What ye are doin'.

What right hae ye to wear braw claes ,
And strut about on holidays
Alang Clyde side, up Cathkin braes,
Or through the Green,
As thochtless as the brutes that graze
Before your e'en?

What right hae ye at e'en to lie
On gude saft beds, baith warm and dry?
You – wha nae better are than kye!
Troth, scarce sae gude –
And yet ye'll daur wi' us to vie –
Ye hoggish brood!

What right, ye wretches, can ye hae
To siccan gudely things as thae?
Boiled beans, burnt yill, horse rugs an' strae,
Wad be mair fittin' –
Wi' gude sharp shears, to stop you frae
Your brat-begettin'.

Sic goodly things alone are ours;
Brose thrice a-day is a' that's yours;
And that's enough to keep your powers
In working play,
As ye've to toil but sixteen hours
Ilk lawfu' day.

And as for Sundays – troth, I think,
Instead o' wasting precious clink
On base bewitching sinfu' drink,
'Twad set you better
To get but twice, that day, a skink
O' meal and water.

For when your hands nae nocht to do,
Your teeth should be as idle too;
Gude troth, it ill sets folk like you,
When earning naething,
To sit and cram your bellies fou,
Or wear braw claithing.

Ye maun retrench, and live mair canny,
And, while it's summer, gather honey;
That is, lay weekly by what money
Ye're used to waste,
To kep a strait that may come on ye
When looked for least.

Ye may be forced to beg when auld.
Ye may be reft o' house and hald,
And be obliged, 'mid winter's cauld,
To sleep out-by;
The dark-brown clouds your curtain's fauld,
Your roof the sky.

Ye may become the beagle's butt,
Ye may be up in prison shut,
Ye may be on the parish put;
(Faith, quietly speaking,
I'd rather see your thrapples cut,
Your base blood reeking).

But to prevent these numerous ills,
Now is the time to help yoursel's ;
Leave aff your drinking sinfu' gills,
And living high,
And learn, although against your wills,
To lay cash by.

And here's the method ye maun tak',
If siller ye wad try to mak',
As ye hae ne'er yet learned the knack
O' taking care o't,
Hand into us ilk orra plack
That ye can spare o't.

And we'll tak' care o't sure enough,
For we're the lads can guide the stuff;
We winna wair't, like you, on snuff,
Or tea or liquor,
Then quick and lay't into our loof,
We'll haud it sicker.

For we've established *Shaving Banks,*
For shaving o' the lower ranks,
For which we claim the gratefu' thanks,
Withouten flattery,
Of you, wha are but useless blanks
In life's great lottery.

(And Lord, we'll shave you if we can,
By auld George Rose's shaving plan,
Whilk shortly will succeed frae 'Dan
Unto Beersheba,'
In shaving ilka labouring man
As clean's a sybo).

Then hear, ye cyphers o' the State,
If ye'd get forward on your gate,
Rise soon to work, and sit up late,
And toil like niggers,
Else, by my saul, ye'll never rate
Amang the figures.

An aye snib aff the ither groat
Frae whisky stoup and porter pot,
Ne'er letting liquor weet your throat,
While water's cheaper,
And soon ye'll come to hae a note
O' gude bank paper.

And when you've scrapit ane thegither,
By bringing a' your bawbees hither,
Quick, work, and scrape, and get anither;
Confound your blood!
What gars ye shake your heads and swither?
'Tis for your good.

Your goods I mean, and chattels, too,
If we durst tell our motive true;
But we'll keep that hid out o' view
As lang's we can,
Else ye might try, ye stubborn crew,
To thwart our plan.

Come, come, my lads, this is nae hoax,
Here are our books – and here's our box,
We'll put your siller in the stocks;
And when it's there,
Confound you for a set o' blocks,
Gin ye see't mair;

What then? – Ye tim'rous, backward set,
The interest ye'll be sure to get,
The stock will help to pay some debt
John Bull is awn,
Or creesh the sair-worn wheels o' State,
To keep them gaun.

For look ye, it is our intent
To cleek you firm to Government;
Then, when your siller a' is lent
To Van & Co.,
Ye'll stick, while ye can draw a cent,
Come weal or woe.

And doubtless ye'll soon see the day
When ye'll be hugged by Cast-ill-ray,
Sad-mouth himsel' will owre you pray,
And grunt a blessing;
The Regent's muckle gouty tae
Ye'll even get kissing.

And that choice chip o' lucky Hunn,
Wha in St. Stephen's plays buffoon,
Will chat to please you – mak' a pun
To shew his wit,
And girn like ony auld baboon
Cracking a nit.

And a' the loyal in the land
Will come and shake you by the hand,
Wi' a' our treason-hatching band
O' moral spies,
Wha serve us aye, upon demand,
Wi' bags o' lies.

That hopeful brood o' true hell game,
Begot upon the bloated frame
O' that auld venerable dame,
Yclep'd Corruption,
By holy *Sid* – frae you will claim
The friendly grip soon.

And we shall leave nae scheme untried
To get ye a' upon our side,
For though your looks we scarce can bide
When ye come near us,
Yet we maun drap our distant pride
When times grow serious.

But we've anither plan forbye,
Which we intend wi' you to try,
And that is, if you e'er apply
For parish aid,
The fient a plack o' such supply
Ye'll e'er be paid.

And if ye daur to raise a fuss,
Or meet the poor laws to discuss,
Then a' your cash belongs to us,
Which we will keep;
Be therefore ye as calm as puss,
And never cheep.

Or if you do, then, by my faith,
And that, ye'll mind, is nae mock aith,
We'll hae the lads in blood-red claith
Again brought in,
Wi' a' their instruments o' death,
To stop your din.

Anither thing we hae in view,
Though it maun ne'er be tauld to you,
We'll see how far taxation's screw
Will thole a thraw yet,
And hence impose some taxes new
By dint o' law yet.

For we're determined – do ye see,
To keep you low as low can be,
To gar you toil like brutes, that we
Like gods may fare,
And shave you o' the last bawbee
That ye can spare.

Sic are our motives, sic our drift,
For trying this bit loopy shift;
And, thanks to gude, ye want the gift
O' common sense,
Else ye our hale design would sift,
And keep your pence.

Stanzas written on reading in an American newspaper an account of the death of Thomas Paine, author of 'Common Sense', 'The Rights of Man', etc.

Tom Paine is dead – Satan, be on thy guard;
Remember he's thy most inveterate foe;
Get thy strong Pandemonian gates well barr'd,
Nor let him enter thy dark realms below.

Else if thou do, prepare to meet thy fate,
Nor longer vainly boast of being king,
But quit thy throne – throw off thy robes of State,
Thy crown and sceptre from thee quickly fling.

For if his levelling doctrines once get ground,
Thy sooty subjects will in fact rebel,
Pull down thy throne, spread Deism around,
Chop off thy head, and make a – France of Hell.

JANET HAMILTON

Crinoline

Auld Scotlan' gangs yirmin an' chanerin' alane;
She wunners whaur a' her trig lassocks ha'e gane;
She's trampit the kintra, an' socht thro' the toons,
An' fan' the fule hizzies – blawn oot like balloons!

Can they be my lassocks – ance cozie an' cosh,
Weel shapit, weel happit – sae stumpy an' tosh?
Twa coats an' a toush, or a goon, ye may ween,
Were boukie aneuch, wi' what nature had gi'en.

They're aye i' my e'e, an' they're aye i' my gate –
At the kirk I am chirtit maist oot o' my seat;
When caul', to the ingle I needna gae ben,
If Kate an' her crinoline's on the fire-en'.

Whan a lad wi' a lassie foregethers yenoo,
It's no her bricht e'en, or her rosie wee mou',
Her snod cockernony, waist jimpy an' fine,
That first tak's his e'e – it's the big crinoline!

To say that he likes it would juist be a lee –
But ye ken that the big thing attracts aye the wee –
An' the lass that cares nocht 'bout her heart an' her heid,
Tak's care that her crinoline's weel spread abreed.

An' say, if dame Nature wad gi'e at her birth
To ilka wee lassie that's born on the yirth
A bouk o' her ain, that grew bigger ilk year,
Ye'd no be sae prood o' the giftie I fear.

Whan a widow was burnt i' the Indian suttees,
To honour the dead, and the fause gods to please,
The puir heathen body I'm pincht to accuse,
Whan I read o' they crinoline deaths i' the news.

Sae aff wi' the whalebone, the cane, an' the steel!
I likena the crinoline, trouth an' atweel;
It's fule-like an' fashous, it's cheatrie an' boss –
I wad juist ha'e yer cleedin' bien, genty, an' doss.

WILLIAM THOM

Whisperings for the Unwashed

'Tyrants make not slaves – slaves make tyrants.'

Scene: A Town in the North. *Time:* Six o'clock morning.

ENTER: TOWN DRUMMER.

Rubadub, rubadub, row-dow-dow!
The sun is glinting on hill and knowe,
An' saft the pillow to the fat man's pow –
Sae fleecy an' warm the guid '*hame-made*,'
An' cozie the happin o' the farmer's bed.
The feast o' yestreen how it oozes through,
In bell an' blab on his burly brow,
Nought recks he o' drum an' bell,
The girnal's fou an' sure the 'sale;'
The laird an' he can crap an keep –
Weel, weel may he laugh in his gowden sleep.
His dream abounds in stots, or full
Of cow an' corn, calf and bull;
Of cattle shows, of dinner speaks –
Toom, torn, and patch'd like weavers' breeks;
An' sic like meaning hae, I trow,
As rubadub, rubadub, row-dow-dow.

Rubadub, rubadub, row-dow-dow!
Hark, how he waukens the Weavers now!
Wha lie belair'd in a dreamy steep –
A mental swither 'tween death an' sleep –
Wi' hungry wame and hopeless breast,
Their food no feeding, their sleep no rest.
Arouse ye, ye sunken, unravel your rags,
No coin in your coffers, no meal in your bags;
Yet cart, barge, and wagon, with load after load,
Creak mockfully, passing your breadless abode.
The stately stalk of Ceres bears,
But not for you, the bursting ears;
In vain to you the lark's lov'd note,
For you no summer breezes float,

Grim winter through your hovel pours –
Dull, din, and healthless vapour yours.
The nobler Spider weaves alone,
And feels the little web his *own,*
His hame, his fortress, foul or fair,
Nor factory whipper swaggers there.
Should ruffian wasp, or flaunting fly
Touch his lov'd lair, *'tis touch and die!*
Supreme in rags, ye weave, in tears,
The shining robe your murderer wears;
Till worn, at last, to very '*waste*,'
A hole to die in, at the best;
And, dead, the session saints begrudge ye
The twa-three deals in death to lodge ye;
They grudge the grave wherein to drap ye,
An' grudge the very *muck* to hap ye.

* * * *

Rubadub, rubadub, row-dow-dow!
The drunkard clasps his aching brow;
And there be they, in their squalor laid,
The supperless brood on loathsome bed;
Where the pallid mother croons to rest,
The withering babe at her milkless breast.
She, wakeful, views the risen day
Break gladless o'er her home's decay,
And God's blest light a ghastly glare
Of grey and deathy dimness there.
In all things near, or sight or sounds,
Sepulchral rottenness abounds;
Yet he, the sovereign filth, will prate,
In stilted terms, of Church and State,
As things that *he* would mould anew –
Could all but his brute self subdue.
Ye vilest of the crawling things,
Lo! how well the fetter clings
To recreant collar! Oh, may all
The self-twined lash unbroken fall,
Nor hold until our land is free'd
Of craven, crouching slugs, that breed
In fetid holes, and, day by day,
Yawn their unliving life away!

But die they will not, cannot – why?
They live not – therefore, cannot die.
In soul's dark deadness dead are they,
Entomb'd in thick corkswollen clay.
What tho' they yield their fulsome breath,
The change but mocks the name of death,
Existence, skulking from the sun,
In misery many, in meanness one.
When brave hearts would the fight renew,
Hope, weeping, withering points to you!

Arouse ye, but neither with bludgeon nor blow,
Let *mind* be your armour, *darkness* your foe;
'Tis not in the ramping of demagogue rage,
Nor yet in the mountebank patriot's page,
In sounding palaver, nor pageant, I ween,
In blasting of trumpet, nor vile tambourine;
For these are but mockful and treacherous things –
The thorns that 'crackle' to sharpen their stings.
When fair Science gleams over city and plain,
When Truth walks abroad all unfetter'd again,
When the breast glows to Love and the brow beams
in Light –
Oh! hasten it Heaven! *Man longs for his right.*

Chaunts for Churls

Ken ye carls howkin' out,
Wha darena howk within,
Holy wark gies your sark,
Yer siller, an' yer sheen.
Gae mak' a fyke to feed the kirk,
Although ye starve yer kin,
An' ye'll be lauchin' lairdies yet,
Youplin in yer yardies yet,
Heich ayont the moon.

We've kirks in ilka corner,
An' wow but we can preach;
Timmer tap, little sap,
Onything for bread.
Their sermons in the draw well,
Drink till ye stretch.
We're clean sairt sookin' at it,
The deil's dazed lookin' at it:
Daud him on the head.

Sawtan said to Sin, 'Bairn,
Whither shall we flee,
Wi' your pit, an' my net,
An' a' our little deils?
Sic musterin' o' ministers,
They'll droon us in the sea;
Wi' their auld taurds whippin' at us,
New brooms sweepin' at us:
Hunted to the heels.'

'Sit siccar on yer seat, Sawtan,
Binna feart o' wark;
In but or ben, heicht or glen,
Ye'll get a deevil nurst;
For priests hae crusht the crousie out,
They're fechtin' in the dark,
An' gouks a' tearin' ither,
Shorin' ither, shearin' ither,
Bannin' like to burst.

'While the black breed's breedin' aye,
Like weel corned beasts,
Out or in sic a din,
Moderate or high,
I'll big a house wi' beadles yet,
An' thack it wi' orra priests;
For they're aye blythe bodies to me,
Aye make roadies to me,
Unco few gae by.'

CHARLES, LORD NEAVES

Let us all be Unhappy on Sunday: A Lyric for Saturday Night

We zealots, made up of stiff clay,
  The sour-looking children of sorrow,
While not over-jolly today,
  Resolve to be wretched tomorrow.
We can't for a certainty tell
  What mirth may molest us on Monday;
But, at least, to begin the week well,
  Let us all be unhappy on Sunday.

That day, the calm season of rest,
  Shall come to us freezing and frigid;
A gloom all our thoughts shall invest,
  Such as Calvin would call over-rigid,
With sermons from morning to night,
  We'll strive to be decent and dreary:
To preachers a praise and delight,
  Who ne'er think that sermons can weary.

All tradesmen cry up their own wares;
  In this they agree well together:
The Mason by stone and lime swears;
  The Tanner is always for leather;
The Smith still for iron would go;
  The Schoolmaster stands up for teaching;
And the Parson would have you to know,
  There's nothing on earth like his preaching.

The face of kind Nature is fair;
  But our system obscures its effulgence:
How sweet is a breath of fresh air!
  But our rules don't allow the indulgence.
These gardens, their walks and green bowers,
  Might be free to the poor man for one day;
But no, the glad plants and gay flowers
  Mustn't bloom or smell sweetly on Sunday.

What though a good precept we strain
  Till hateful and hurtful we make it!
What though, in thus pulling the rein,
  We may draw it as tight as to break it!
Abroad we forbid folks to roam,
  For fear they get social or frisky;
But of course they can sit still at home,
  And get dismally drunk upon whisky.

Then, though we can't certainly tell
  How mirth may molest us on Monday;
At least, to begin the week well,
  Let us all be unhappy on Sunday.

ROBERT LOUIS STEVENSON

The Counterblast Ironical

It's strange that God should fash to frame
The yearth and lift sae hie,
An' clean forget to explain the same
To a gentleman like me.

They gutsy, donnered ither folk,
Their weird they weel may dree;
But why present a pig in a poke
To a gentleman like me?

They ither folk their parritch eat
An' sup their sugared tea;
But the mind is no to be wyled wi' meat
Wi' a gentleman like me.

They ither folk, they court their joes
At gloamin' on the lea;
But they're made of a commoner clay, I suppose,
Than a gentleman like me.

They ither folk, for richt or wrang,
They suffer, bleed, or dee;
But a' thir things are an emp'y sang
To a gentleman like me.

It's a different thing that I demand,
Tho' humble as can be –
A statement fair in my Maker's hand
To a gentleman like me:

A clear account writ fair an' broad,
An' a plain apologie;
Or the deevil a ceevil word to God
From a gentleman like me.

JOHN DAVIDSON

The Crystal Palace

Contraption, – that's the bizarre, proper slang,
Eclectic word, for this portentous toy,
The flying-machine, that gyrates stiffly, arms
A-kimbo, so to say, and baskets slung
From every elbow, skating in the air.
Irreverent, we; but Tartars from Thibet
May deem Sir Hiram the Grandest Lama, deem
His volatile machinery best, and most
Magnific, rotatory engine, meant
For penitence and prayer combined, whereby
Petitioner as well as orison
Are spun about in space: a solemn rite
Before the portal of that fane unique,
Victorian temple of commercialism,
Our very own eighth wonder of the world,
The Crystal Palace.

So sublime! Like some
Immense crustacean's gannoid skeleton,
Unearthed, and cleansed, and polished! Were it so
Our paleontological respect
Would shield it from derision; but when a shed,
Intended for a palace, looks as like
The fossil of a giant myriapod! . . .
'Twas Isabey – sarcastic wretch! – who told
A young aspirant, studying tandem art
And medicine, that he certainly was born
To be a surgeon: 'When you try,' he said,
'To paint a boat you paint a tumour.'

No
Idea of its purpose, and no mood
Can make your glass and iron beautiful.
Colossal ugliness may fascinate
If something be expressed; and time adopts
Ungainliest stone and brick and ruins them
To beauty; but a building lacking life,

A house that must not mellow or decay? –
'Tis nature's outcast. Moss and lichen? Stains
Of weather? From the first Nature said 'No!
Shine there unblessed, a witness of my scorn!
I love the ashlar and the well-baked clay;
My seasons can adorn them sumptuously:
But you shall stand rebuked till men ashamed,
Abhor you, and destroy you and repent!'

But come: here's crowd; here's mob; a gala day!
The walks are black with people: no one hastes;
They all pursue their purpose business-like –
The polo-ground, the cycle-track; but most
Invade the palace glumly once again.
It is 'again'; you feel it in the air –
Resigned habitués on every hand:
And yet agog; abandoned, yet concerned!
They can't tell why they come; they only know
They must shove through the holiday somehow.

In the main floor the fretful multitude
Circulates from the north nave to the south
Across the central transept – swish and tread
And murmur, like a seaboard's mingled sound.
About the sideshows eddies swirl and swing:
Distorting mirrors; waltzing-tops – wherein
Couples are wildly spun contrariwise
To your revolving platform; biographs,
Or rifle-ranges; panoramas: choose!

As stupid as it was last holiday?
They think so – every whit! Outside, perhaps?
A spice of danger in the flying-machine?
A few who passed that whirligig, their hopes
On higher things, return disconsolate
To try the Tartar's volant oratory.
Others again, no more anticipant
Of any active business in their own
Diversion, joining stalwart folk who sought
At once the polo-ground, the cycle-track,
Accept the ineludible; while some

(Insidious anti-climax here) frequent
The water-entertainments – shallops, chutes
And rivers subterrene: – thus, passive, all,
Like savages bewitched, submit at last
To be the dupes of pleasure, sadly gay –
Victims, and not companions, of delight.

Not all! The garden-terrace: – hark, behold,
Music and dancing! People by themselves
Attempting happiness! A box of reeds –
Accordion, concertina, seraphine –
And practised fingers charm advertent feet!
The girls can dance; but, O their heavy-shod,
Unwieldy swains! – No matter: – hatless heads,
With hair undone, eyes shut and cheeks aglow
On blissful shoulders lie: – such solemn youths
Sustaining ravished donahs! Round they swing,
In time or out, but unashamed and all
Enchanted with the glory of the world.
And look! – Among the laurels on the lawns
Torn coats and ragged skirts, starved faces flushed
With passion and with wonder! – hid away
Avowedly; but seen – and yet not seen!
None laugh; none point; none notice: multitude
Remembers and forgives; unwisest love
Is sacrosanct upon a holiday.
Out of the slums, into the open air
Let loose for once, their scant economies
Already spent, what was there left to do?
O sweetly, tenderly, devoutly think,
Shepherd and shepherdess in Arcady!

A heavy shower; the Palace fills; begins
The business and the office of the day,
The eating and the drinking – only real
Enjoyment to be had, they tell you straight
Now that the shifty weather fails them too.
But what's the pother here, the blank dismay?
Money has lost its value at the bars:
Like tavern-tokens when the Boar's Head rang
With laughter and the Mermaid swam in wine,

Tickets are now the only currency.
Before the buffets, metal tables packed
As closely as mosaic, with peopled chairs
Cementing them, where damsels in and out
Attend with food, like disembodied things
That traverse rock as easily as air –
These are the havens, these the happy isles!
A dozen people fight for every seat –
Without a quarrel, unturbently: O,
A peaceable, a tame, a timorous crowd!
And yet relentless: this they know they need;
Here have they money's worth – some food, some drink;
And so alone, in couples, families, groups,
Consuming and consumed – for as they munch
Their victuals all their vitals ennui gnaws –
They sit and sit, and fain would sit it out
In tedious gormandize till firework-time.
But business beats them: those who sit must eat.
Tickets are purchased at besieged Kiosks,
And when their value's spent – with such a grudge! –
They rise to buy again, and lose their seats;
For this is Mob, unhappy locust-swarm,
Instinctive, apathetic, ravenous.

Beyond a doubt a most unhappy crowd!
Some scores of thousands searching up and down
The north nave and the south nave hungrily
For space to sit and rest to eat and drink:
Or captives in a labyrinth, or herds
Imprisoned in a vast arena; here
A moment clustered; there entangled; now
In reaches sped and now in whirlpools spun
With noises like the wind and like the sea,
But silent vocally: they hate to speak:
Crowd; Mob; a blur of faces featureless,
Of forms inane; a stranded shoal of folk.

Astounding in the midst of this to meet
Voltaire, the man who worshipped first, who made
Indeed, the only god men reverence now,
Public Opinion. There he sits alert –

A cast of Houdon's smiling philosophe.
Old lion-fox, old tiger-ape – what names
They gave him! – better charactered by one
Who was his heir: 'The amiable and gay.'
So said the pessimist who called life sour
And drank it to the dregs. Enough: Voltaire –
About to speak: hands of a mummy clutch
The fauteuil's arms; he listens to the last
Before reply; one foot advanced; a new
Idea radiant in his wrinkled face.

Lunch in the grill-room for the well-to-do,
The spendthrifts and the connoisseurs of food –
Gourmet, gourmand, bezonian, epicure.
Reserved seats at the window? – Surely; you
And I must have the best place everywhere.
A deluge smudges out the landscape. Watch
The waiters since the scenery's not on view.
A harvest-day with them, our Switzers – knights
Of the napkin! How they balance loaded trays
And though they push each other spill no drop!
And how they glare at lazy lunchers, snatch
Unfinished plates sans 'by your leave', and fling
The next dish down, before the dazzled lout
(The Switzer knows his man) has time to con
The menu, every tip precisely gauged,
Precisely earned, no service thrown away.
Sign of an extra douceur, reprimand
Is welcomed, and the valetudinous
Voluptuary served devoutly: he
With cauteries on his cranium; dyed moustache;
Teeth like a sea-wolf's, each a work of art
Numbered and valued singly; copper skin;
And nether eyelids pouched: – why, he alone
Is worth a half-day's wage! Waiters for him
Are pensioners of indigestion, paid
As secret criminals disburse blackmail,
As Attic gluttons sacrificed a cock
To Esculapius to propitiate
Hygeia – if the classic flourish serves!

'Grilled soles?' – for us: – Kidneys to follow. – Now,
Your sole, sir; eat it with profound respect.
A little salt with one side; – scarce a pinch!
The other side with lemon; – tenderly!
Don't crush the starred bisection; – count the drops!
Those who begin with lemon miss the true
Aroma: quicken sense with salt, and then
The subtle, poignant, citric savour tunes
The delicate texture of the foam-white fish,
Evolving palatable harmony
That music might by happy chance express.
A crust of bread – (eat slowly: thirty chews,
Gladstonian rumination) – to change the key.
And now the wine – a well-decanted, choice
Chateau, *bon per*; a decade old; not more;
A velvet claret, piously unchilled.
A boiled potato with the kidney . . . No!
Barbarian! Vandal! Sauce? 'Twould ruin all!
The kidney's the potato's sauce. Perpend:
You taste the esoteric attribute
In food; and know that all necessity
Is beauty's essence. Fill your glass: salute
The memory of the happy neolith
Who had the luck to hit on roast and boiled.
Finish the claret. – Now the rain has gone
The clouds are winnowed by the sighing south,
And hidden sunbeams through a silver woof
A warp of pallid bronze in secret ply.

Cigars and coffee in the billiard-room.
No soul here save the marker, eating chops;
The waiter and the damsel at the bar,
In listless talk. A most uncanny thing,
To enter suddenly a desolate cave
Upon the margent of the sounding Mob!
A hundred thousand people, class and mass,
In and about the palace, and not a pair
To play a hundred up! The billiard-room's
The smoking-room; and spacious too, like all
The apartments of the Palace: – why
Unused on holidays? The marker: aged;

Short, broad, but of a presence; reticent
And self-respecting; not at all the type: –
'O well,' says he; 'the business of the room
Fluctuates very little, year in, year out.
My customers are seasons mostly.' One
On the instant enters: a curate, very much
At ease in Zion – and in Sydenham.
He tells two funny stories – not of the room;
And talks about the stage. 'In London now,'
He thinks, 'the play's the thing. He undertakes
To entertain and not to preach: you see,
It's with the theatre and the music-hall,
Actor and artiste, the parson must compete.
Every bank-holiday and special day
The Crystal Palace sees him. Yes; he feels
His hand's upon the public pulse on such
Occasions.' O, a sanguine clergyman!

Heard in the billiard-room the sound of Mob,
Occult and ominous, besets the mind:
Something gigantic, something terrible
Passes without; repasses; lingers; goes;
Returns and on the threshold pants in doubt
Whether to knock and enter, or burst the door,
In hope of treasure and a living prey.
The vainest fantasy! Rejoin the crowd:
At once the sound depreciates. Up and down
The north nave and the south nave hastily
Some tens of thousands walk, silent and sad,
A most unhappy people. – Hereabout
Cellini's Perseus ought to be. Not that;
That's stucco – and Canova's: a stupid thing;
The face and posture of a governess –
A nursery governess who's had the nerve
To pick a dead mouse up. It used to stand
Beside the billiard-room, against the wall,
A cast of Benvenuto's masterpiece –
That came out lame, as he foretold, despite
His dinner dishes in the foundry flung.
They shift their sculpture here haphazard. – That?
King Francis – by Clesinger; – on a horse.

Absurd: most mounted statues are. — And this?
Verrocchio's Colleone. Not absurd:
Grotesque and strong, the battle-harlot rides
A stallion; fore and aft, his saddle, peaked
Like a mitre, grips him as in a vice.
In heavy armour mailed; his lifted helm
Reveals his dreadful look; his brows are drawn;
Four wrinkles deeply trench his muscular face;
His left arm half-extended, and the reins
Held carelessly, although the gesture's tense;
His right hand wields a sword invisible;
Remorseless pressure of his lips protrudes
His mouth; he would decapitate the world.

The light is artificial now; the place
Phantasmal like a beach in hell where souls
Are ground together by an unseen sea.
A dense throng in the central transept, wedged
So tightly they can neither clap nor stamp,
Shouting applause at something, goad themselves
In sheer despair to think it rather fine;
'We came here to enjoy ourselves. Bravo,
Then! Are we not?' Courageous folk beneath
The brows of Michael Angelo's Moses dance
A cakewalk in the dim Renascence Court.
Three people in the silent Reading-room
Regard us darkly as we enter: three
Come in with us, stare vacantly about,
Look from the window and withdraw at once.
A drama; a balloon; a Beauty Show: —
People have seen them doubtless; but none of those
Deluded myriads walking up and down
The north nave and the south nave anxiously —
And aimlessly, so silent and so sad.

The day wears; twilight ends; the night comes down.
A ruddy targelike moon in a purple sky,
And the crowd waiting on the fireworks. Come:
Enough of Mob for one while. This way out —
Past Linacre and Chatham, the second Charles,
Venus and Victory — and Sir William Jones

In placid contemplation of a State! –
Down the long corridor to the district train.

CHARLES MURRAY

Dockens afore his Peers
(Exemption Tribunal) March 1916.

Nae sign o' thow yet. Ay, that's me, John Watt o' Dockenhill:
We've had the war throu' han' afore, at markets owre a gill.
O ay, I'll sit, birze ben a bit. Hae, Briggie, pass the snuff;
Ye winna hinner lang wi' me, an' speer a lot o' buff,
For I've to see the saiddler yet, an' Watchie, honest stock,
To gar him sen' his prentice up to sort the muckle knock,
Syne cry upo' the banker's wife an' leave some settin' eggs,
An' tell the ferrier o' the quake that's vrang aboot the legs.
It's yafa wedder, Mains, for Mairch, wi' snaw an' frost an' win',
The ploos are roustin' i' the fur, an' a' the wark's ahin'.
Ye've grun yersels an' ken the tyauve it is to wirk a ferm,
An' a' the fash we've had wi' fouk gyaun aff afore the term;
We've nane to spare for sojerin', that's nae oor wark ava,
We've rents to pey, an' beasts to feed, an' corn to sell an' saw;
Oonless we get the seed in seen, faur will we be for meal?
An' faur will London get the beef they leuk for aye at Yeel?
There's men aneuch in sooters' shops, an' chiels in masons' yards,
An' coonter-loupers, sklaters, vrichts, an' quarrymen, an' cyaurds,
To fill a reg'ment in a week, withoot gyaun vera far,
Jist shove them in ahin' the pipes, an' tell them that it's 'War';
For gin aul' Scotland's at the bit, there's naething for't but list.
Some mayna like it vera sair, but never heed, insist.
Bit, feich, I'm haverin' on like this, an' a' I need's a line
To say there's men that maun be left, an' ye've exemptit mine.
Fat said ye? Fatna fouk hae I enoo' at Dockenhill?
It's just a wastrie o' your time, to rin them throu', but still –

First there's the wife – 'Pass her,' ye say. Saul! had she been a lass
Ye hadna rappit oot sae quick, young laird, to lat her pass,
That may be hoo ye spak' the streen, fan ye was playin' cairds,
But seein' tenants tak' at times their menners fae their lairds,
I'll tell ye this, for sense an' thrift, for skeel wi' hens an' caur,
Gin ye'd her marrow for a wife, ye woudna be the waur.
Oor maiden's neist, ye've heard o' her, new hame fae buirdin' squeel,
Faur she saw mair o' beuks than broth, an' noo she's never weel,
But fan she's playin' ben the hoose, there's little wird o' dwaams,
For she's the rin o' a' the tunes, strathspeys, an' sangs, an' psalms;
O' 'Evan' an' 'Neander' baith, ye seen can hae aneuch,
But 'Hobble Jennie' gars me loup, an' crack my thooms, an' hooch.
Weel, syne we hae the kitchie deem, that milks an' mak's the maet,
She disna aft haud doon the deese, she's at it ear' an' late,
She cairries seed, an' braks the muck, an' gies a han' to hyow,
An' churns, an' bakes, an' syes the so'ens, an' fyles there's peats to rowe.
An' fan the maiden's friens cry in, she'll mask a cup o' tay,
An' butter scones, an' dicht her face, an' cairry ben the tray.
She's big an' brosy, reid and roch, an' swippert as she's stoot,
Gie her a kilt instead o' cotts, an' thon's the gran' recruit.
There's Francie syne, oor auldest loon, we pat him on for grieve,
An', fegs, we would be in a soss, gin he should up an' leave;
He's eident, an' has lots o' can, an' cheery wi' the men,
An' I'm sae muckle oot aboot wi' markets till atten'.
We've twa chaps syne to wirk the horse, as sweir as sweir can be,

They fussle better than they ploo, they're aul' an' mairret tee,
An' baith hae hooses on the ferm, an' Francie never kens
Foo muckle corn gyangs hame at nicht, to fatten up their hens.
The baillie syne, a peer-hoose geet, nae better than a feel,
He slivvers, an' has sic a mant, an' ae clog-fit as weel;
He's barely sense to muck the byre, an' cairry in the scull,
An' park the kye, an' cogue the caur, an' scutter wi' the bull.
Weel, that's them a' – I didna hear – the laadie i' the gig?
That's Johnnie, he's a littlan jist, for a' he leuks sae big,
Fy na, he isna twenty yet – ay, weel, he's maybe near't;
Owre young to lippen wi' a gun, the crater would be fear't.
He's hardly throu' his squeelin' yet, an' noo we hae a plan
To lat him simmer i' the toon, an' learn to mizzer lan'.
Far? Gar him list! Oor laadie list? 'Twould kill his mither, that,
To think o' Johnnie in a trench awa' in fat-ye-ca't;
We would hae sic a miss at hame, gin he was hine awa',
We'd raither lat ye clean the toon o' ony ither twa;
Ay, tak the wife, the dother, deem, the baillie wi' the mant,
Tak' Francie, an' the mairret men, but John we canna want.
Fat does he dee? Ye micht as weel speir fat I dee mysel',
The things he hasna time to dee is easier to tell;
He dells the yard, an' wi' the scythe cuts tansies on the brae,
An' fan a ruck gyangs throu' the mull, he's thrang at wispin' strae,
He sits aside me at the mart, an' fan a feeder's sell't
Taks doon the wecht, an' leuks the beuk for fat it's worth fan fell't;
He helps me to redd up the dask, he taks a han' at loo,
An' sorts the shalt, an' yokes the gig, an' drives me fan I'm fou.
Hoot, Mains, hae mind, I'm doon for you some sma' thing wi' the bank;
Aul' Larickleys, I saw you throu', an' this is a' my thank;
An' Gutteryloan, that time ye broke, to Dockenhill ye cam'—
'Total Exemption.' Thank ye, sirs. Fat say ye till a dram?

J. M. CAIE

The Puddock

A puddock sat by the lochan's brim,
An' he thocht there was never a puddock like him.
He sat on his hurdies, he waggled his legs,
An' cockit his heid as he glowered throu' the seggs.
The bigsy wee cratur' was feelin' that prood
He gapit his mou' an' he croakit oot lood:
'Gin ye'd a' like tae see a richt puddock,' quo' he,
'Ye'll never, I'll sweer, get a better nor me.
I've fem'lies an' wives an' a weel-plenished hame,
Wi' drink for my thrapple an' meat for my wame.
The lasses aye thocht me a fine strappin' chiel,
An' I ken I'm a rale bonny singer as weel.
I'm nae gyaun tae blaw, but the truth I maun tell –
I believe I'm the verra MacPuddock himsel'.'

. . . . . .

A heron was hungry an' needin' tae sup,
Sae he nabbit th' puddock and gollup't him up;
Syne runkled his feathers: 'A peer thing,' quo' he,
'But – puddocks is nae fat they eesed tae be.'

HUGH MacDIARMID

Crowdieknowe

Oh to be at Crowdieknowe
When the last trumpet blaws,
An' see the deid come loupin' owre
The auld grey wa's.

Muckle men wi' tousled beards,
I grat at as a bairn
'll scramble frae the croodit clay
Wi' feck o' swearin'.

An' glower at God an' a' his gang
O' angels i' the lift
– Thae trashy bleezin' French-like folk
Wha gar'd them shift!

Fain the weemun-folk'll seek
To mak' them haud their row
– Fegs, God's no blate gin he stirs up
The men o' Crowdieknowe!

From
A Drunk Man Looks at the Thistle

I amna' fou' sae muckle as tired – deid dune.
It's gey and hard wark coupin' gless for gless
Wi' Cruivie and Gilsanquhar and the like,
And I'm no' juist as bauld as aince I wes.

The elbuck fankles in the coorse o' time,
The sheckle's no' sae souple, and the thrapple
Grows deef and dour: nae langer up and doun
Gleg as a squirrel speils the Adam's apple.

Forbye, the stuffies's no' the real Mackay,
The sun's sel' aince, as sune as ye began it,
Riz in your vera saul: but what keeks in
Noo is in truth the vilest 'saxpenny planet.'

And as the worth's gane doun the cost has risen.
Yin canna thow the cockles o' yin's hert
Wi'oot ha'en' cauld feet noo, jalousin' what
The wife'll say (I dinna blame her fur't).

It's robbin' Peter to pey Paul at least. . . .
And a' that's Scotch aboot it is the name,
Like a' thing else ca'd Scottish nooadays
– A' destitute o' speerit juist the same.

(To prove my saul is Scots I maun begin
Wi' what's still deemed Scots and the folk expect,
And spire up syne by visible degrees
To heichts whereo' the fules ha'e never recked.

But aince I get them there I'll whummle them
And souse the craturs in the nether deeps,
– For it's nae choice, and ony man s'ud wish
To dree the goat's weird tae as weel's the sheep's!)

Heifetz in tartan, and Sir Harry Lauder!
Whaur's Isadora Duncan dancin' noo?
Is Mary Garden in Chicago still
And Duncan Grant in Paris – and me fou'?

Sic transit gloria Scotiae – a' the floo'ers
O' the Forest are wede awa'. (A blin' bird's nest
Is aiblins biggin' in the thistle tho'? . . .
And better blin' if'ts brood is like the rest!)

You canna gang to a Burns supper even
Wi'oot some wizened scrunt o' a knock-knee
Chinee turns roon to say 'Him Haggis – velly goot!'
And ten to wan the piper is a Cockney.

No' wan in fifty kens a wurd Burns wrote
But misapplied is a'body's property,
And gin there was his like alive the day
They'd be the last a kennin' haund to gi'e –

Croose London Scotties wi' their braw shirt fronts
And a' their fancy freen's, rejoicin'

That similah gatherings in Timbuctoo,
Bagdad – and Hell, nae doot – are voicin'

Burns' sentiments o' universal love,
In pidgin' English or in wild-fowl Scots,
And toastin' ane wha's nocht to them but an
Excuse for faitherin' Genius wi' *their* thochts.

A' *they've* to say was aften said afore
A lad was born in Kyle to blaw aboot.
What unco fate mak's *him* the dumpin'-grun'
For a' the sloppy rubbish they jaw oot?

Mair nonsense has been uttered in his name
Than in ony's barrin' liberty and Christ.
If this keeps spreedin' as the drink declines,
Syne turns to tea, wae's me for the *Zeitgeist*!

Rabbie, wad'st thou wert here – the warld hath need,
And Scotland mair sae, o' the likes o' thee!
The whisky that aince moved your lyre's become
A laxative for a' loquacity.

O gin they'd stegh their guts and haud their wheesht
I'd thole it, for ' a man's a man,' I ken,
But though the feck ha'e plenty o' the ' a' that,'
They're nocht but zoologically men.

I'm haverin', Rabbie, but ye understaun'
It gets my dander up to see your star
A bauble in Babel, banged like a saxpence
'Twixt Burbank's Baedeker and Bleistein's cigar.

There's nane sae ignorant but think they can
Expatiate on *you*, if on nae ither.
The sumphs ha'e ta'en you at your wurd, and, fegs!
The foziest o' them claims to be a – Brither!

Syne 'Here's the cheenge' – the star o' Rabbie Burns.
Sma' cheenge, 'Twinkle, Twinkle.' The memory slips
As G. K. Chesterton heaves up to gi'e
'The Immortal Memory' in a huge eclipse,

Or somebody else as famous if less fat.
You left the like in Embro in a scunner
To booze wi' thieveless cronies sic as me.
I'se warrant you'd shy clear o' a' the hunner

Odd Burns Clubs tae, or ninety-nine o' them,
And haud your birthday in a different kip
Whaur your name isna ta'en in vain – as Christ
Gied a' Jerusalem's Pharisees the slip,

– Christ wha'd ha'e been Chief Rabbi gin he'd lik't! –
Wi' publicans and sinners to foregather,
But, losh! the publicans noo are Pharisees,
And I'm no' shair o' maist the sinners either.

But that's aside the point! I've got fair waun'ert.
It's no' that I'm sae fou' as juist deid dune,
And dinna ken as muckle's whaur I am
Or hoo I've come to sprawl here 'neth the mune.

That's it! It isna me that's fou' at a',
But the fu' mune, the doited jade, that's led
Me fer agley, or 'mogrified the warld.
– For a' I ken I'm safe in my ain bed.

Jean! Jean! Gin *she's* no' here it's no' *oor* bed,
Or else I'm dreamin' deep and canna wauken,
But it's a fell queer dream if this is no'
A real hillside – and thae things thistles and bracken!

It's hard wark haud'n' by a thocht worth ha'en'
And harder speakin't, and no' for ilka man;
Maist Thocht's like whisky – a thoosan' under proof,
And a sair price is pitten on't even than.

As Kirks wi' Christianity ha'e dune,
Burns Clubs wi' Burns – wi' a' thing it's the same.
The core o' ocht is only for the few,
Scorned by the mony, thrang wi'ts empty name.

And a' the names in History mean nocht
To maist folk but 'ideas o' their ain,'

The vera opposite o' onything
The Deid 'ud awn gin they cam' back again.

A greater Christ, a greater Burns, may come.
The maist they'll dae is to gi'e bigger pegs
To folly and conceit to hank their rubbish on.
They'll cheenge folks' talk but no' their natures, fegs!

From
To Circumjack Cencrastus

Tell me the auld, auld story
O' hoo the Union brocht
Puir Scotland into being
As a country worth a thocht.
England, frae whom a' blessings flow
What could we dae withoot ye?
Then dinna threip it doon oor throats
As gin we e'er could doot ye!
My feelings lang wi' gratitude
Ha'e been sae sairly harrowed
That dod! I think it's time
The claith was owre the parrot!

Tell me o' Scottish enterprise
And canniness and thrift,
And hoo we're baith less Scots and mair
Than ever under George the Fifth,
And hoo to 'wider interests'
Oor ain we sacrifice
And yet tine naething by it
As aye the parrot cries.
Syne gi'e's a chance to think it oot
Aince we're a' weel awaur o't,
For, losh, I think it's time
The claith was owre the parrot!

Tell me o' love o' country
Content to see't decay,
And ony ither paradox

Ye think o' by the way.
I doot it needs a Hegel
Sic opposites to fuse;
Oor education's failin'
And canna gi'e's the views
That were peculiar to us
Afore oor vision narrowed
And gar'd us think it time
The claith was owre the parrot!

A parrot's weel eneuch at times
But whiles we'd liefer hear
A blackbird or a mavis
Singin' fu' blythe and clear.
Fetch ony native Scottish bird
Frae the eagle to the wren,
And faith! you'd hear a different sang
Frae this painted foreigner's then.
The marine that brocht it owre
Believed its every word
– But we're a' deeved to daith
Wi' his infernal bird.

It's possible that Scotland yet
May hear its ain voice speak
If only we can silence
This endless-yatterin' beak.
The blessing wi' the black
Selvedge is the clout!
It's silenced Scotland lang eneuch,
Gi'e England turn aboot.
For the puir bird needs its rest –
Wha else'll be the waur o't?
And it's lang past the time
The claith was owre the parrot!

And gin that disna dae, lads,
We e'en maun draw its neck
And heist its body on a stick
A' ither pests to check.
I'd raither keep't alive, and whiles

Let bairns keek in and hear
What the Balliol accent used to be
Frae the Predominant Pairtner here!
— But save to please the bairns
I'd absolutely bar it
For fegs, it's aye high time
The claith was owre the parrot!

An Apprentice Angel

To L. M. W.

I

Try on your wings; I ken vera weel
It wadna look seemly if ony ane saw
A Glasgow Divine ga'en flutherin' aboot
In his study like a drunk craw.

But it 'ud look waur if you'd to bide
In an awkward squad for a month or mair
Learnin' to flee afore you could join
Heaven's air gymkhana aince you get there.

Try on your wings, and gi'e a bit flap,
Pot belly and a', what does it maitter?
Seriously prepare for your future state
— Tho' that's never been in your natur'!

II

As the dragonfly's hideous larva creeps
Oot o' the ditch whaur it was spawned
And straight is turned to the splendid fly,
Nae doot by Death's belated hand
You'll be changed in a similar way,
But as frae that livin' flash o' licht
The cruel features and crawlin' legs
O' its former state never vanish quite
I fancy your Presbyterian Heaven
'll be haunted tae wi' a hellish leaven.

Prayer for a Second Flood

There'd ha'e to be nae warnin'. Times ha'e changed
And Noahs are owre numerous nooadays,
(And them the vera folk to benefit maist!)
Knock the feet frae under them, O Lord, wha praise
Your unsearchable ways sae muckle and yet hope
  To keep within knowledgeable scope!

Ding a' their trumpery show to blauds again.
Their measure is the thimblefu' o' Esk in spate.
Like whisky the tittlin' craturs mete oot your poo'ers
Aince a week for bawbees in the kirk-door plate,
– And pit their umbrellas up when they come oot
  If mair than a pulpitfu' o' You's aboot!

O arselins wi' them! Whummle them again!
Coup them heels-owre-gowdy in a storm sae gundy
That mony a lang fog-theekit face I ken
'll be sooked richt doon under through a cundy
In the High Street, afore you get weel-sterted
  And are still hauf-herted!

Then flush the world in earnest. Let yoursel' gang,
Scour't to the bones, and mak' its marrow holes
Toom as a whistle as they used to be
In days I mind o' ere men fidged wi' souls,
But naething had forgotten you as yet,
  Nor you forgotten it.

Up then and at them, ye Gairds o' Heaven.
The Divine Retreat is owre. Like a tidal bore
Boil in among them; let the lang lugs nourished
On the milk o' the word at last hear the roar
O' human shingle; and replenish the salt o' the earth
  In the place o' their birth.

Glasgow, 1960

Returning to Glasgow after long exile
Nothing seemed to me to have changed its style.
Buses and trams all labelled 'To Ibrox'
Swung past packed tight as they'd hold with folks.
Football match, I concluded, but just to make sure
I asked; and the man looked at me fell dour,
Then said, 'Where in God's name are *you* frae, sir?
It'll be a record gate, but the cause o' the stir
Is a debate on "la loi de l'effort converti"
Between Professor MacFadyen and a Spainish pairty.'
I gasped. The newsboys came running along,
'Special! Turkish Poet's Abstruse New Song.
Scottish Authors' Opinions' – and, holy snakes,
I saw the edition sell like hot cakes!

WILLIAM SOUTAR

Empery

Alexander was greetin
Ahint the tent's flap-door:
'Heh!' speer'd the keekin trollop:
'What are ye greetin for?'

'Am I no Alexander
Wi' the hale world on my back?
But noo that I've taen the world
There's naething mair to tak.'

'Blubber awa!' yapp't the baggage:
'Gin it does ye onie guid:
I thocht ye were maybe minded
O' the braw lads that are dead.'

Franciscan Episode

Francis, wha thocht the gospel-words
Guid-news for ilka body,
Aince preach'd a sermon to the birds
And catechis'd a cuddie.

He was the haliest saint o' a'
Be grace and be affliction;
And kent God's craturs, great or sma',
Were ane in their election.

But ae day, whan he was fell thrang
Confabbin wi' a gander,
A course gleg stug him sic a stang
As fair rous'd up his dander.

'Be aff!' yapp't Francis wi' a yowt,
'To Beelzebub your maister:'
And gied the gutsy beast a clowt
To gar it gang the faster.

The Hungry Mauchs

There was a moupit, mither mauch
Wha hadna onie meat;
And a' her bairns, aye gleg to lauch,
Were gether'd round to greet.

'O mither, mither, wha was yon
That breisted on through bluid:
Wha crackit crouns, and wrackit touns,
And was our faithers' pride?

O mither, mither, wha was yon
That was sae frack and fell?'
'My loves, it was Napoleon
But he's sma' brok himsel'.'

'Noo lat us a' lowt on our knees,'
The spunkiest shaver said:
'And prig upon the Lord to gie's
Napoleon frae the dead.'

The mither mauch began to lauch:
'Ye needna fash nor wurn:
He's clappit doun, and happit roun',
And in a kist o' airn.'

'O whaur, O whaur's my faither gaen?'
The peeriest bairn outspak.
'Wheesht, wheesht, ye wee bit looniekin,
He'll fetch a ferlie back.'

'Will he bring hame Napoleon's head
To cockle up my kite?'
'He'll bring ye hame the wuff o' bluid
That's reid and rinnin yet.'

A Whigmaleerie

There was an Auchtergaven mouse
(I canna mind his name)
Wha met in wi' a hirplin louse
Sair trauchl'd for her hame.

'My friend, I'm hippit; and nae doot
Ye'll heist me on my wey.'
The mouse but squinted doun his snoot
And wi' a breenge was by.

Or lang he cam to his ain door
Doun be a condie-hole;
And thocht, as he was stappin owre:
Vermin are ill to thole.

The Philosophic Taed

There was a taed wha thocht sae lang
On sanctity and sin;
On what was richt, and what was wrang,
And what was in atween –
That he gat naething dune.

The wind micht blaw, the snaw micht snaw,
He didna mind a wheet;
Nor kent the derk'nin frae the daw,
The wulfire frae the weet;
Nor fuggage frae his feet.

His wife and weans frae time to time,
As they gaed by the cratur,
Wud haut to hae a gowk at him
And shak their pows, or natter:
'He's no like growin better.'

It maun be twenty year or mair
Sin thocht's been a' his trade:
And naebody can tell for shair
Whether this unco taed
Is dead, or thinks he's dead.

GEORGE BRUCE

Transplant

'Christ!' said the surgeon, 'It's not there.' Though why
he should have expected it, considering
my heart has been in my mouth for years.
So there they were scouting around,
pulling up the tripes, chasing along the gut,
digging the bowels, hugging the liver,
freaking out the lungs, inspecting the duodenum –
and nothing in sight. Zero hour and the trumpets
sounding. 'Christ!' said the surgeon, still doing
his nut on the wrong track. The trouble was
semantics. Shouldn't he have known
– O Lamp of Licht –
Christus Victus, Christus Victor,
Kyrie Eleison – the water of Babylon.

Somewhere along the computerised line an omission.
Feedback. Reprogram: LLLLLLLLLLLLLLLLLLLLL
libliblibliblibliblibliblibliblibliblibliblibliblibli
'Got it' he said. LIBERAL STUDIES.

ROBERT GARIOCH

Embro to the Ploy

In simmer, whan aa sorts foregether
in Embro to the ploy,
folk seek out friens to hae a blether,
or faes they'd fain annoy;
smorit wi British Railways' reek
frae Glesca or Glen Roy
or Wick, they come to hae a week
of cultivatit joy,
or three,
in Embro to the ploy.

Americans wi routh of dollars,
wha drink our whisky neat,
wi Sasunachs and Oxford Scholars
are eydent for the treat
of music sedulously high-tie
at thirty-bob a seat;
Wop opera performed in Eytie
to them's richt up their street,
they say,
in Embro to the ploy.

Furthgangan Embro folk come hame
for three weeks in the year,
and find Auld Reekie no the same,
fu sturrit in a steir.
The stane-faced biggins whaur they froze
and suppit puirshous leir
of cultural cauld-kale and brose
see cantraips unco queer
thae days
in Embro to the ploy.

The tartan tred wad gar ye lauch;
nae problem is owre teuch.
Your surname needna end in *-och*;
they'll cleik ye up the cleuch.

A puckle dollar bills will aye
preive Hiram Teufelsdrockh
a septary of Clan McKay,
it's maybe richt eneuch,
                    verfluch!
in Embro to the ploy.

The auld High Schule, whaur monie a skelp
of triple-tonguit tawse
has gien a hyst-up and a help
towards Doctorates of Laws,
nou hears, for Ramsay's cantie rhyme,
loud pawmies of applause
frae folk that pey a pund a time
to sit on wudden raws
                    gey hard
in Embro to the ploy.

The haly kirk's Assembly-haa
nou fairly coups the creel
wi Lindsay's Three Estaitis, braw
devices of the Deil.
About our heids the satire stots
like hailstanes till we reel;
the bawrs are in auld-farrant Scots,
it's maybe jist as weill,
                    imphm,
in Embro to the ploy.

The Epworth Haa wi wunner did
behold a pipers' bicker;
wi *hadarid* and *hindarid*
the air gat thick and thicker.
Cumha na Cloinne pleyed on strings
torments a piper quicker
to get his dander up, by jings,
than thirty u. p. liquor,
                    hooch aye!
in Embro to the ploy.

The Northern British Embro Whigs
that stayed in Charlotte Square,
they fairly wad hae tined their wigs
to see the Stuarts there,
the bleidan Earl of Moray and aa
weill-pentit and gey bare;
Our Queen and Princess, buskit braw,
enjoyed the hale affair
(see Press)
in Embro to the ploy.

Whan day's anomalies are cled
in decent shades of nicht,
the Castle is transmogrified
by braw electric licht.
The toure that bields the Bruce's croun
presents an unco sicht
mair sib to Wardour Street nor Scone,
wae's me for Scotland's micht,
says I
in Embro to the ploy.

A happening, incident, or splore
affrontit them that saw
a thing they'd never seen afore –
in the McEwan Haa:
a lassie in a wheelie-chair
wi' naething on at aa,
jist like my luck! I wasna there,
it's no the thing ava,
tut-tut,
in Embro to the ploy.

The Café Royal and Abbotsford
are filled wi orra folk
whaes stock-in-trade's the scrievit word,
or twicet-scrievit joke.
Brains, weak or strang, in heavy beer,
or ordinary, soak.
Quo yin: This yill is aafie dear,
I hae nae clinks in poke,

nor fauldan-money,
in Embro to the ploy.

The auld Assembly-rooms, whaur Scott
foregethert wi his fiers,
nou see a gey kenspeckle lot
ablow the chandeliers.
Til Embro drouths the Festival Club
a richt godsend appears;
it's something new to find a pub
that gaes on sairvan beers
eftir hours
in Embro to the ploy.

Jist pitten-out, the drucken mobs
frae howffs in Potterraw,
fleean, to hob-nob wi the Nobs,
ran to this Music Haa,
Register Rachel, Cougait Kate,
nae-neb Nellie and aa
stauchert about amang the Great,
what fun! I never saw
the like,
in Embro to the ploy.

They toddle hame doun lit-up streets
filled wi synthetic joy;
aweill, the year brings few sic treats
and muckle to annoy.
There's monie hartsom braw high-jinks
mixed up in this alloy
in simmer, whan aa sorts foregether
in Embro to the ploy.

Did Ye See Me?

I'll tell ye of ane great occasioun:
I tuk pairt in a graund receptioun.
Ye cannae hae the least perceptioun
hou pleased I was to get the invitatioun

tae assist at ane dedicatioun.
And richtlie sae; frae its inceptioun
the hale ploy was my ain conceptioun;
I was asked to gie a dissertatioun.

The functioun was held in the aipen air,
a peety, that; the keelies of the toun,
a toozie lot, gat word of the affair.

We cudnae stop it: they jist gaithert roun
to mak sarcastic cracks and grin and stare.
I wisht I hadnae worn my M. A. goun.

And They Were Richt

I went to see 'Ane Tryall of Hereticks'
by Fionn MacColla, treatit as a play;
a wycelike wark, but what I want to say
is mair taen-up wi halie politics

nor wi the piece itsel; the kinna tricks
the unco-guid get up til whan they hae
their wey. Yon late-nicht ploy on Setturday
was thrang wi Protestants and Catholics,

an eydent audience, wi fowth of bricht
arguments wad hae kept them gaun till Monday.
It seemed discussion wad last out the nicht,

hadna the poliss, sent by Mrs Grundy
pitten us out at twelve. And they were richt!
Wha daur debait religion on a Sunday?

Twa Festival Sketches

I

I wes passing a convertit kirk –
   Whit's that ye say?
A convertit kirk, plenty o thaim about;

the kirks yuistae convert the sinners,
bit nou the sinners convert the kirks.
Weill oniewey, here wes this convertit kirk
wi bills stuck owre the front
and folk queuin up to git in
to hear the Po-etic Gems
o William McGonagall.
On the pavement outside
there wes a richt rammie gaun on,
folk millin about, ken?
And in the middle o this rammie
wes a man that wes gittin Moved On –
   Whit fir? –
He'd been sellin broadsheets
o poems, Gode help him!
o his ain composition.

II

At the Tattoo
they hae twa-three collapsible cot-houssis.
We behold a typical Hieland Scena:
a typical blacksmith dingan on his stiddie,
and a typical drouth boozan at the nappie –
the usquebaugh, I should say –
   et cetera.
Alang comes the Duchess o Gordon on horseback.
She wants sodgers
and the Hielands are fou o Hielandmen.
She gies til each recruit a blue-bluidit kiss.
Nou the boozan has ceased.
The smiddie-fire is out.
The Duchess o Gordon has gien them
the Kiss o Daith.

Sisyphus

Bumpity doun in the corrie gaed whuddran the pitiless
   whun stane.
Sisyphus, pechan and sweitan, disjaskit, forfeuchan and
   broun'd-aff,

sat on the heather a hanlawhile, houpan the Boss didna spy him,
seean the terms of his contract includit nae mention of tea-breaks,
syne at the muckle big scunnersom boulder he trauchlit aince mair.
Ach! hou kenspeckle it was, that he ken'd ilka spreckle and blotch on't.
Heavan awa at its wecht, he manhaunnlit the bruitt up the brae-face,
takkan the easiest gait he had fand in a fudder of dour years,
haudan awa frae the craigs had affrichtit him maist in his youth-heid,
feelan his years aa the same, he gaed cannily, tenty of slipped discs.
Eftir an hour and a quarter he warslit his wey to the brae's heid,
hystit his boulder richt up on the tap of the cairn – and it stude there!
streikit his length on the chuckie-stanes, houpan the Boss wadna spy him,
had a wee look at the scenery, feenisht a pie and a cheese-piece.
Whit was he thinkan about, that he jist gied the boulder a wee shove?
Bumpity doun in the corrie gaed whuddran the pitiless whun stane,
Sisyphus dodderan eftir it, shair of his cheque at the month's end.

NORMAN MacCAIG

Street Preacher

Every Sunday evening at seven o'clock
He howls outside my window. He howls about God.
No tattered prophet: a rosy bourgeois, he lifts
His head and howls. He addresses me as friend.

One day I'll open the window and howl at him
And so betray his Enemy. I'll call him Brother.
Who'd laugh the louder, the Devil or God, to see
Two rosy bourgeois howling at each other?

When he goes coughing home, does he speak to his wife
Of the good fight well fought, the shaft well sped,
Before he puts God's teeth in a glass and, taking
His sensible underclothes off, rolls into bed?

Milne's Bar

Cigarette smoke floated
in an Eastern way
a yard above the slopped tables.

The solid man thought
nothing could hurt him
as long as he didn't show it –

a stoicism of a kind. I
was inclined to agree with him,
having had a classical education.

To prove it, he went on telling
of terrible things that had
happened to him –

so boringly, my mind
skipped away among the glasses
and floated, in an Eastern way,

a yard above the slopped
table; when it looked down,
the solid man

was crying into his own mouth.
I caught sight of myself
in a mirror

and stared, rather admiring
the look of suffering
in my middle-aged eyes.

Wild Oats

Every day I see from my window
pigeons, up on a roof ledge – the males
are wobbling gyroscopes of lust.

Last week a stranger joined them, a snowwhite
pouting fantail,
Mae West in the Women's Guild.
What becks, what croo-croos, what
demented pirouetting, what a lack
of moustaches to stroke.

The females – no need to be one of them
to know
exactly what they were thinking – pretended
she wasn't there
and went dowdily on with whatever
pigeons do when they're knitting.

DOUGLAS YOUNG

Last Lauch

The Minister said it wald dee,
  the cypress buss I plantit.
But the buss grew til a tree,
  naething dauntit.

It's growan stark and heich,
  derk and straucht and sinister,
kirkyairdie-like and dreich.
  But whaur's the Minister?

On a North British Devolutionary

They libbit William Wallace,
  he gart them bleed.
They dinna libb MacFoozle,
  they dinna need.

SYDNEY GOODSIR SMITH

The Grace of God and the Meth-Drinker

There ye gang, ye daft
And doitit dotterel, ye saft
Crazed outland skalrag saul
In your bits and ends o winnockie duds
Your fyled and fozie-fousome clouts
As fou's a fish, crackt and craftie-drunk
Wi bleerit reid-rimmed
Ee and slaveran crozie mou
Dwaiblan owre the causie like a ship
Storm-toss't i' the Bay of Biscay O
At-sea indeed and hauf-seas-owre
Up-til-the-thrapple's-pap
Or up-til-the-crosstrees-sunk –
    Wha kens? Wha racks?
Hidderie-hetterie stouteran in a dozie dwaum
O' ramsh reid-biddie – Christ!
        The stink
O' jake ahint him, a mephitic
Rouk o miserie, like some unco exotic
Perfume o the Orient no juist sae easilie tholit
By the bleak barbarians o the Wast
But subtil, acrid, jaggan the nebstrous
Wi 'n owrehailan ugsome guff, maist delicat,
Like in scent til the streel o a randie gib . . .
        O-hone-a-ree!

His toothless gums, his lips, bricht cramasie
A schere-bricht slash o bluid
A schene like the leaman gleid o rubies
Throu the gray-white stibble
O' his blank unrazit chafts, a hangman's
Heid, droolie wi gob, the bricht een
Sichtless, cannie, blythe, and slee –
                                        Unkennan.

Ay,
Puir gangrel!
There
– But for the undeemous glorie and grace
O' a mercifu ominpotent majestic God
Superne eterne and sceptred in the firmament
Whartil the praises o the leal rise
Like incense aye about Your throne,
Ayebydan, thochtless, and eternallie hauf-drunk
Wi nectar, Athole-brose, ambrosia – nae jake for
You –
God there! –
But for the 'bunesaid unsocht grace, unprayed-for,
Undeserved –
Gangs,
Unregenerate,
Me.

The Years of the Crocodile
A Dirge

In the years o the maytree
The hevins were bricht
In thc ycars o thc crocodile
Nicht wantan licht.

In the years o the lilie
I loed wiout loss
In the years o the crocodile
Tosspots I toss.

In the years o the rose
I read aa the bukes
In the years o the crocodile
I lossit my looks.

In the years o solesequium
I secutit the sun
In the years o the crocodile
I sat on my bum.

In the years o the vine
I'd a horse for the wish
In the years o the crocodile
I drank like a fish.

In the years o the lotus
I wore a lum hat
In the years o the crocodile
I sat doun and grat.

O the tears o the crocodile
Fill the Waters o Leith
And the glent o the gourmand
Sheens on his teeth.

O the tears o the crocodile
Greit for us aa
Wi a grin o content
He lowsens his jaw.

TOM SCOTT

Jay
(Garrulus Glandarius)

No for him the lyric gift o sang
Alane identifees the outwaled bard:
Yon bird's a realist, and his voice
A harsk and realistic skriek
Like linoleum tearan,
Tho whiles he chuckles and clucks
As owre some private joke,
Or wheeples and pyow-myows in his neb.

But tho nae Orpheus in voice he hes an ee
A bead o slaty-blue
That glints warily out
And misses little:
A clever ee that jays the world
Intil a world o his ain conceit.

He's kittle, mak na dout,
A sleekit, aggressive sidewinder o a bird,
Fit for tricks and treacheries,
Preferran the shade o a wuid til open fields,
As weel he micht, because,
Tho rife eneuch in England,
Here the breed is herried for its habits
By keepers o game, and by game fishers
For its fly feathers.

Whiles his pagan tones are heard
Deep in the mirk o a wuid
Whaur ither birds are scant,
Caain owre his individual notes, emulatin
Nae ither sound but his ain original skraak;
Nae traditionist he, to sit at the feet o the masters,
Yet, tho he claitters awa in wearie repetition,
Self-imitation,
On aucht that really maitters til the race
The fient a word he hes to say but 'skraak'.

Owre lourd on the wing for lang flights,
He's agile eneuch in the trees,
Climbs and clings weel on brainches,
Is cliquish, fond o bickeran pairties.
Nae dangerous liver, he nests aye near the grund,
Well-eneuch established, weel-eneuch theekit –
He hauds his ain in life, and even Gets On.

Aa birds are worth some study,
And sae is he for whom,
His meisurements carefully booked,
I've tailor-made this suitably tuneless ode:
For under the gaudy disguise,
The gew-gaw glitter and the modish feathers,
Yon taxidermist's pet
Is just anither craw.

MAURICE LINDSAY

The Vacant Chair

Suddenly, they broke out
of the discipline of absorbing facts
as if there really were such things.
Suddenly, they wanted to ask,
and have answered, the awkward questions.

Why scientists calculated
the cheapest form of total explosion?
Why children's bellies distended
with the needless obscenity of hunger?
Priests be permitted to father poverty
under the bedclothes of superstition?
Why those whom age had cataracted
with inoperable complacency
should profess to teach each generation
as if such blindness didn't exist?

A reasonable line was taken
by public and Press for a little while.
But at last they whom the blindness most
affected began to get angry. Who
were the young to expect answers for questions,
actions for needs? Why couldn't they stay
closed in their studies, leaving life
to settle at its own level,
accepting the absence of solutions?
After all, what they wanted
was, clearly, a Chair of Impossibilities.

And who could they have found to fill it?

One Day at Shieldaig

Behind rolled Vauxhall windows
two women, sealed in homely Aran sweaters,
knitted their fingers into sweated Arans.

Two men, cast off for
'a breath of air' (discreetly to water themselves),
came sweating back, two strolling Arans homing.

Even the clouds and mountains
got knitted up in patterns of each other,
the sea's fingers glinting incredibly.

EDWIN MORGAN

The Flowers of Scotland

Yes, it is too cold in Scotland for flower people; in any case
who would be handed a thistle?
What are our flowers? Locked swings and private rivers –
and the island of Staffa for sale in the open market, which
no one questions or thinks strange–
and lads o' pairts that run to London and Buffalo without a
backward look while their elders say Who'd blame them–
and bonny fechters kneedeep in dead ducks with all the
thrawn intentness of the incorrigible professional Scot–
and a Kirk Assembly that excels itself in the bad old rhetoric
and tries to stamp out every glow of charity and change,
most wrong when it thinks most loudly it is most right–
and a Scottish National Party that refuses to discuss Viet-
nam and is even applauded for doing so, do they think
no lesson is to be learned from what is going on there?–
and the unholy power of Grouse-moor and Broad-acres to
prevent the smoke of useful industry from sullying Inver-
gordon or setting up linear cities among the whaups–
and the banning of Beardsley and Joyce but not of course
of 'Monster on the Campus' or 'Curse of the Undead'–
those who think the former are the more degrading,
what are their values?–
and the steady creep of the preservationist societies,
wearing their pens out for slums with good leaded
lights–if they could buy all the amber in the Baltic and
melt it over Edinburgh would they be happy then?–the
skeleton is well-proportioned–
and by contrast the massive indifference to the slow death
of the Clyde estuary, decline of resorts, loss of steamers,
anaemia of yachting, cancer of monstrous installations
of a foreign power and an acquiescent government–
what is the smell of death on a child's spade, any more
than rats to leaded lights?–
and dissidence crying in the wilderness to a moor of
boulders and two ospreys–
these are the flowers of Scotland.

School's Out

I

A colonnade, binding light in fasces
of striped stone and shadow, suited Plato.
'Tight reins,' he used to say, 'all training
is restraint.' Are boys like horses then?
Stupid questions got no answer, but
a thin smile came and went, left no trace.
We were born into Utopia:
cold baths, porridge and Pythagoras,
Pythagoras, porridge and cold baths.
We never exactly hated the routine
but felt there must be something else. He said
life should be in the Dorian mode, sober
as a shepherd's pipe, and 'hell take all
Bacchantes and Assyrian kettledrums',
which was strong words for him. Looking back,
it seems as if the discuses we threw
to swing our muscles into harmonies
'like the deep universe's harmonies'
were no more solid than the wrestling-oil
that seeped into the sand, or watery songs
of how the gods are good as gold. We did
our sums, deaf to the music of the spheres,
        and came out into chaos,
        blood, shrieks, kettledrums.

II

Milton thought a country house was best,
'at once both school and university',
and he'd have acres to do marvels in.
He was really pure theatre. I don't forget
his first words: 'Open your mouths, let me hear
a clear vowel from now on, stop mumbling
just because there's mist in Buckinghamshire.'
We thought he must be mad, but practical,
and it's no secret his model was Prince Hamlet
(bating the royal appurtenances).
We sweated swordplay, strategy and tactics,
as well as sonnets and the vocative.

We groaned through Hebrew but we knew the stars.
I could put on a splint, survey a field,
ride a horse and play the organ. Poachers,
pedlars, smiths he made us learn from, for
'you never know what might help the commonwealth'.
It's all gone now of course. The king came back.
Rigour was no longer *de rigueur*.
I sometimes wonder what it was all for –
and then I remember that sardonic voice
pausing in its anatomy lesson to say
        why heads of kings come
        off so easily.

III

Whatever did we learn at Summerhill?
No maths, no hangups; how to play *Dear Brutus*.
It wasn't doing barbola on the mantelpiece
with red-hot pokers, breaking windows all day
or maidenheads all night – though you'd think so
to hear the critics. And did Neill set us free?
You never know with voluntary lessons,
they crouch there in your path like friendly enemies,
you pat them or you sidle past, knowing
you can't play truant when you're free already.
School government was on our hunkers, noisy,
fizzing, seesawing, Neill won, we won, no one won
while the long shadows gathered on the chintz.
We were Hitler's autobahns in reverse,
anti-Stakhanovites, our trains would never
run on time. 'If I create a millionaire'
cried Neill 'I've failed!' But capitalism
slid on its way despite our lost repressions.
We tinkered in the workshop, made toy guns
but never robbed a bank or even knew
half Europe had been robbed. Now if you ask
what I think of it I honestly don't know,
        it was great but I
        honestly don't know.

IV

Ivan Illich bought a big new broom.
'Most people learn most things out of school.'
Why not junk the institution then?
The point was we had reached the stage we could.
Access! Access! was his cry, and timetables, textbooks,
exams, walls, bells were as much garbage
as last year's Cadillac. Plug in! playback!
tapespond! the electronic network longs
to set you free. The what and where and when
of learning's in your own hands now. Deschool.
Decamp. Disperse. The player and the game
are one, nobody prods men to the board.
– So we were the first tape and data children,
we've been through the tube, come out, still cool.
We know how Armstrong landed, bleeps call us
in our breast-pockets everywhere we go,
we've got cassettes of Basque folk-songs, slides
of the water-flea, microfilm drips from us
in clusters, if there's music of the spheres
we've heard it. I've been talking to the dolphins
in California, and they say they've seen
a school (which I know is impossible)
        far out in the bay.
        Whales, whales, you fool.

Letters of Mr Lonelyhearts

I

Little Mr Lonelyhearts
picked at the sofa,
hating the horsehair
but there it was.
Dear Disappointed,
he wrote, I think
you must forget
the bad baking.
A burnt scone is
a burnt scone, but
marriage is more

than a tearful plateful
– or even two –
of carbonized baps.
You spoke of a kitchen
of smoke and a kick
at the gateleg and glad
for a beer with the boys
but now go
easy, chum,
your mother burnt
her rice in her time
so don't cast
that up.
A hard potato
is not cruelty
and anyway she cried.
So remember your bride
who tries to please you
running to the door
with her floury apron
and a bun in the oven.
Remember that.
Be thankful for that.

II

Mr Lonelyhearts loosened his tie
with a great sigh, closed the marshmallows.
He took a turn about the room, spoke
sharply to his budgerigar, stared out
at nothing passing, came back
and with a last marshmallow grimly
settled to type. Dear Puzzled, it went,
Look, you got back your monkey, so
what's all the fuss? I've got broken hearts,
roofs collapsing, no month's rent, I've got
crazy wills, incest, grandmothers locked out–
and so I'm to lose sleep over a monkey?
You say it's not safe to leave one in the streets,
and you've lost all trust in your fellow-men.
Grow up and get a sense of proportion.
You say you hardly knew this man

in Kent Street, with his one brown eye
and one blue eye – are you making it up,
I don't know why I answer letters –
and yet you left this – Judy, you call her?
with him, red suit, chain, banana,
the lot, and went for your car, right?
I don't get it. I don't get it.
Meanwhile your rainbow-eyed china – some china –
passed on this vagrant marmoset
to a third party, did he just get tired
of holding her? All right, I'll believe you.
But then this third man, in whom lies the crunch,
thought he had been left holding the baby
– more edifying all round if it *had* been a baby,
baby – and took her home for the night.
Now what puzzles *me*, friend Puzzled, is simply
what you were up to all this time,
did your car have a flat, or perhaps
you really were trying to leave your monkey
on somebody's doorstep? Oh yes I admit
you went after her, you unravelled the string
of accidents, touching reunion
I'm sure, with the red hat and all. But –
why don't you just come off it, quietly?
Stick to bitter lemon. I won't have
two-eyed men in this column, or
unintelligible organ-grinders.

III

The thunder broke, and Mr Lonelyhearts
seized a sheet like lightning. Dear Rosie,
he wrote, Kill him. For a man
who'd take a snake basket
on his honeymoon, divorce
is peanuts. Shoot him,
get yourself a night's sleep.

Instamatic Translunar Space March 1972

The interior of Pioneer-10,
as it courses smoothly beyond the Moon
at 31,000 miles an hour,
is calm and full of instruments.
No crew for the two-year trip to Jupiter,
but in the middle of the picture
a gold plaque, six inches by nine,
remedies the omission. Against a diagram
of the planets and pulsars of our solar system and galaxy,
and superimposed on an outline of the spacecraft
in which they are not travelling
(and would not be as they are shown
even if they were) two quaint nude figures
face the camera. A deodorized American man
with apologetic genitals and no pubic hair
holds up a banana-like right hand
in Indian greeting, at his side a woman,
smaller, and also with no pubic hair,
is not allowed to hold up her hand,
stands with one leg off-centre, and
is obviously an inferior sort
of the same species. However,
the male chauvinist pig
has a sullen expression, and the woman
is faintly smiling, so
interplanetary intelligences may still have homework.
Meanwhile, on to the Red Spot,
Pluto, and eternity.

ALEXANDER SCOTT

Til John Maclean 23/73
(Eftir the anniversary celebrations)

Ye saltired the reid flag
and connached condemned
as a double daftie.

Fifty year on (and on)
ye're a double messiah,
baith scarlet and blue.

But wha hae the reidest faces
and wha the bluest
o aa your converts?

They praise ye wi pentecost voices,
gifted – but girnan,
the t'ane at the t'ither.

you lie in your voiceless lair
wi ae colour,
the mirk o the mools.

There's fient the resurrection.

Ballade of Beauties

Miss Israel Nineteen-Sixty-Eight is new,
A fresh-poured form her swimsuit moulds to sleekness,
Legs long, breasts high, the shoulders firm and true,
The waist a lily wand without a weakness,
The hair, *en brosse* and black, is shorn to bleakness,
Yet shines as stars can make the midnight do –
But still my mind recalls more maiden meekness,
Miss Warsaw Ghetto Nineteen-Forty-Two.

Her masters filmed her kneeling stripped to sue
The mercy barred as mere unmanning weakness,

Or raking rubbish-dumps for crusts to chew,
Or licking boots to prove her slavish meekness,
Or baring loins to lie beneath the bleakness
Of conqueror's lust (and forced to smile it through),
Her starving flesh a spoil preferred ro sleekness,
Miss Warsaw Ghetto Nineteen-Forty-Two.

The prize she won was given not to few
But countless thousands, paid the price of meekness,
And paid in full, with far too high a due,
By sadist dreams transformed to functioned sleekness,
A pervert prophet's weakling hate of weakness
Constructing a mad machine that seized and slew,
The grave her last reward, the final bleakness,
Miss Warsaw Ghetto Nineteen-Forty-Two.

Princesses, pale in death or sunned in sleekness,
I dedicate these loving lines to you,
Miss Israel Sixty-Eight and (murdered meekness)
Miss Warsaw Ghetto Nineteen-Forty-Two.

Lament for a Makar
(I.M.Douglas Young)

Ye dee'd in Dixie – yon's
a queer 'last lauch'
on a mockan makar
whas sang o the sterk cypress
leuch at the minister's lair –
there's you that tholit the jyle
afore ye'd thole the Union,
yet failed sae far at tholan
our ain owre thankless country
as flee intil exile,
no for a tint cause
(the cause o this connached fowk)
but ettlan for aince to win
instead o forever wantan,
and preean the prize

o the tap title, 'Prof,'
and a puckle dollars.

And nou ye're deid in Dixie,
exiled, but aye
in a connached country
wi fowk like ours that fell
til the strang stranger
– a fikey fate,
and sair, sair to thole.

Your ain epigram's end
was hardly sae coorse a caution.

Heart of Stone
(A Poem on Aberdeen)
(extract)

Bonnieness-blind, thae fowk, for aa their birr!
Wha else, i the stanie straucht o Union Street,
Wi only the ae brig til open space,
Wad block thon brichtness out wi shargar shoppies?
What ither toun can blaw its blastie tooter
For siccan a rowth o temples til the Muses
(A pictur-hous for ilk ten thousan heid)?
Whaur else are fowk sae daft on 'the modern drama'
That time-woorn Hamlet plays til a toom haa
While even courtan couples howder in queues
Gin X sud mark the spot – and X aye marks it –
For spang-new Nocht-Nocht-Seeven?
Whaur else wad Wallace pynt the finger o scorn
At a theatre thrang wi a clyter o Scoatch coamics,
Kilted tenors, and cantrips frae Agatha Christie?
Whaur else wad Gordon tak sic a hint frae the toun
And turn til the Art Gall'ry a gallus back?
Whaur else wad Burns far leifer glower at's gowan
Nor look his brither Scots i the ee – and lauch?
Na, na, he's nae amused – like vogie Victoria,
The cross queen stuid standan at Queen's Cross,

And even she, her face til the fike o Balmoral,
Feels mair at hame in an artless airt nor Burns.

Ahint his back auld men find school-the-board
A cantier ploy nor onie poetry clavers,
And neives that aince had haudden cleek or spad
Are grippit nou for a game
In a green howe at the hert o the granite toun,
Nae mair nor a sclim o steps frae the stane centre
Whaur business breeds in banks its paper bairns
And hous-insurance biggs its hames in haas
Abune the heids o leddies wi smaa leisure
(And smaa-er cheenge) that jink frae shop til store
In het pursuit o twa for the price o the t'ane,
Their ae fond dwaum the mak o a braw bargain,
Bonnier far nor a ballant threepit by Burns,
Thon daisy-daffer, deid in a thratch o debt.

Gin onie debt be here, it's haudden dern,
Happed ahin stanes that sclent the speak o siller
Frae raw on hauchty raw o terraced houses
Whiter nor whited sepulchres daur decore,
Their snawie fronts as clean as a banker's credit
And cauld as his arctic hert, a cranreuch beauty
Born frae the frore skinkle o iceberg stane,
The rock itsel (far mair nor the men that wrocht it),
The rock steekan its ain sterk style
On fowk whas foremaist fancy was biggan cheap
In hame-owre stane that speired the least o siller
To howk frae a hole out-by and bike in bields,
Syne fand themsels a fowk whas granite een
Were claucht in an icy wab o granite graithing,
A cauldrife charm they never meant to mak
But hytered on by chance, the luck o the land.
Yet syne they socht to suit thon chancy charm
Til notions stown frae beuks on 'aht end beauteh' –
Save us, a bonnie soss! Our sins in stane,
The graveyairds sprauchle gantan, their granite teeth
Asclent wi a deid skinkle, a gless girn
At nichtgouned angels far owre lourd to flie,
And nappied cherubs far owre cauld to flichter,

And whim-wham scrolls, and whigmaleerie urns,
The haill jing-bang bumbazed in a sacred scutter
To fleg the deid wi a fate that's waur nor death.

But fient the fate has pouer to ding sic fauters,
In life they looked wi never a blink o the ee
At horror mair profane nor the pynes o hell,
Thon maister-monsterpiece the Marischal College,
A Gothic nichtmare, granite steered like glaur
Til ferlie frills and fancy flichtmaflethers,
Stookie insteid o stane,
Whaur sterkness, strength, the granite's only graces,
Are raxed and rived til pranksome prettifications,
The fraiky shots at grace o a graceless fowk.

Nae grace ava i the howder o growsome houses
Biggit as bargains – and ilkane bad –
Whan Sassenach brick and Swedish timmer,
Bocht for a groatsworth less nor the sillerie stane,
Got pride o place and connached pride o place
Wi street eftir street o the same subtopian slaur,
Less fit to stand by granite's stey gramultion
Nor fremmit mountain-dew by the real Mackay,
A wersh bourach o bawbee braws,
A clyter o menseless clart.

But neither auld mistaks nor new mishanters
Can steerach the fine fettle o ferlie stane,
The adamant face that nocht can fyle,
Nae rain, nae reek,
Fowr-square til aa the elements, fine or foul,
She stares back straucht at the skimmeran scaud o the su
Or bares her brou til the bite o the brashy gale,
Riven frae raw rock, and rockie-rooted,
A breem bield o steive biggins,
A hard hauld, a sterk steid
Whaur bonnie fechters bolden at ilka ferlie,
The city streets a warld o wild stramash
Frae clintie seas and bens as coorse as brine
For fowk sae fit to daur the dunt o storms
Wi faces stobbed by the stang o saut

Or callered by country winds
In a teuch toun whaur even the strand maks siller,
Rugged frae the iron faem and the stanie swaws
As the sweel o the same saut tide
Clanjamfries crans and kirks by thrang causeys
Whaur cushat's croudle mells wi sea-maw's skirl,
And hirplan hame hauf-drouned wi the weicht o herrin
The trauchled trawler waffs in her wake
A flaffer o wings – a flash o faem-white feathers –
As the sea-maw spires i the stane-gray lift
Owre sworlan swaws o the stane-gray sea
And sclents til the sea-gray toun, the hert o stane.

Scotched
(extracts)

Scotch God
Kent His
Faither.

Scotch Religion
Damn
Aa.

Scotch Education
I tellt ye
I tellt ye.

Scotch Queers
Wha peys wha
– For what?

Scotch Prostitution
Dear,
Dear.

Scotch Liberty
Agree
Wi me.

Scotch Equality
Kaa the feet frae
Thon big bastard.

Scotch Fraternity
Our mob uses
The same razor.

Scotch Optimism
Through a gless,
Darkly.

Scotch Pessimism
Nae
Gless.

Scotch Initiative
Eftir
You.

Scotch Generosity
Eftir
Me.

Scotch Sex
In atween
Drinks.

Scotch Passion
Forgot
Mysel.

Scotch Free-Love
Canna be
Worth much.

Scotch Lovebirds
Cheap
Cheap.

Scotch Fractions
A hauf
'n' a hauf.

Scotch Afternoon-Tea
Masked
Pot.

Scotch Drink
Nip
Trip.

Scotch Poets
Wha's the
T'ither?

GEORGE MACKAY BROWN

Ikey on the People of Hellya

Rognvald who stalks round Corse with his stick
I do not love.
His dog has a loud sharp mouth.
The wood of his door is very hard.
Once, tangled in his barbed wire
(I was paying respects to his hens, stroking a wing)
He laid his stick on me.
That was out of a hard forest also.

Mansie at Quoy is a biddable man.
Ask for water, he gives you rum.
I strip his scarecrow April by April.
Ask for a scattering of straw in his byre
He lays you down
Under a quilt as long and light as heaven.
Then only his raging woman spoils our peace.

Gray the fisherman is no trouble now
Who quoted me the vagrancy laws
In a voice slippery as seaweed under the kirkyard.
I rigged his boat with the seven curses.
Occasionally still, for encouragement,
I put the knife in his net.

Though she has black peats and a yellow hill
And fifty silken cattle
I do not go near Merran and her cats.
Rather break a crust on a tombstone.
Her great-great-grandmother
Wore the red coat at Gallowsha.

The thousand rabbits of Hollandsay
Keep Simpson's corn short,
Whereby comes much cruelty, gas and gunshot.
Tonight I have lit a small fire.
I have stained my knife red.
I have peeled a round turnip.

And I pray the Lord
To preserve those nine hundred and ninety nine innocents.

Finally in Folscroft lives Jeems,
Tailor and undertaker, a crosser of limbs,
One tape for the living and the dead.
He brings a needle to my rags in winter,
And he guards, against my stillness
The seven white boards
I got from the Danish wreck one winter.

ALASTAIR MACKIE

In Absentia

‘We’ve no heard frae God this while,’
said ane o the angels.
It was at a synod
o the metaphors.

Cam a wind;
it was aabody speirin
‘Wha?’
intill themsels.

It was heard by the sauls
o Baudelaire and Pascal.
They fell thro the muckle hole
opened by the question.

I the boddom Jesus sweatit
‘Consummatum est.’
And Nietzsche
hou he laucht and laucht.

The maist o fowk bein neither
philosophers or theologians
kept gaun tae the kirk.
Whiles, like.

Syne God said: ‘Noo I’m awa,
mak a kirk or a mill o’t.’

And God gaed tae the back o beyond
i the midst o aathing.

Beethoven's Chunty

'Picture to yourself . . . a rather ancient grand piano . . . Under it–I do not exaggerate–an unemptied chamber-pot.' *Baron de Trémont on a visit to Beethoven in 1809*

'The chaumer's like a muck-midden.'
And he steppit atween the aidle-peels on the flair.
'It's a gey and queer rain, gin it be rain.
Herr Beethoven
maun hae a deef neb forby.'

Brakfest and denner on the cheers.
A sark sleeve plytered amang soup.
Priein the fat
the flees joukit in and oot the soss.

On the tap o the grand piana
a smirr o stew.
Note-books. A jumble o blads;
sang-notes briered atween the furs o the staves.
'The makkins o a symphony? The seeventh?
The baron near fylt himsel to speir.

Aa o a sudden he saw't.

'Losh be here!
The chunty's no been teemed.'

It stood ablow the piana
as hamely as a joug on the brod,
as the leavins in the shet.

He'd sat on't and he'd birsed.
It had saired its turn.
A body eats and drinks and kichs.
In atween times there were airels in his heid.
A place for ilkie thing
ilkie thing in its place.

The baron wrote hame–
'I dinna exaggerate . . .'

He wrote truer nor he kent.

Scots Pegasus

Oor Scots Pegasus
is a timmer naig
wi a humphy back and cockle een.

He ettles tae flee
but his intimmers are fu o the deid-chack.
Gin he rins ava
he pechs sair.
And spales drap aff like sharn.

he's fed on bruck
scranned frae aa the airts.
This gies him the belly thraw
and yon etten and spewed look.

Makars whiles
fling a leg ower his rig-bane
and crank the hunnle on his spauld.

He taks a turn roon the park
but niver gets aff the grun
or oot o the bit.
This mishanter's caad
in some stables –
'A new voice in Lallans.'

Ithers, brither Scots
gie him the hee-haw.

The hert o the nut is this –
naebody, dammt, kens the horseman's wird.

W. PRICE TURNER

Fable from Life

Eight hundred telephone directories
will bulletproof a truck, claims
a fruit company in South America.
Think of a bullet with so many numbers
on it, stopping nothing. Bandits,
clamped to their rocks like wild posies,
leap up, banging and screeching.
The desert bristles with rifles
and vexed moustaches. After all
that fuss, the truck bumps on.
Fruitless compliments to the patron saint
of bad luck; then a clutter of big hats
raises a thin oasis of ritual smoke.
El Moroso, who once broke a tooth
on his own bullet in the first bite
of cool plunder, savours the loss.
Clearly, the moral is to have no truck
with thick-skinned civilizations.

Hard Times

A dealer in second-hand delusions
swears that the bottom dropped out of the market
as soon as the magic lamp clicked.
Time was you could sell them anything
if the packaging was right. Whatever
they didn't want to buy they'd go broke trying to win
if you maddened them with balloons and squeakers.
It's different now. They're just about immune
to lotus blossom; you have to tempt them
by subtler stuff, like sweating to fix up Junior
with a Chair of Nugatory Equivocation,
or Moving With The Times into a New Era
of technological streamlined aimlessness.
Trouble is, when they're on a regular overdose
of shadow passion, they tend to fall back

on guilt-edged securities like IOU's to God,
the pies Mother used to bake, the holiday camp
at the bottom of the bottle, logical analysis,
or If-I-didn't-do-it-someone-else-would.
Once they start making their own there's no holding them,
so where's the percentage in manufacturing
the stuff, with everyone hooked on his own bait?
You might as well try to interest them in
reality, one day at a time. Can
you see them queuing for guaranteed
involvement, slow uncertain developments,
sudden letdowns, chances, lulls and challenges?
Neither can I. Besides, my subscription
to the ulcer society lapsed long ago.
How are you fixed for allegories?

Wig Block

Polystyrene heads,
going at twenty-nine pence!
I must have one of those.

Such purity. White, odourless;
dense as the texture of critical prose,
yet featherweight enough
to contain millions of sterile cells
in puffed tensions, an immobile foam
shaped in egghead form
to appease the arcadian dream
sealed in the tomb
of the unknown economist.

Let this be my surrogate
at public opinion polls
and let it occupy my pillow
when my bed
is otherwise empty.
The umpteen ageing plots
of a thousand prosperous novelists
have less substance

than this smooth beauty.
Later I'll buy two wigs
to keep her warm, and a set
of best quality mink eyelashes.
With all this accomplished
no one will ever guess
how inadequate I do not feel
owning only one pair of shoes
and two feet to fit in them,
not even a single hat,
but a solitary head
and not enough hair to cover that.

Colour Supplement

If, when you turn on the tap,
blood chortles out, hawking and snorting
into a sluggish glottal flow,
there's no need to be alarmed
providing you keep a pint bottle
of fresh milk handy to rinse the sink.

It's best to draw just enough
for immediate needs, though a full glass
will keep fairly well overnight. Don't
throw away the skin. Shredded
through mayonnaise it adds piquancy
to even the humblest of salads.

For soup, about a quart, straight
into the pot. Slice an onion, add
a pinch of tarragon and simmer
gently: serves four. For cocktails,
always chill before serving and mix
well. Try it with vodka for new zest.

A Few Novelties from our Extensive Range

The coffin as sentry-box beside the bed,
or the coffin on wheels, a perspex coffin.

The coffin as bed itself, with ox-tripe sheets,
or the coffin as bath, and plastic lotus.

A connoisseur's coffin, limited edition,
champagne cork lining, cigar-band crest.

A coffin of marzipan, with sugared rivets,
or the stainless steel coffin, Teflon-lined.

The do-it-yourself coffin, collapsible,
the rubber and leather one, with chains.

The progressive coffin, computerised
to champ its way down and belch flowers.

Box-file coffins, government surplus,
stackable coffins, room-dividers.

The rockabye gilt-edged for security,
the happening, for your own Thing.

IAIN CRICHTON SMITH

The Visit of the Inspectors

The inspectors come to inspect.
The inspected wait by their beds.

The trumpets sound. Man is on his way
through a tangle of paper, through a forest of pens,
through a trembling of cloth.
The inspectors fasten a button.
The inspectors notice a 2
missing from a memorandum
about what is expected from
an old typewriter
in the atomic age.

The office cleaner is hidden in a cupboard
because she is dirty
and smells like a cloud of dung
when you approach her:
similarly the office clerk
who has been here for fifty years
and reports absurd tales
of loyalty, honesty, sincerity,
who is, in relation to the inspectors,
indecipherable blotting paper.

Stand by your beds!
Hear the notes of the paper bugles.
The shepherds on the green hillsides
spit lazily as they talk.
Soon they will be unable to play.
For the paper mounts and mounts
and the illiterate inspectors
have their notebooks open.

Ah, poor shepherds, stand by your sheep!
You have to account for every moment
you dozed there, absorbing the sun.
And also those times you played cards

when you should have been watching
the position of the grass in the field,
and noting the temperature.

What have you done with your flutes?
The inspectors will want to know.
They are not educated men
but they know what they like
such as scenes showing harvests
and men toiling beautifully under the sun.
They will not speak proper grammar
and they wear blue shiny suits
and finally let me tell you they hate you
for being so idle.

They don't know anything about sheep
but they know about inspections
and their words are as definite as death.
They use language differently from you. Know that.
They do not suffer as you do
but they are human.

Your job therefore is to watch them
standing there with straws in your mouths.
Remember the blue suits, the thin wives,
the ladders of diamonds.
Remember it and put it in your music
which should be solid as the stones
that lie out on the hillsides
and after all ought to be here
when you are both gone.

TOM BUCHAN

Scotland the wee

Scotland the wee, crèche of the soul,
of thee I sing

land of the millionaire draper, whisky vomit
and the Hillman Imp

staked out with church halls, gaelic sangs
and the pan loaf

eventide home for teachers and christians,
nirvana of the keelie imagination

Stenhousemuir, Glenrothes, Auchterarder, Renton
– one way street to the coup of the mind.

The Weekend Naturalist

My humanoid friend, myself, a limited animal
in love with the planet
escapes across the dumb topographies of Assynt
with his maps and compass
taking incorrect fixes on anonymous Bens
staring into bog-pools

entertaining himself with half-baked notions
of a utilitarian character
and applying his ragbag of ecological data
to flowers which he recognises
with difficulty as if they were old friends
he was unable to place

timidly leaping backwards at the green skeleton
of a ewe
scared out of his wits by an equally terrified stag
and always very much conscious
of his wet socks, deaf ear, balding pate
and overfilled gut

but retaining even here persistent after-images
of his bank-statement
the impersonal malevolence of the minor officials
the pretensions
of well-paid academics, the untrustworthiness
of friends, shopkeepers and politicians

until the speculative fountain of his vague ideas
coalesces into irritability
and the innocent towers of darkening gneiss
stand over him like tax-inspectors
as he stumbles on a delinquent peat
and falls on his face.

Letter from a Partisan

Up here in the orgone stream our muscular
armour relaxes com-
pletely, pinetrees shimmy
like dildos on their moist pelvic
floor and oxygenated water
cascades past our sensitized ears.

In our mountain command post
our synapses are in full spasm suffused
with invisible telepathic
vibrations as we plan the lib-
eration of Scotland
from the puritanical conformist unionist hordes.

Our cap-
tain (confined to his sleeping-bag
with a painful bout of genital
cramp) issues his orders in curt quiet tones:
you can hear the copper clunk of bullets, the plop
of rain on a mapcase.

Message boys slip away through the bracken
to contact our suburban groupuscules: they
travel on foot hitching occasional lifts

from unsuspecting lairds and suspicious ministers
stopping only at lonely Highland mo-
tels for a lay and a sip of the cratur.

At the head of the Black
Loch we ambush a file of artificial insemination
technologists. We entertain com-
rades from Truro – for them
our uniformed girls open their soft
parts as a gesture of interfraternal sol-

idarity. We question an agent
provocateur from St Andrew's House nearly
yanking his balls off. It's a hard
life but a good one
up here in the mountains. Tell Charlie
thanks for the truss. Scotland for ever!

DUNCAN GLEN

Progress

Is not nature wonderful

The goose walks oot and gets its mither
baith schooled and weel conditioned

Is not nature wonderful

We come oot head first   get a slap
and oor mither tongue

Is not nature wonderful

They gae walkin oot ane ahint the ither

Is not nature wonderful

Hush a bye baby on a tree top
A wash and sang and then to sleep

Is not progress wonderful

Ane and ane mak twa
And Jack gaes up the hill

Is not progress wonderful

Jack. Jack. Jack.
That's my guid boy.
Thief. Thief. Thief.
Jack. Jack. Jack.
That's my guid boy.

Is not progress wonderful

And soon in fine condition for schoolin

Is not progress wonderful

And the goose walks oot and gets
a box on a string

Is not nature wonderful

Dresst to Kill

We're dresst to kill.
It's a white tie and tails affair.

There's nae bare breists here.
Nae drinkin frae the finger bowl.

Aa's talk and polisht siller.
We ken the ceremony.

We staun in lines wi pride in oor weys.
We toast oor peers – oor heids thrown back.

Let in the lang-haired ane.
Let her roll naukit on the table.
Bring in the scabby heid.
The hairy-breistit ane.
The ane-leggit dwarf.

The stiff protectin fronts are burst.
Thocht's broken doun wi its sophistication.
Reid-breistit emotion's in the drivin seat.
Aa's nuclear pooer and lynch-mob gane wud.

We're faur ayont ony chimps' tea-pairty.
We'll tear the stuffin oot ony fremit doll.

ALAN JACKSON

Knox (1)

the old scots grim man
with the chin
eats an apple on the bus

he hides it in his pocket between bites

for fear of the animal
for fear of the people

Knox (2)
(second half to 'Johnny Lad')

in the pub
where the hundred fastest women in Glasgow go
to get Americans
I put my hand round my girlfriend's breast.
Quick as a flash the barman comes up and says:
'Cut that out, son. This is a public bar'.

O Knox he was a bad man
he split the Scottish mind.
The one half he made cruel
and the other half unkind.
As for you, as for you, as for you, auld Jesus lad,
gawn dance the nails fae oot yer taes, an
try an be mair glad.

Wifie

This wifie wi a shoppin basket,
A goes up tae her an says
Hey wifie, see, there's the wild Pentlands
Just behind ye.

She drapped it.

And so it goes on

and the wife is the mother
and the wife is the house
and the wife is the cooking pot
cooking glue

and the husband is the son
he makes a journey every morning
and makes it back every night
not an hour late
not a minute late
not a second late
is best

the mother grub is waiting on the table

Young Politician

What a lovely, lovely moon.
And it's in the constituency too.

Edinburgh Scene

we used to be typists
but the hell wi' that
now we live with these boys
in a two room flat

we've never washed for ages
we sleep on bits of sack
we've baith lost wir pants
and wi dinnae want them back

the boys are a' big beardies
they think we're awfy sweet
we never know which one we're with
that's what it means to be beat

The Worstest Beast

the worstest beast that swims in the sea
is man with his bathing trunks down to his knee

the worstest beast that goes through the air
is man with his comb to tidy his hair

the worstest beast that bores through soil
is man with his uses for metal and oil

the worstest beast that hunts for meat
is man who kills and does not eat

the worstest beast that suckles its young
is man who's scared of nipples and dung

the worstest beast that copulates
is man who's mixed his loves and hates

the worstest beast that has warm skin
is man who stones himself with sin

he's the worstest beast because he's won
it's a master race and it's almost run

DONALD CAMPBELL

Vietnam on my Mind

Gaun doun one Sunday tae the back-green
tae tak hir washin in, my wife was raped
up the back-passage by an unseen
unkent sex-maniac wha'd seeminly escaped
frae some near-haun loony-bin or ither

My puir wee laddie, worrit for his mither
rushed tae the windae when he heard her yell
an, raxan up, managed fine tae lowse the sneck
but in the lowsan tint his balance an syne fell
the full fifteen feet – an aa but broke his neck!

Loupan tae my feet when I heard the crash
o my son's body bringan baith o us tae earth
I gaed owre tae the windae an heard the sair stramash
o my lassie screaman 'Murder!!!!!'
                                        for aa that she was warth. . . .

An I jaloused that (aiblins) I'd neglectit my ain kind
sittan at the fireside – wi Vietnam on my mind.

TOM LEONARD

The Voyeur

what's your favourite word dearie
is it wee
I hope it's wee
wee's such a nice wee word
like a wee hairy dog
with two wee eyes
such a nice wee word to play with dearie
you can say it quickly
with a wee smile
and a wee glance to the side
or you can say it slowly dearie
with your mouth a wee bit open
and a wee sigh dearie
a wee sigh
put your wee head on my shoulder dearie
oh my
a great wee word
and Scottish
it makes you proud

NOTES

Place of publication is London unless otherwise indicated. The abbreviation S.T.S. refers to the Scottish Text Society.

ANONYMOUS POEMS

These poems of the fifteenth and sixteenth centuries are found in the Bannatyne MS (1568), except for 'The Bewteis of the Fute-ball' which comes from the Maitland Folio MS (c.1580).

Ane anser to ane Inglis railar

During the period of national independence, the Scots were understandably irritated by the British national legend fostered by historians and myth-makers south of the border. This snapping sonnet attacks Geoffrey of Monmouth's account of the Trojan Brut(us), great-grandson of Aeneas and eponymous founder of Britain, by blacking Brut's character; Geoffrey says he killed his father accidentally (*Historia Regum Britanniae*, I.iii). The poet also mocks Bede's story of how Pope Gregory, noticing some handsome English slaves on sale in Rome, said they were well named—angels rather than Angles (*Historia Ecclesiastica Gentis Anglorum*, II.1). Not so, says the poet; the Angle's haunt is the Angulus (angle, shady nook, lurking-place).

See: *Bannatyne MS*, ed. W. T. Ritchie, S.T.S., 4 vols., Edinburgh and London, 1928-34.
Maitland Folio MS, ed. W. A. Craigie, S.T.S., 2 vols., Edinburgh and London, 1919-27.
Select Remains of the Ancient Popular and Romance Poetry of Scotland, ed. D. Laing and J. Small, Edinburgh and London, 1885.

ROBERT HENRYSON

Almost nothing is known about Henryson, though the tradition is that he was a schoolmaster in Dunfermline. There are different early versions of his *Morall Fabillis*, and the text is in some dispute. Standard modern editions tend to be based on the Bassandyne printed edition of 1571, with a few corrective readings from the Bannatyne MS (1568). Professor John MacQueen argues in his book on Henryson (listed below) that the Bannatyne texts are generally superior and should be used as the basis. Without being convinced by all of MacQueen's argument, I append the two most important passages from 'The Fox and the Wolf' where Bannatyne's version may be preferred.

My destany, and eik my werd I watt,
Myn evintour is cleirly to me kend;
With mischeif mynyet is my mortall fait,
My mysleving the soner bot I men(d).

(36-39)

This suddane deid and unprovisit end
Off this fals tod, without contritioun,
Exemple is exhortand folk to mend,
For dreid of sic a lyke conclusioun:
For monye gois now to confessioun
Can nocht repent, nor for thair synnis greit,
Becaus thai think thair lustye lyfe so sweit.

(162-8)

See: *The Poems of Robert Henryson*, ed. G. G. Smith, S.T.S., 3 vols., Edinburgh and London, 1906-14.
The Poems and Fables of Robert Henryson, ed. H. H. Wood, Edinburgh, 1933, 1958.
Robert Henryson: *Poems*, ed. C. Elliott, Oxford, 1963, 1974.
M. W. Stearns, *Robert Henryson*, New York, 1949.
J. MacQueen, *Robert Henryson: A Study of the Major Narrative Poems*, Oxford, 1967.

WILLIAM DUNBAR

Very little that is factual is known about Dunbar's life. He held some unspecified position at the court of James IV (1488-1513). His royal pension of £10, granted in 1500, was raised to £20 by 1507 and £80 by 1510. He had taken priestly orders by 1504. The rest of his 'biography' is mainly conjecture based on his poems.

The Fenyeit Freir of Tungland

The 'feigned friar' was John Damian, an Italian adventurer, doctor, and alchemist who won the favour of James IV, being made Abbot of Tungland (Tongland, near Kirkcudbright) in 1504, and receiving many payments, recorded in the Treasurer's Accounts, for the furthering of his scientific experiments. In 1507 he strapped on a pair of wings, tried to fly from the battlements of Stirling Castle, fell and broke his thigh, but survived.

To the Merchantis of Edinburgh

The 'stinking school' (l.15) has not been identified; the 'parish kirk' (l.16) is St Giles; the 'high cross' (l.22) is the Mercat Cross, north-east of St Giles; the 'stinking style' (l.38) is probably the Old-Kirk Style, a lane running through the Luckenbooths (shops) north of St Giles. In the last line a word is missing in the only MS of the poem.

See: *The Poems of William Dunbar*, ed. J. Small, A. J. G. Mackay, and W. Gregor, S.T.S., 3 vols., Edinburgh and London, 1884-93.
The Poems of William Dunbar, ed. W. M. Mackenzie, Edinburgh, 1932; London, 1960.
The Poems of William Dunbar, ed. J. Kinsley, Oxford, 1979.
J. W. Baxter, *William Dunbar: A Biographical Study*, Edinburgh and London, 1952.

T. Scott, *Dunbar: A Critical Exposition of the Poems*, Edinburgh and London, 1966.

SIR DAVID LYNDSAY

Lyndsay was the eldest son of David Lyndsay of the Mount, an estate near Cupar, Fife. It is not known where he was educated, but records show that by 1511 he had some position at the court of James IV. After James's death at Flodden in 1513, he became usher to the infant James V. Although he lost this post during the ascendancy of the Earl of Angus (1524-28), he later returned to favour, being made a herald by 1530, and receiving his knighthood and appointment as Lyon King of Arms about 1542. His post as herald, which involved the arrangements of pageants and masques, encouraged the development of his sense of theatre, and an early version of his *Satyre* was played in Linlithgow Palace in 1540. It was presented in extended form at the Castle Hill in Cupar in 1552, and on Calton Hill in Edinburgh in 1554. There have been highly successful revivals in recent years at the Edinburgh Festival and at Glasgow University.

The first of the two extracts included here comes from the comic interlude between the two main parts of the play. In Part I the young King Humanity is led astray by flatterers and by Lady Sensuality, and is warned by Divine Correction that he must summon a parliament of the estates of the realm. In Part II the parliament is convened, and John the Commonweil states his case against the widespread abuses and corruptions in church and state, the ecclesiastics in particular being exposed by condemning themselves out of their own mouths, as in the second of the present extracts. Lyndsay's sympathies are strongly on the side of reform, though his final position as 'Catholic' or 'Protestant' may be less than clearcut.

The Pardoner's references, in best music-hall tradition, are an interesting mixture of the legendary and the contemporary, the far-flung and the local: the Irish giant Finn MacCool (l.50) and the Khan of Tartary (l.44) rub shoulders with reformers like Martin Luther, Heinrich Bullinger, and Philip Melanchthon (ll.34-35), or with the border reiver Johnny Armstrong hanged by James V.

See: *The Works of Sir David Lindsay*, ed. D. Hamer, S.T.S., 4 vols., Edinburgh and London, 1931-6.
Ane Satyre of the Thrie Estaits, ed. J. Kinsley, 1954.
A Satire of the Three Estates (abridged acting text), ed. R. Kemp and M. McDiarmid, 1967.
W. Murison, *Sir David Lyndsay: Poet, and Satirist of the Old Church in Scotland*, Cambridge, 1938.
J.S.Kantrowitz, *Dramatic Allegory: Lindsay's 'Ane Satyre of the Thrie Estaitis'*, Lincoln, Nebraska, 1975.

ALEXANDER MONTGOMERIE

Much of the evidence relating to Montgomerie's life is tantalizing, obscure, or even contradictory. Although his rough dates would tend to be given as c.1545-c.1610, dates nearer 1550-1597 would be argued by some interpreters of facts recently discovered, even if this still leaves unsolved problems. He was a soldier of fortune, a pirate, a Catholic spy, involved in Catholic conspiracies in Europe and at home, imprisoned and outlawed, yet he also had some happy years at the court of the young James VI and enjoyed his favour, intermittently at least. James, a kinsman as well as an admirer of 'belovit Sandirs', quotes from his 'Flyting' in *Ane Schort Treatise, Conteining som Reulis and Cautelis to be observit and eschewit in Scottis Poesie* (1584), and the flyting with Sir Patrick Hume of Polwarth probably took place as a reading or performance at court about 1582. As Montgomerie says in his 27th Sonnet:

I love the King,
Whose Highness laughed som tym for to look
Hou I chaist Polwart from the chimney nook.

l.23: there is probably some word-play in the name Powmathorne. There is a Pomathorn in Midlothian, though Polwarth is in Berwickshire.

l.150: Caithness and the Canonry of Ross were parts of northern Scotland strongly associated with witches.

See: *The Poems of Alexander Montgomerie*, ed. J. Cranstoun, S.T.S., Edinburgh and London, 1887; Supplementary Volume, ed. G. Stevenson, 1910.
Alexander Montgomerie: A Selection from his Songs and Poems, ed. H. M. Shire, Edinburgh, 1960.

WILLIAM DRUMMOND

Drummond's father was the laird of Hawthornden, an estate near Lasswade in Midlothian, and held a minor position at the court of James VI. The poet was educated at Edinburgh University, and later studied in France. He was learned in many languages, built up a fine library, and lived the life of a country gentleman at Hawthornden. He died a few months after the execution of Charles I in 1649. Drummond has been rather emasculated by literary historians, and a revaluation of his work is under way. The prevailing image of the refined, melancholy lyricist has to face the fact that he also wrote political pamphlets, and satirical and scurrilous verse, some of it of remarkable virulence. He was a conservatist and a royalist, stung into satire by the growth of militant presbyterianism and the eruption of the Civil War.

A Character of the Anti-Covenanter

Drummond ironically attacks himself, or the beliefs of someone like himself, through the voice of a Covenanter. A 'Malignant' was the name given to a royalist by the parliamentarians. The 'Tables' (l.13) were a permanent committee formed in Edinburgh in 1637 to defend presbyterianism. An 'Armenian' (i.e. Arminian, l.18) rejected strict Calvinist doctrine and emphasized continuity with the pre-Reformation church. Lines 68-70 probably refer to the Catholic League, and to the deaths of Henry III and Henry IV of France, both assassinated by religious fanatics.

On Pime

John Pym (1584-1643) was the leading English parliamentarian and opposer of Charles I. He was active in confirming the Anglo-Scottish alliance after English acceptance of the Scottish Solemn League and Covenant of 1643, which provided for the establishment of a presbyterian state church in England and Ireland as well as in Scotland.

See: *The Poetical Works of William Drummond of Hawthornden*, ed. L. E. Kastner, S.T.S., 2 vols., Edinburgh and London, 1913.
William Drummond of Hawthornden: Poems and Prose, ed. R. H. MacDonald, Edinburgh and London, 1976.
D. Masson, *Drummond of Hawthornden: The Story of his Life and Writings*, 1873 (reprinted New York, 1969).
F. R. Fogle, *A Critical Study of William Drummond of Hawthornden*, New York, 1952.
R. H. MacDonald (ed.), *The Library of Drummond of Hawthornden*, Edinburgh, 1971.

ALLAN RAMSAY

Ramsay was born at Leadhills in Lanarkshire and became first a wigmaker in Edinburgh, and later a bookseller and publisher. He opened the first British circulating library, was a founder-member of an art school, and did his best to start a theatre. His strong national feeling made him the instigator of a revival of writing in Scots, his own contribution showing in his *Poems* of 1721 and 1728, and the earlier tradition being gathered up in his anthologies, *The Tea-Table Miscellany* (1723-37) and *The Ever Green* (1724).

Lucky Spence's Last Advice

Ramsay's own note on the title reads: 'Lucky [i.e. bawd, alewife—Ed.] *Spence*, a famous bawd who flourished for several Years about the Beginning of the Eighteenth Century; she had her Lodgings near *Holyrood-house*; she made many a benefit Night to herself, by putting a Trade in the Hands of young Lasses that had a little Pertness, strong Passions, Abundance of Laziness, and no Fore-thought.'

l.41: Ramsay explains as follows: 'Delate them to the Kirk-Treasurer. *Hale the Dools* is a Phrase used at Foot-ball, where the Party that gains the *Goal* or *Dool* is said to hail it or win the Game, and so draws the Stake.'

See: *The Works of Allan Ramsay*, ed. B Martin, J. W. Oliver, A. M. Kinghorn and A. Law, S.T.S., 6 vols., Edinburgh and London, 1951-74.
Poems by Allan Ramsay and Robert Fergusson, ed. A. M. Kinghorn and A. Law, Edinburgh and London, 1974.
B. Martin, *Allan Ramsay: A Study of his Life and Works*, Cambridge, Mass., 1931 (reprinted Westport, Conn., 1973).

ROBERT FERGUSSON

'Poor Bob Fergusson', as Burns called him, was born in Edinburgh, and educated at Edinburgh High School, Dundee Grammar School, and St Andrews University. He worked in Edinburgh as a copying clerk, but in his leisure time showed his passion for music and theatre and for the vivacious drinking-club ambience of the city. During the last year of his short life he suffered from a psychotic depressive illness, and died as a 'pauper lunatic' in the appalling cells of the Edinburgh Bedlam.

Hame Content

l.60: the idea is of a weakling succeeding to an inheritance.

ll.89-96: 'Leader haughs an' Yarrow braes', 'Tweeda's banks', and 'Cowdenknows' refer to popular songs.

l.107: William Hamilton of Bangour (1704-54), poet, author of the song 'The Braes of Yarrow'.

To the Principal and Professors

The superb treat took place on 19 August 1773, and Johnson wrote later that he was 'entertained with all the elegance of lettered hospitality'; Boswell, more blunt, said it was 'a very good dinner'.

l.10: the River Eden enters the sea at St Andrews.

ll.61-64: in the opening lines of 'Polemo-Middinia', a macaronic poem attributed to William Drummond and probably by him; the poem deals with a burlesque fight in Fife.

ll.65-66: alluding to two songs, 'The Roast Beef of Old England' and 'The East Neuk of Fife'.

ll.83-98: Fergusson had been challenged to a duel by a man in Dunfermline who objected to his uncomplimentary poem 'An Expedition to Fife and the Island of May'.

See: *The Poems of Robert Fergusson*, ed. M. P. McDiarmid, S.T.S., 2 vols., Edinburgh and London, 1954-56.
Poems by Allan Ramsay and Robert Fergusson, ed. A. M. Kinghorn and A. Law, Edinburgh and London, 1974.
S. G. Smith (ed.), *Robert Fergusson 1750-1774: Essays by Various Hands to Commemorate the Bicentenary of his Birth*, Edinburgh, 1952.
A. H. MacLaine, *Robert Fergusson*, New York, 1965.

ROBERT BURNS

Burns was born at Alloway in Ayrshire. His father was a gardener and later an unlucky and unsuccessful farmer. Burns had an unsettled education in the formal sense, as the family moved from farm to farm, but was a voracious reader and made himself a well-informed and very articulate man. After the success of the Kilmarnock edition of his poems in 1786 he went to be lionized in Edinburgh, but returned to the countryside to farm in Dumfriesshire, with no more satisfaction in that job than his father had had. In his last years he worked as an exciseman in Dumfries, where he died.

The Twa Dogs

ll.1-2: the district of Kyle in Ayrshire.
ll.11-12: Newfoundland.
l.27: in James Macpherson's Ossianic poems.

Holy Willie's Prayer

The epigraph, from *The Rape of the Lock*, IV.64, comes in a catalogue of actions caused by the spirit of Spleen. Holy Willie's real name was William Fisher, and the 'Sessional process' refers to the questioning of Gavin Hamilton in 1785 for alleged inadequacy in church attendance. Hamilton was a liberal-minded solicitor and a friend of Burns. 'Father Auld' was William Auld, parish minister in Mauchline. Robert Aiken was a patron of Burns who helped him to get subscribers for the Kilmarnock edition.
l.17: 4004 B.C. was the traditional date of the Creation.

Address to the Deil

The epigraph is from *Paradise Lost*, I.128-9, Beelzebub addressing Satan.
l.101: Job.
l.111: during the war in Heaven (*Paradise Lost*, VI.320-34).

Address of Beelzebub

Burns takes up an unexpected viewpoint in this poem, since it is usual to commiserate with the Highlanders who in the late eighteenth and early nineteenth centuries were forced to emigrate, on being evicted from their homes and holdings to make way for sheep. But he is concerned less with the Highland Clearances as such than with what he sees as aristocratic tyranny trying to foil democratic will. John Prebble thinks that Burns's insight failed him in this instance, if he 'could believe with the gentry that the people were going willingly and happily to the other side of the world' (*The Highland Clearances*, 1963). Whether or not this is so, Burns's feeling in the poem is extremely strong.

ll.13-16: John Hancock, Benjamin Franklin, George Washington, and Richard Montgomery were charismatic figures of the American struggle to gain independence from Britain.

ll.21-24: Lord North, Lord George Sackville, Sir William Howe, and Sir Henry Clinton were, from Burns's point of view, an anti-charismatic British quartet to match the above.

l.58: Polycrates was tyrant of Samos in the 6th century B.C.

l.60: Diego D'Almagro served under Francisco Pizarro during the sixteenth-century conquest of Peru, and was put to death by him.

l.64: Beelzebub does not care to call the date Anno Domini 1786.

When princes and prelates

l.9: the Duke of Brunswick led Prussian and Austrian troops against France in 1792, but was defeated.

l.15: Frederick William II of Prussia.

ll.21-22: Catherine the Great of Russia placed her ex-lover Stanislaus Poniatowski on the throne of Poland in 1763, and Poland was later partitioned between Russia and Prussia.

See: *The Poems and Songs of Robert Burns*, ed. J. Kinsley, 3 vols., Oxford, 1968.
The Songs of Robert Burns, ed. J. C. Dick, 1903 (reprinted Hatboro, Penn., 1962).
The Merry Muses of Caledonia, ed. J. Barke and S. G. Smith, Edinburgh, 1959.
The Letters of Robert Burns, ed. J. De L. Ferguson, 2 vols., Oxford, 1931.
F. B. Snyder, *The Life of Robert Burns*, New York, 1932 (reprinted Hamden, Conn., 1968).
H. Hecht, *Robert Burns: The Man and his Work*, London, Edinburgh, and Glasgow, 1936.
De L. Ferguson, *Pride and Passion: Robert Burns 1759-1796*, New York, 1939.
D. Daiches, *Robert Burns*, 1952.
T. Crawford, *Burns: A Study of the Poems and Songs*, Edinburgh and London, 1960.
M. Lindsay, *The Burns Encyclopedia*, 2nd edn., 1970.
M. Lindsay, *Robert Burns: The Man, his Work, the Legend*, 2nd edn., 1968.
R. T. Fitzhugh, *Robert Burns: The Man and the Poet*, New York, 1970.
D. A. Low (ed.), *Critical Essays on Robert Burns*, 1975.

JAMES HOGG

The 'Ettrick Shepherd' was indeed a shepherd, and the son of a shepherd, and was born at Ettrickhall farm in the parish of Ettrick in the Scottish borders. He had hardly any formal schooling, but read much, and had his imagination filled with songs, stories, and ballads from local and general Scottish tradition. After encouragement by Walter Scott, and after a number of disastrous farming ventures, he moved to Edinburgh in 1810 to become a professional writer, and gained fame as a poet, though today he is more highly regarded as the novelist of *Confessions of a Justified Sinner*.

Sir Morgan O'Doherty's Farewell to Scotland

Hogg wrote a 'Reply to Sir Morgan O'Doherty's Farewell to Scotland', which is unfortunately much less spirited than the attack.

l.15: the River Sark runs into the Solway Firth.

l.21: Cadwall(ad)er was a semi-legendary seventh-century Welsh king and national hero.

See: *The Works of the Ettrick Shepherd*, ed. T. Thomson, 2 vols., London, Glasgow, and Edinburgh, 1865.
James Hogg: Selected Poems, ed. D. S. Mack, Oxford, 1970.
E. C. Batho, *The Ettrick Shepherd*, Cambridge, 1927.
A. L. Strout, *The Life and Letters of James Hogg*, Vol. 1. (1770-1825) (no more published), Lubbock, Texas, 1946.
L. Simpson, *James Hogg: A Critical Study*, Edinburgh and London, 1962.
D. S. Mack, 'The Development of Hogg's Poetry', *Scottish Literary News*, Vol.3, No. 1, April 1973, pp.1-8.
D. Gifford, *James Hogg*, Edinburgh, 1976.

SIR WALTER SCOTT

Born in Edinburgh, where his father was a Writer to the Signet, Scott likewise studied law, and was called to the bar in 1792. His passion for the Scottish ballad, and for Scottish history and legend, was roused in his boyhood and never left him, giving him themes for many of the best of his novels and poems. The long poems which first made his name—*The Lay of the Last Minstrel*, *Marmion*, *The Lady of the Lake*—are verse romances, with some fine cumulative large-scale effects but insufficient care or concentration in the writing. He achieved a tighter poetry in the short song-like or ballad-like pieces found in his novels.

Proud Maisie

Although it stands perfectly well by itself, the poem should also be seen in the context where it appears (*The Heart of Midlothian*, chap.10), where it is the last of four snatches of song uttered on her deathbed by the crazed Madge Wildfire, in a scene of great power. There is an interesting discussion of the poem in the book by Robin Mayhead listed below (pp.117-22).

See: *The Poetical Works of Sir Walter Scott*, ed. J. L. Robertson, 1904.
Sir Walter Scott: Selected Poems, ed. T. Crawford, Oxford, 1972.
J. W. Oliver, 'Scottish Poetry in the Earlier Nineteenth Century', in *Scottish Poetry: A Critical Survey*, ed. J. Kinsley, 1955.
D. Davie, 'The Poetry of Sir Walter Scott', *Proceedings of the British Academy*, Vol.47, 1961, pp.60-75.
T. Crawford, *Scott*, Edinburgh and London, 1965.
E. Johnson, *Sir Walter Scott: The Great Unknown*, 2 vols., 1970.
R. Mayhead, *Walter Scott*, Cambridge, 1973.

ALLAN CUNNINGHAM

Cunningham was born in a cottage near Blackwood House in Nithsdale, Dumfriesshire, and trained as a stonemason. His father, a factor and sometime farmer, was an acquaintance of Burns, and he himself was a friend of James Hogg. His literary interest centred on traditional ballad and song, and many of his poems were imitations of traditional ballad style. 'Honest Allan', as Walter Scott perhaps unwisely called him, delighted in deceiving innocent ballad-collector, but he did not deceive the experts. He captures admirably, in the present 'Jacobite' poem, the general unpopularity of the new Hanoverian dynasty as well as the more specific Scottish slant of the Jacobite threat.

See: *Poems and Songs*, ed. P. Cunningham, 1847.
D. Hogg, *Life of Allan Cunningham, with Selections from his Work and Correspondence*, Dumfries, 1875.
F. Miller, *The Poets of Dumfriesshire*, Glasgow, 1910.

ALEXANDER RODGER

Born in East Calder, Midlothian, Rodger lived most of his life in Glasgow and was known as a 'Glasgow Radical' poet. He was variously employed as silversmith, weaver, cloth-inspector, music-teacher, and journalist. Although he was a part-editor of the sentimental *Whistle-Binkie* anthologies, and contributed to them, he shows a greater vigour in his satirical work, which has been unduly neglected.

Sawney, now the King's come

Explained in a footnote by Rodger's editor, Robert Ford: 'When, in 1822, George IV visited Scotland, Sir Walter Scott was largely in evidence, and produced for the occasion, as everybody knows, his celebrated poem—"Carle, now the King's Come," Rodger sounded quite another note—not less spirited; and almost simultaneously with the appearance of Sir Walter Scott's well-known poem, and, in point of fact, just as His Majesty was enriching his Scottish subjects with the first glint of his royal person, the *London Examiner* made its appearance in Auld Reekie containing the above satirical lyric, "Sawney, now the King's Come," which caused scarcely less sensation. It certainly greatly annoyed the sensitive loyalty of the author of "Waverley," and speculation ran wild as to the identity of the author, until, by and by, Rodger chose to reveal himself.' To which it may be added that Scott was himself, as he wrote, adding 'new words to an auld spring', the song being much older.

l.1: Sawney (Sandy, Alexander) is a derisory term for a Scotsman.

l.43: the 'forty-twa' was a public lavatory in Edinburgh with forty-two cubicles.

Shaving Banks

The first savings bank, or at least the first to be organized on sound business principles, is generally agreed to be Scottish, and to have opened in Ruthwell, Dumfriesshire, in 1810. Although savings banks spread rapidly in the next decades, they were regarded with great suspicion by radicals, as clever and far-seeing devices for a new sort of enslavement of working people. The 'Matthew' of the subtitle, or Matthew the Cyclops as he is called in an earlier version of the poem, is one of a series of grotesquely caricatured ministers set out in an anti-clerical poem, 'Advice to the Priest-ridden', written about the same time. No doubt Rodger does not forget that the Ruthwell Savings Bank was the brainchild of a minister, the Rev. Henry Duncan. The occasion of the satire was the opening of a savings bank at Calton in the east end of Glasgow.

ll.27-28: Cathkin Braes and Glasgow Green are open parks in Glasgow.

l.104: George Rose, M.P., fathered the Savings Bank Act of 1817. As a wealthy man with many sinecures, he was strongly attacked by William Cobbett and other radicals.

ll.105-6: 'from one end of the country to the other'.

l.148: Nicholas Vansittart, M.P., was Chancellor of the Exchequer.

ll.152-3: Viscount Castlereagh and Viscount Sidmouth were statesmen whose repressive domestic policies made their names anathema to radicals.

l.155: the Prince Regent, later George IV.

l.157: George Canning, anti-radical statesman and poet.

l.158: St Stephen's Chapel at Westminster was the old House of Commons.

l.173: i.e. Sidmouth.

Stanzas written on reading of the death of Thomas Paine

Thomas Paine (1737-1809) wrote in support of the American and French Revolutions and died in New York. Rodger interestingly inverts the customary Romantic exaltation of Satan as a figure of liberating opposition to the divine tyranny.

See: A. Rodger, *Scotch Poetry: consisting of Songs, Odes, Anthems, and Epigrams*, 1821.

Peter Cornclips, A Tale of Real Life, with other Poems and Songs, Glasgow, 1827.

Stray Leaves from the Portfolios of Alisander the Seer, Andrew Whaup, and Humphrey Henkeckle, Glasgow, 1842.

Poems and Songs, Humorous, Serious, and Satirical, ed. R. Ford, Paisley, 1897; enlarged edn. 1901, including 'Peter Cornclips'.

JANET HAMILTON

A remarkable self-educated woman, daughter of a shoemaker, Janet Hamilton was born at Carshill near Shotts in Lanarkshire. In her hard life—she was married at thirteen, raised a large family, went blind—she wrote poetry on a great variety of subjects from Italian and Polish politics to colliery disasters and the role of women in society. Her prose essays, especially 'Scottish Peasant Life and Character in Days of Auld Langsyne', 'Sketches of a Scottish Roadside Village Sixty Years Since', and 'Reminiscences of the Radical Times in 1819-20', are vivid and informative.

See: *Poems Sketches and Essays by Janet Hamilton* (ed. J. Hamilton, with essays by G. Gilfillan and A. Wallace), New Edition, Glasgow, 1885.
J. Young, *Pictures in Prose and Verse, or, Personal Recollections of the late Janet Hamilton, Langloan*, Glasgow, 1877.

WILLIAM THOM

Thom was born in an Aberdeen slum, and became a weaver; he had little schooling. In a life of much poverty and hardship, with many moves from place to place in search of work, he had a brief period of fame in London. Like so many minor poets of the time in Scotland, he lacked discerning critics, and wasted a lot of his effort on undistinguished sentimental verse when he should have been developing his real talent for the satirical and the grotesque.

Whisperings for the Unwashed

l.1: Thom's footnote reads: 'In most of the small boroughs of the north of Scotland there is a town drummer, who parades at five in the summer and six o'clock in the winter. In Nairn a man blows a cow-horn.'

Chants for Churls

Written on the Disruption in the Church of Scotland in 1843, when the Free Church was formed.

See: *Rhymes and Recollections of a Hand-Loom Weaver*, by William Thom, ed. W. Skinner, Paisley, 1880.
R. Bruce, *William Thom, The Inverurie Poet—A New Look*, Aberdeen, 1970.

CHARLES, LORD NEAVES

Born in Edinburgh, the son of a solicitor, Neaves was educated at the Royal High School and Edinburgh University. Called to the bar in 1822, he was made a judge in the court of session in 1854. He was a philologist, a translator, and a regular contributor to *Blackwood's Magazine*. His 'Songs and Verses', whether one calls them poetry or light verse, are sprightly and stimulating, and cover a wide range of subjects, biological, religious, philosophical, social, linguistic, and literary.

See: *Songs and Verses, Social and Scientific*, 4th edn., enlarged, Edinburgh and London, 1875.

ROBERT LOUIS STEVENSON

Stevenson was born in Edinburgh, the son of a civil engineer. After studying engineering and later law at Edinburgh University, he travelled in France, Switzerland, and America, and eventually sailed for the South Seas in 1889, settling on an estate in Samoa, where he died.

The Counterblast Ironical

Last of a trio of poems, of which the first two are called 'The Blast–1875' and 'The Counterblast–1886'. The first jocularly curses God for perversely upsetting human plans and expectations; the second argues for moderation, for acceptance of the mixed state of things here below. Both poems are rather commonplace. But the third, with the bite of its irony, stands out, as if Stevenson had felt the need for something sharper.

See: *Robert Louis Stevenson: Collected Poems*, ed. J. A. Smith, 2nd edn., 1971.
H. W. Garrod, 'The Poetry of R. L. Stevenson', in *Essays Mainly on the Nineteenth Century Presented to Sir Humphrey Milford*, 1948.
D. Young, 'Scottish Poetry in the Later Nineteenth Century', in *Scottish Poetry: A Critical Survey*, ed. J. Kinsley, 1955.
S. Saposnik, *Robert Louis Stevenson*, New York, 1974.
E. Morgan, 'The Poetry of Robert Louis Stevenson', in *Essays*, Cheadle, Cheshire, 1974.

JOHN DAVIDSON

Davidson was born in Barrhead, Renfrewshire, the son of a minister of the Evangelical Union. After trying a variety of jobs–working in a chemical laboratory, clerking, teaching–he moved south to London, to make writing his profession, in 1889. An ambitious output of novels, plays, and essays, as well as poems, failed to gain him the full recognition he sought, and a certain megalomania spread in his writing and no doubt contributed to his eventual suicide. The strength of his impact on later poets may be gauged from the tributes by T. S. Eliot and Hugh MacDiarmid included in the book by Maurice Lindsay listed below.

The Crystal Palace

The Crystal Palace, erected in Hyde Park for the Great Exhibition of 1851, was moved to Sydenham in south London in 1854; almost destroyed by fire in 1936, it was demolished in 1941. The huge glass and iron structure, much admired by architectural historians, is satirized by Davidson for its unyielding, unweathering quality–'A house that must not mellow or decay –but the detail and brilliant vigour of his mocking description argue an underlying attraction.

l.7: Sir Hiram Maxim (1840-1916), American inventor of a famous machine-gun, also took an early interest in aircraft design.

l.23: Jean Baptiste Isabey (1767-1855), French portrait-painter and miniaturist.

l.150: Jean-Antoine Houdon (1741-1828). French sculptor.

l.154: Schopenhauer referred to 'the gay and amiable Voltaire' in *The World as Will and Idea*, Book 4, Supplementary chapter 'On Death'.

ll.187-8: Aesculapius, god of medicine; Hyg(i)eia, goddess of health.

l.203: *bon per*, so far unexplained, may be a misprint for *bonpré*, a kind of Bordeaux wine.

l.258: Benvenuto Cellini (1500-71), Italian sculptor and metalsmith.

l.259: Antonio Canova (1757-1822), Italian sculptor.

l.268: Jean Baptiste Auguste Clésinger (1814-43), French sculptor.

l.270: Andrea del Verrocchio (1435-88), Italian sculptor and painter.

l.306: Thomas Linacre (c.1460-1524), humanist and physician; William Pitt the Elder, Earl of Chatham (1708-78), statesman.

l.307: Sir William Jones (1746-94), philologist and jurist.

See: *The Poems of John Davidson*, ed. A. Turnbull, 2 vols., Edinburgh and London, 1973.
John Davidson: A Selection of his Poems, ed. M. Lindsay, 1961.
J. B. Townsend, *John Davidson: Poet of Armageddon*, New Haven, 1961.
C. V. Peterson, *John Davidson*, New York, 1972.

CHARLES MURRAY

Born at Alford, Aberdeenshire, Murray trained as a civil engineer and surveyor and spent most of his working life in South Africa, becoming Secretary for Public Works in that country in 1910. His supple and persuasive use of spoken Aberdeenshire Scots comes just before Hugh MacDiarmid was to push Scots in a different direction—towards a more general, synthetic, literary language. The argument between 'spoken' and 'literary' Scots has continued.

Dockens afore his Peers

Published in his collection of poems of the First World War, *A Sough o' War* (1917).

See: *Hamewith: The Complete Poems of Charles Murray* (with introduction by N. Shepherd), Aberdeen, 1979.

J. M. CAIE

Caie was born at Banchory-Devenick in Kincardineshire and educated at Aberdeen University and the North of Scotland College of Agriculture, becoming eventually Deputy Secretary of the Department of Agriculture.

See: J. M. Caie, *The Kindly North: Verse in Scots and English* (with introduction by P. Giles), Aberdeen, 1934.

HUGH MACDIARMID

Christopher Murray Grieve ('Hugh MacDiarmid') was born at Langholm in Dumfriesshire, where his father was a postman. After being educated at Langholm Academy and the Broughton Junior Students' Centre in Edinburgh, he worked as a journalist in various parts of Scotland, and later of England, and took a practical part in politics. He was a founder-member of the National Party of Scotland, and had a stormy relationship with that party and also with the Communist Party. He served with the Royal Army Medical Corps during the First World War and as an engineer in the Merchant Service during the Second. He was the driving force behind the 20th-century revival of Scottish Poetry.

Crowdieknowe

Crowdieknowe is a graveyard near Langholm.

A Drunk Man Looks at the Thistle

The opening section of a long poem in which the image of a drunk man, sprawling in the moonlight and gazing at what he sees as the metamorphoses of a giant thistle, is used to present a kaleidoscopic vision of Scotland in the context of history and eternity.

l.29: a kilted Polish violinist would be no more ridiculous, in MacDiarmid's view, than the kilted Scottish comedian.

ll.30-32: Duncan: American dancer, with Scottish ancestry; Garden and Grant: Scottish soprano and painter respectively, who made their names outside Scotland.

l.54: 'There was a lad was born in Kyle' is an autobiographical song by Burns.

ll.66-67: 'A man's a man for a' that' is a refrain line in Burns's song 'Is there, for honest poverty'.

l.72: decadent cosmopolitanism is echoed in T. S. Eliot's poem 'Burbank with a Baedeker: Bleistein with a Cigar'.

ll.70, 77: a popular but maudlin song like 'The Star o' Rabbie Burns' is indeed small change for a nation to receive.

To Circumjack Cencrastus

The title of this long poem ('to enfold the curly snake') refers to its rather intermittently pursued theme of catching the winding and elusive serpent of wisdom. The poem is a loose mosaic, where many sub-themes, like that of Scottish independence as in the present extract, shoot off from the main search.

An Apprentice Angel

The dedicatee, the Very Rev. Lauchlan Maclean Watt, was a minor poet and literary essayist who was also Minister of Glasgow Cathedral and later Moderator of the General Assembly of the Church of Scotland. He died in 1957. He had reviewed MacDiarmid's *To Circumjack Cencrastus* in dismissive and vulgar terms ('it sounds like Homer after he had swallowed his false teeth'), and the poet pillories him in his autobiography *Lucky Poet*, but takes a more poetic revenge in 'An Apprentice Angel'.

Prayer for a Second Flood

l.8: the Esk is a Scottish border river familiar to MacDiarmid from his childhood.

Glasgow 1960

First published 1935.

l.3: Ibrox Park, ground of Rangers Football Club.

See: *Hugh MacDiarmid: Complete Poems 1920-1976*, ed. M. Grieve and W. R. Aitken, 2 vols., 1978.
The Uncanny Scot: A Selection of Prose by Hugh MacDiarmid, ed. K. Buthlay, 1968.
Selected Essays of Hugh MacDiarmid, ed. D. Glen, 1969.
Hugh MacDiarmid, *Lucky Poet: A Self-Study in Literature and Political Ideas,* 1943 (reprinted 1972).
Hugh MacDiarmid: A festschrift, ed. K. D. Duval and S. G. Smith, Edinburgh, 1962.
Hugh MacDiarmid: A Critical Survey, ed. D. Glen, Edinburgh and London, 1972.
D. Glen, *Hugh MacDiarmid and the Scottish Renaissance*, Edinburgh and London, 1964.
K. Buthlay, *Hugh MacDiarmid*, Edinburgh and London, 1964.
R. Watson, *Hugh MacDiarmid*, Milton Keynes, 1976.
E. Morgan, *Hugh MacDiarmid*, 1976.
Akros 34-35 (MacDiarmid double number), August 1977.
Scottish Literary Journal, Vol.5, No. 2 (MacDiarmid memorial number), December 1978.

WILLIAM SOUTAR

Born in Perth, the son of a joiner, Soutar was educated at the Southern District School and Perth Academy. After serving in the Navy (1917-18), he entered Edinburgh University to study medicine, but transferred to English and graduated in 1923. He was attacked by a form of spondylitis, and spent the last thirteen years of his life immobilized in bed.

Empery

Alexander the Great wept, the story goes, because he had no more worlds left to conquer. Soutar's answer is like Brecht's in a poem written about the same time, 'Questions from a worker, reading': 'The young Alexander took India. / By himself?'

A Whigmaleerie

l.1: Auchtergavan is a village in Perthshire.

See: *William Soutar: Collected Poems*, ed. H. MacDiarmid, 1948.
Poems in Scots and English by William Soutar, ed. W. R. Aitken, Edinburgh, 1961.
Diaries of a Dying Man by William Soutar, ed. A. Scott, Edinburgh and London, 1954.

A. Scott, *Still Life: William Soutar 1898-1943*, Edinburgh and London, 1958.

GEORGE BRUCE

Bruce was born in Fraserburgh, Aberdeenshire, where his father ran a herring-curing firm. He was educated at Fraserburgh Academy and Aberdeen University. After teaching English and history at Dundee High School, he became a B.B.C. producer (1946-70) and was responsible for a vigorous output of Scottish cultural and documentary programmes. After 1970 he held various creative writing fellowships and visiting professorships in Britain and America.

See: *The Complete Poems of George Bruce*, Edinburgh, 1971.
G. Bruce, 'The Boy on the Roof', in *As I Remember*, ed. M. Lindsay, 1979.
A. Scott, 'Myth-Maker: The Poetry of George Bruce', *Akros* 29, December 1975, pp.25-40.

ROBERT GARIOCH

Robert Garioch Sutherland, to give him his full name, was born in Edinburgh and educated at the Royal High School and Edinburgh University. He was a teacher for many years, in Scotland and England; served with the Royal Corps of Signals during the Second World War and was taken prisoner; and worked on the *Dictionary of the Older Scottish Tongue* and at the School of Scottish Studies in Edinburgh.

Embro to the Ploy

This satire on the Edinburgh Festival uses the 'bob-wheel' stanza often employed by earlier Scottish poets, and especially by the anonymous medieval author (possibly James I) of *Peblis to the Play*, a poem of May Day celebrations in Peebles.

And They Were Richt

ll.1-2: 'Fionn Mac Colla', pen-name of novelist Thomas Douglas MacDonald (1906-75); *Ane Tryall of Heretiks* (his spelling) is a chapter of a historical novel which was presented as a dramatic dialogue at the 1962 Edinburgh Festival.

See: R. Garioch, *Collected Poems*, Edinburgh, 1977 and Manchester, 1980.
The Masque of Edinburgh, Edinburgh, 1954.
Two Men and a Blanket: Memoirs of Captivity, Edinburgh, 1975.
'Early Days in Edinburgh', in *As I Remember*, ed. M. Lindsay, 1979.
D. M. Black, 'Robert Garioch', *Lines Review* 23, Spring 1967, pp.8-15.

R. Watson, 'The Speaker in the Gairdens: The Poetry of Robert Garioch', *Akros* 16, April 1971, pp.69-76.
D. Campbell, 'Another Side to Robert Garioch, or, A Glisk of Near-Forgotten Hell', *Akros* 33, April 1977, pp.47-52.

NORMAN MACCAIG

Born in Edinburgh and educated at the Royal High School and at Edinburgh University, where he took Classics, MacCaig spent most of his career as a teacher and latterly headmaster. Since 1970 he has been Fellow in Creative Writing at Edinburgh University and Reader in Poetry at Stirling University.

See: N. MacCaig, *Old Maps and New: Selected Poems*, 1978.
Tree of Strings, 1977.
'My Way of It', in *As I Remember*, ed. M. Lindsay, 1979.
Akros 7, March 1968 (special MacCaig issue).
M. J. W. Scott, 'Neoclassical MacCaig', *Studies in Scottish Literature*, Vol. 10, No. 3, January 1973, pp.135-44.
R. Fulton, *Contemporary Scottish Poetry: Individuals and Contexts*, Edinburgh, 1974, pp.69-87.
W. S. Porter, 'The Poetry of Norman MacCaig', *Akros* 32, December 1976, pp.37-53.
E. Frykman, *'Unemphatic Marvels': A Study of Norman MacCaig's Poetry*, Göteborg, 1977.

DOUGLAS YOUNG

Young was born in Tayport, Fife, and educated at Merchiston Castle School in Edinburgh. He went on to study Classics at St Andrews and Oxford, and then to teach that subject at various universities in Scotland, America, and Canada, becoming Paddison Professor of Greek at the University of North Carolina in 1970. He was Chairman of the Scottish National Party 1942-45. A linguist, translator, and scholar, he called himself with fair accuracy 'an intermittent, but sometimes quite accomplished, minor poet'.

Last Lauch

Perhaps a further 'last laugh' has now emerged in the fact that the poem itself has become a memorial object, carved on a paving-stone in Glenrothes where pedestrians may meditate on it or stamp on it according to choice.

See: *A Clear Voice: Douglas Young, Poet and Polymath: A Selection from his Writings with a Memoir*, ed. C. Young and D. Murison, Edinburgh, 1977.
D. Young, *Auntran Blads: An Outwale o Verses*, Glasgow, 1943.

D. Young, *A Braird o Thristles: Scots Poems*, Glasgow, 1947.
Chasing an Ancient Greek: Discursive Reminiscences of an European Journey, 1950.

SYDNEY GOODSIR SMITH

Born in Wellington, New Zealand, of a Scottish mother, Smith was educated at Malvern College and at the universities of Oxford and Edinburgh. His father held the Chair of Forensic Medicine at Edinburgh University. Smith was a literary editor, playwright, novelist, painter, and art critic as well as poet. Although the Scots medium he developed was eclectic and idiosyncratic, he identified himself very wholeheartedly with the movement to revive the use of Scots.

See: S. G. Smith, *Collected Poems 1941-1975* (with introduction by Hugh MacDiarmid), 1975.
The Wallace: A Triumph in Five Acts, Edinburgh and London, 1960.
Carotid Cornucopius, Glasgow, 1947 (revised and enlarged edn., Edinburgh, 1964).
A. Scott, 'Daylight and the Dark: Edinburgh in the Poetry of Robert Fergusson and Sydney Goodsir Smith', *Lines* 3, Summer 1953 (S.G. Smith number), pp.9-13.
N. MacCaig, 'The Poetry of Sydney Goodsir Smith', *Saltire Review*, Vol. 1, No.1, April 1954, pp.14-19.
Akros 10, May 1969 (S.G. Smith number).
T. Crawford, 'The Poetry of Sydney Goodsir Smith', *Studies in Scottish Literature*, Vol 7, Nos. 1-2, July-October 1969, pp.40-59.
E. Gold, *Sydney Goodsir Smith's 'Under the Eildon Tree': An Essay*, Preston, Lancashire, 1975.
Scotia Review 9, April 1975 (memorial number).
For Sydney Goodsir Smith (memorial miscellany), Edinburgh, 1975.
K. Buthlay, 'Sydney Goodsir Smith: Makar Macironical', *Akros* 31, August 1976, pp. 46-56.

TOM SCOTT

Scott was born in Glasgow and educated at Hyndland Secondary School, Madras College (St Andrews), and (much later) at Edinburgh University where he took a doctorate. His father was a boilermaker and later a builder's labourer, and Scott himself worked at the latter job. He served with the Royal Army Pay Corps in England and Nigeria (1939-44), and after the war lived for some years in London before finally settling in Edinburgh. He has edited various anthologies, and published a study of William Dunbar.

See: T. Scott, *An Ode til New Jerusalem*, Edinburgh, 1956.
The Ship and Ither Poems, 1963.
At the Shrine o the Unkent Sodger: A Poem for Recitation, Preston, Lancashire, 1968.
Brand the Builder, 1975.
The Tree, Dunfermline, 1977.
J. Herdman, 'Towards New Jerusalem: The Poetry of Tom Scott', *Akros* 16, April 1971, pp.43-49.
T. Crawford, 'Tom Scott: From Apocalypse to Brand', *Akros* 31, August 1976, pp.57-69.
Scotia Review 13-14, August-November 1976 (T. Scott double issue).

MAURICE LINDSAY

Born in Glasgow, where his father was an insurance manager, Lindsay was educated at Glasgow Academy and the Scottish National Academy of Music (now the Royal Scottish Academy of Music and Drama). An arm injury put an end to his hoped-for career as a violinist, but he led a varied and busy life as drama and music critic, broadcaster, editor, anthologist, TV programme controller, and (from 1967) Director of the Scottish Civic Trust. During the Second World War he served in the Cameronians (Scottish Rifles). He has published travel books, books on Burns, and a history of Scottish literature.

One Day at Shieldaig

Shieldaig is a village in Wester Ross.

See: M. Lindsay, *Collected Poems* (with introduction by A. Scott), Edinburgh, 1979.
Selected Poems 1942-1972, 1973.
Walking Without an Overcoat: Poems 1972-76, 1977.
'I Belong to Glasgow', in *As I Remember*, ed. M Lindsay, 1979.
D. Campbell, 'A Different Way of Being Right: The Poetry of Maurice Lindsay', *Akros* 24, April 1974, pp.22-26.

EDWIN MORGAN

Born in Glasgow, where his father was a clerk with a firm of iron and steel scrap merchants, and later a director with the same firm, Morgan was educated at Rutherglen Academy, Glasgow High School, and Glasgow University. He served with the Royal Army Medical Corps, mostly in the Middle East, 1940-46. After taking a degree in English in 1947, he lectured in that subject at Glasgow University, where he was made Titular Professor in 1975. He has published or exhibited concrete/visual poems, has written a number of opera librettos, and has worked as translator, editor, and anthologist.

The Flowers of Scotland

Written in 1967, the year of the great anti-Vietnam demonstration in Washington, when (to quote Norman Mailer) 'posed against the lines of soldiers, already some historic flowers were being placed insouciantly, insolently, and tenderly in gun barrels by boys and girls' (*The Armies of the Night*). Other references in the poem—the sale of Staffa, a particularly reactionary annual meeting of the General Assembly of the Church of Scotland, the banning of an Aubrey Beardsley exhibition and of the film of Joyce's *Ulysses*—were also topical in the Scotland of that year.

School's Out

1.49: Summerhill was the school founded in 1921 at Leiston, Suffolk, by the progressive Scottish educationalist A. S. Neill.

1.73: Ivan Illich, American educationalist, published his book *Deschooling Society* in 1971.

See: E. Morgan, *The Second Life*, Edinburgh, 1968.
Instamatic Poems, 1972.
From Glasgow To Saturn, Cheadle, Cheshire, 1973.
Essays, Cheadle, Cheshire, 1974.
The New Divan, Manchester, 1977.
R. Fulton, 'Two Scottish Poets: Edwin Morgan and Iain Crichton Smith', *Stand* Vol. 10, No.4, 1969, pp.60-68.
R. Fulton, *Contemporary Scottish Poetry: Individuals and Contexts*, Edinburgh, 1974, pp.13-40.
J. Rillie, 'Wrinkles of the Shrinking World', *Lines Review* 57, March 1976, pp. 14-21.
M. Walker, *Edwin Morgan: An Interview*, Preston, Lancashire, (reprinted from *Akros* 32, December 1976), 1977.
M. Schmidt, *Fifty Modern British Poets*, 1979, pp.314-20.

ALEXANDER SCOTT

Scott was born in Aberdeen, the son of a power-loom tuner, and educated at Aberdeen Academy and Aberdeen University, where he graduated in English in 1947. During the war he was in the Royal Artillery and the Gordon Highlanders, serving in north-western Europe and winning the Military Cross. He lectured briefly at Edinburgh University in English, and since 1948 has taught Scottish Literature at Glasgow University, where he was made Head of Department of Scottish Literature in 1971. He has been playwright, editor, biographer, and anthologist as well as poet, and has been very active in extending the knowledge and study of Scottish literature.

Til John Maclean

John Maclean (1879-1923) was a Glasgow teacher and communist revolutionary who also wanted to see a Scottish republic. As the first line of the poem says, he added the blue-and-white saltire of the Scottish flag to the red flag of international communism—unacceptably, as it turned out, to both socialists and nationalists in Scotland, who remained divided.

Lament for a Makar

ll.6-7: Douglas Young was jailed for refusing war service in an army that was British, not Scottish.

Heart of Stone

Written for a B.B.C. television film in 1966.

l.16: a statue of General Gordon of Khartoum.

l.67: the present neo-Gothic façade of Marischal College (a part of Aberdeen University) dates from 1906.

See: A. Scott, *Mouth Music: Poems and Diversions*, Edinburgh, 1954.
Cantrips, Preston, Lancashire, 1968.
Greek Fire: A Sequence of Poems, Preston, Lancashire, 1971.
Double Agent: Poems in English and Scots, Preston, Lancashire, 1972.
Selected Poems 1943-1974, Preston, Lancashire, 1975.
The MacDiarmid Makars 1923-1972 (with appendix 'The Poetry of Alexander Scott' by G. Bruce), Preston, Lancashire, 1972.
'Growing Up with Granite', in *As I Remember*, ed. M. Lindsay, 1979.
N. MacCaig, review of *Cantrips* in *Akros* 9, January 1969, pp.67-69.
L. Macintyre, 'Alexander Scott, Makar Extraordinary', *Akros* 25, August 1974, pp.71-78.
L. Mason, *Two North-East Makars: Alexander Scott and Alastair Mackie: A Study of their Scots Poetry*, Preston, Lancashire, 1975.
R. Lennox, 'The Poetry of Alexander Scott', *Akros* 33, April 1977, pp.60-68.

GEORGE MACKAY BROWN

Born in Stromness, Orkney, the son of a postman who was also a part-time tailor, Brown was educated at Stromness Academy, at Newbattle Abbey College (when Edwin Muir was warden), and at Edinburgh University. He has published short stories, novels, plays and essays as well as poetry. Almost all his writing is about Orkney, where he has continued to live.

Ikey on the People of Hellya

The figure of Ikey the tinker recurs in a number of Brown's poems—disgracefully irrepressible. Hellya is an imaginary island, used by Brown also in his novel *Greenvoe* and his play *A Spell for Green Corn*.

See: G. M. Brown, *Loaves and Fishes*, 1959.
The Year of the Whale, 1965.
Fishermen with Ploughs, 1971.
Winterfold, 1976.
Selected Poems, 1977.
An Orkney Tapestry, 1969 (prose).
Letters from Hamnavoe, 1975 (prose).

G. M. Brown, 'An Autobiographical Essay', in *As I Remember*, ed. M. Lindsay, 1979.
D. Dunn, ' "Finished Fragrance": The Poetry of George Mackay Brown', *Poetry Nation* 2, 1974, pp.80-92.
P. Pacey, 'The Fire of Images: The Poetry of George Mackay Brown', *Akros* 32, December 1976, pp.61-71.
D. Jones, 'Swatches from the Weave of Time: The Work of George Mackay Brown', *Planet* 40, November 1977, pp.38-44.
A. Bold, *George Mackay Brown*, Edinburgh, 1978.

ALASTAIR MACKIE

Born in Aberdeen and educated at Skene Square School, Robert Gordon's College, and Aberdeen University, Mackie served in the Royal Air Force and Royal Navy during the war, and has been an English teacher at Stromness and at Anstruther. Like MacDiarmid, he has tried (in his own words) to 'work for a more extended canon of Scots in order to give Scots poetry bulk and variety'.

See: A. Mackie, *Soundings*, Preston, Lancashire, 1966.
Clytach, Preston, Lancashire, 1972.
At the Heich Kirk-yaird: A Hielant Sequence, Preston, Lancashire, 1974.
'Change and Continuity in Modern Scottish Poetry', *Akros* 33, April 1977, pp.13-40.
R. Garioch, review of *Clytach* in *Lines Review* 42-43, September 1972-February 1973, pp.143-6.
J. Herdman, 'The Progress of Scots', *Akros* 20, December 1972, pp.31-42.
A. Scott, *The MacDiarmid Makars 1923-1972*, Preston, Lancashire, 1972.
L. Mason, *Two North-East Makars: Alexander Scott and Alastair Mackie: A Study of their Scots Poetry*, Preston, Lancashire, 1975.
G. Bruce, 'The Poetry of Alastair Mackie, or, Feet on the Grun', *Akros* 33, April 1977, pp.76-86.

W. PRICE TURNER

Born in York, of Scottish parents, and educated in Glasgow at Whitehill Secondary School, Turner served in the Royal Engineers 1945-47. He has written novels and radio plays as well as poetry, has edited a poetry magazine, and has worked as a journalist, a B.B.C. floor manager, and a tutor and fellow in creative writing.

See: W. P. Turner, *First Offence*, Bristol, 1955.
The Rudiment of an Eye, 1955.

W. P. Turner, *The Flying Corset*, 1962.
Fables from Life, Newcastle-upon-Tyne, 1966.
More Fables from Life, Portrush, N. Ireland, 1969.
The Moral Rocking-Horse, 1970.
Thistles, Malvern, Worcestershire, 1979.
K. Smith, review of *The Flying Corset*, *Stand*, Vol.6, No.4, 1964, pp. 71-72.
M. Butler, review of *The Moral Rocking-Horse*, *Samphire* 11, January 1971, pp.22-23.
R. Fisher, review of *The Moral Rocking-Horse*, *Birmingham Post*, 31 July 1971, p.11.

IAIN CRICHTON SMITH

Born on the island of Lewis, Smith was educated at the Nicolson Institute, Stornoway, and Aberdeen University. After serving in the Royal Army Educational Corps, he taught English at Clydebank and Oban. Since 1977 he has been a free-lance writer. He is the author of novels, short stories, plays, translations, and criticism, in addition to poetry, and is bilingual in Gaelic and English.

See: I. C. Smith, *The Long River*, Edinburgh, 1955.
Thistles and Roses, 1961.
The Law and the Grace, 1965.
From Bourgeois Land, 1969.
Selected Poems, 1970.
Hamlet in Autumn, Edinburgh, 1972.
Love Poems and Elegies, 1972.
The Notebooks of Robinson Crusoe, 1975.
In the Middle, 1977.
'Between Sea and Moor', in *As I Remember*, ed. M. Lindsay, 1979.
Akros 29, June 1969 (I. C. Smith number).
L. Macintyre, 'Poet in Bourgeois Land' (interview with I. C. Smith), *Scottish International Review*, September 1971, pp.22-27.
R. Fulton, 'The Poetry of Iain Crichton Smith', *Lines Review* 42-43, September 1972-February 1973, pp.92-116.
E. Morgan, 'The Raging and the Grace: Some Notes on the Poetry of Iain Crichton Smith', in *Essays*, Cheadle, Cheshire, 1974.
F. Lindsay, 'Disputed Angels: The Poetry of Iain Crichton Smith', *Akros* 36, December 1977, pp.15-26.

TOM BUCHAN

Born in Glasgow, the son of a doctor, Buchan was educated at Jordanhill College School, Balfron High School, Aberdeen Grammar School, and

Glasgow University. He has worked as a teacher of English and drama in schools and colleges in Scotland and India; has been associated with the Iona Community; and has been a theatre director and an organizer of festivals and community projects. He collaborated with the comedian Billy Connolly in the writing of *The Great Northern Welly Boot Show*, produced in Glasgow and in London in 1972.

Scotland the Wee

l.9: towns in Stirlingshire, Fife, Perthshire, and Dunbartonshire respectively.

The Weekend Naturalist

l.3: Assynt is a mountainous region in Sutherland.

See: T. Buchan, *Ikons*, Madras, 1958.
Dolphins at Cochin, 1969.
Exorcism, Glasgow, 1972.
Poems 1969-1972, Edinburgh, 1972.
Forwords, Glasgow, 1977.
'Double Profile: Tom McGrath and Tom Buchan', *Scottish International Review*, Vol. 5, No.2, February 1972, pp.29-32.

DUNCAN GLEN

Born in Cambuslang, Lanarkshire, Glen was educated at West Coats School, Cambuslang, Rutherglen Academy, Heriot-Watt College, Edinburgh, and Edinburgh College of Art. He served in the Royal Air Force 1956-58. He is a typographic designer, and has taught and administered that subject at Watford, Preston, and Nottingham. He has been very active as publisher, editor, anthologist and bibliographer, and has devoted his energies particularly to making available and publicizing the work of Hugh MacDiarmid.

See: D. Glen, *Idols: When Alexander our King was Dead*, Preston, Lancashire, 1967.
Kythings, Thurso, Caithness, 1969.
In Appearances, Preston, Lancashire, 1971.
Mr & Mrs J.L. Stoddart at Home, Preston, Lancashire, 1975.
Buits and Wellies: or, sui generis: A Sequence o Poems, Preston, Lancashire, 1976.
Follow! Follow! Follow!, Preston, Lancashire, 1976.
Traivellin Man: A Sequence o Poems, Preston, Lancashire, 1977.
In Place of Wark: or, Man of Art, Preston, Lancashire, 1977.
Gaitherings: Poems in Scots, Preston, Lancashire, 1977 (collects *Feres*, 1971; *Clydesdale*, 1971; *A Cled Score*, 1974).
Of Philosophers and Tinks: A Sequence of Poems, Preston, Lancashire, 1977.
The Individual and the Twentieth-Century Scottish Literary Tradition, Preston, Lancashire, 1971.
J. C. Weston, review of *In Appearances*, *Akros* 16, April 1971, pp. 77-80.

A. Cluysenaar, review of *In Appearances, Stand,* Vol. 12, No. 4, 1971, p. 73.
W. Perrie, 'Meaning and Self', *Chapman*, Vol. 2, No. 1, Spring 1972, pp.9-11.
J. Herdman, 'The Progress of Scots', *Akros* 20, December 1972, pp.31-42.
T. S. Law, 'At Home with "Mr and Mrs J. L. Stoddart at Home"', *Akros* 29, December 1975, pp.57-74.
L. Mason, *Two Younger Poets: Duncan Glen and Donald Campbell: A Study of their Scots Poetry*, Preston, Lancashire, 1976.
P. Pacey, 'The Poetry of Duncan Glen, or, Lallans and Heich Places', *Akros* 33, April 1977, pp.91-102.

ALAN JACKSON

Born in Liverpool, Jackson was educated at the Royal High School, Edinburgh, and Edinburgh University, where he left without taking a degree. He has worked as a labourer and as a trainee psychiatric nurse, and was active in developing poetry readings in Scotland in the 1960s.

See: A .Jackson, *Underwater Wedding*, Edinburgh, 1961.
Sixpenny Poems, Bristol, 1962.
Well Ye Ken Noo, Bristol, 1963.
All Fall Down, Edinburgh, 1965.
The Worstest Beast, Edinburgh, 1967.
The Grim Wayfarer, 1969.
Idiots are Freelance, Dyce, Aberdeenshire, 1973.
'The Knitted Claymore: An Essay on Culture and Nationalism', issued as *Lines Review* 37, June 1971 (special number).
D. Eadie, 'Alan Jackson: Poet with a Choice to make', *Glasgow Herald*, 28 September 1968, p.8.
R. Gardner, 'Out of the Foetal Underground: Interview with Alan Jackson', *Guardian*, 26 May 1970, p.8.

DONALD CAMPBELL

Born in Wick, Caithness, and educated at Boroughmuir Senior Secondary School, Edinburgh, Campbell has worked as an accounts clerk and as a writer-in-residence to Edinburgh schools. He has written several successful plays.

See: D. Campbell, *Poems*, Preston, Lancashire, 1971.
Rhymes 'n Reasons (with introduction by Hugh MacDiarmid), Edinburgh, 1972.
Murals, Edinburgh, 1975.
Blether, Nottingham, 1979.

D. Campbell, 'Art and Society', *Q*, June 1976, pp.17-18.
'Four Figures in a Personal Landscape', in *Jock Tamson's Bairns*, ed. T. Royle, 1977.
J. Herdman, 'The Progress of Scots', *Akros* 20, December 1972, pp.31-42.
A. Scott, *The MacDiarmid Makars*, Preston, Lancashire, 1972.
Scotia Review 11, December 1975 (interview), pp.2-8.

TOM LEONARD

Born in Glasgow and educated at Lourdes Secondary School, Glasgow, and Glasgow University, Leonard has worked in a bookshop and as a dole clerk and has done postgraduate research on James ('B. V.') Thomson. He writes in English and in Glasgow patois, and has a particular interest in 'voice', which has led him to radio drama and to sound-poetry.

See: T. Leonard, *Six Glasgow Poems*, Glasgow, 1969.
A Priest Came On at Merkland Street, Glasgow, 1970.
Poems, Dublin, 1973.
Bunnit Husslin, Glasgow, 1975.
Three Glasgow Writers (with Alex Hamilton and James Kelman), Glasgow, 1976.
My Name Is Tom, 1978.
If Only Bunty Was Here: A Drama Sequence of Totally Undramatic Non-sequiturs, Glasgow, 1979.
'The Proof of the Mince Pie', *Scottish International Review*, December 1973, pp.20-23.
'Tom Leonard in Conversation with David Drever' (interview), *Oasis* (Glasgow), Vol. 1., No.3, 1976, pp. 15-17.
'The Locust Tree in Flower, and Why it had Difficulty Flowering in Britain', *Poetry Information* 16, Winter 1976-77, pp.9-14.
E. Morgan, review of *Poems* in *Eboracum* (York) 17, Winter 1973, p.14.
T. McGrath, 'Tom Leonard: Man with Two Heads', *Akros* 24, April 1974, pp.40-49.
G. Rosie, 'Noo lissenty mi toknty yi', *Radio Times*, 12-18 February 1977, p.14.

GLOSSARY

Aa, a': all
aabody: everybody
aafie: awfully
abasit: dismayed
ablow: below
abread, abreed: abroad
abune, abone: above
ae: one, only
aff: off
affrichtit: frightened
aft: often
agley: astray
ahin(t): behind
aiblins: perhaps
aidle-peels: urine-pools
aikand: aching
ain: own
a(i)nce, anes, anis: once
aipen: open
aiprim: (?)apron
airels: musical tones
airn: iron
airt: quarter, direction; art
aits: oats
aittand: eating
aixis: ague fit
alhaill: altogether
alkin: all kinds of
allther: of all
almous-hous oster: almshouse oyster
almry: cupboard
alrege: eldritch, uncanny
als: also
amland: ambling
ane: a, one, alone
anew: enough
angilberreis: excrescences on feet of cattle
annamalit: enamelled, embellished
ark: large chest
arselins: backwards
asclent: askew
Athole-brose: whisky with honey and oatmeal
attour: over
atweel: truly
aul(d): old
auld-farrant: old-fashioned
Auld Reekie: Edinburgh
ava: at all
aver, avoir: cart-horse
awn: own, owed
ay(e): always, still
ayebydan: immortal
ayont: beyond

Baid: waiting
bailie: city magistrate
baill: evil, torment
baillie: cattle-boy
bainespavin: bone-spavin (callous growth on horse's leg)
bair: uncover, clear; boar
bairn, berne: child
baith: both
ballant: ballad, poem
ballingaris: ships
band: bound; cursed; agreement (or the b. makin—before the agreement was signed)
ban(e): swear, curse
bane: bone
baneschaw: sciatica
bang: cram
bannet: bonnet
barbillis: tongue disease of horses and cattle
baret, barrat: strife, trouble
barkit: tanned
battis: botts, bot-fly disease in horses
bauchles: (?)documents
bauk: strip of untilled land
bauld: fit, bold
baw: lull

bawbee: halfpenny
bawch: feeble
bawis: balls
bawr: joke
baws'nt: brindled
be: by, by the time that
beagle: sheriff's officer
beek, beik: bask, warm
beese: vermin
behud: had to
beid: bed
beild: suppurated
beir: barley; outcry
beit: supply
bek: bow of respect
belair'd: buried, stuck
beld: bald
bell: bubble
bellithraw, belly-thraw: stomach-ache, colic
belyf, belyve: suddenly, at once
ben: mountain; inner room, inside
bend: 'ben', into the kitchen
ben our: over in towards
bent: grass, heath
bernis: men
beswik: deceive
beuche, bewch: bough
bewrie: reveal
bezonian: raw recruit, beginner
bicker: drinking-cup
bield: shelter, home
bien: comfortable
bigg: build
biggins: buildings
bigsy: uppish
bike: assemble
bill: bull
billie: young fellow
binge: bow
binna: don't be
birky: fellow
birr: energy
birs, birsies: bristles, hair
birse, birze: squeeze, press
birsel: scorch
bissart: buzzard
bit: but
bizz: flurry
blab: blob
blae: pallid
blainis: pustules, pimples
blasnit: (?)
blastie: shrivelled, wretched; wretch
blast(i)et: accursed
blate: backward
bla(u)ds: leaves, bits of manuscript, fragments
blaw: boast
bledder: bladder
bledoch: buttermilk
bleeze: blaze
bleids: haemorrhage
bleirit: blear-eyed
blenkis: leers, glances
blent: glanced
blynis: ceases
bo: make a face
bodin: prepared, furnished out
Boece: Boethius
bogill: goblin
bo(i)che: eruptive disease
boll: measure of grain
boord: surface
boortrie, bowrtrie: shrub-elder
borowstown: borough town
boss: hollow, empty
botch: tumour
bouk: body, bulk
boukie: bulky
boun: ready
bour: boudoir, bedroom
bourach: crowd, heap
bourd: joke
bowdyn: swollen
bow(i)s: (papal) bulls
bowkaill: cabbage
bowtt: bolt
brachart: brat

brae: slope
braid: lifted
braks the muck: forks the dung
brand: brawned
brankand: swaggering
brankit: primped and pranced
brashy: stormy
brat: wrap
braw: fine
brawnis: muscles
braws: fine clothes
brechame: horse-collar
breeks: trousers
breem: strong, fierce, bleak
breenge: rush, dash
breid (on b.): abroad
breid of erd: inch of ground
brier(d): sprout
brig: bridge
brissit: bruised, torn
brize: (?) bristle, splutter
broch: clasp, brooch
bro(c)k: odds and ends, rubbish, remnants
brod: board
broddit: goaded
brogue: trick
broidsuis: brood-sows
broke: went bankrupt
brose: porridge
brosy: stout
bruck: odds and ends, rubbish
bruik: boil, tumour
bruikit: streaked with dirt
bruitt: brute
bruke: enjoy
brukill: brittle, frail
brunstane: brimstone
brydill-renye: bridle-rein
brym: fierce
buddis: bribes (for all the b. of Johne Blunt—promises! promises!)
buff: nonsense
buir: bore, carried
buird: council; board, table
buirdin squeel: boarding school
buirdly: stalwart, well-built
bukill: tackle
bukky: whelk-shell
buklit: mounted
bum: hum
bumbart: drone
bumbazed: confounded
bum-clock: cockchafer
bunwyd: flax-stalk
burrow landis: town-houses
busk: dress, adorn; bush
buss: bush
but: outer room, outside; without
bute: help
buthman: merchant
buttock-maill: fine imposed for fornication
byke: nest
byllis: boils

Ca(a): call; whistle; drive, knock
cabeld: haltered
caff: chaff
caiche: tennis
caird: card for dressing hemp or wool
cairt: chart
caller: fresh, cool
callered: freshened
came: comb
camscheocht: crooked (one)
can: ability
Cane: Khan
canker'd: bad-tempered
cannae: can't
Cannogait breikis: venereal disease
cannoun: canonical
canton: secede
cantr(a)ips: capers, magic spells
canty, cantie: pleasant, cheerful
cap: drinking-cup
cappill: horse
capriellis: capers
caption: order to pay debts

carl(e): man, fellow
carline, carling: old woman
carpit: chatted
Carrick to Carraill: from one side of Scotland to the other (Carrick in Argyll, Crail in Fife)
cart(e)s: cards
carybald: monster
cassin: cast
cast: lot, fate
cattaris: catarrh
caul(d): cold
cauld-kale: cabbage soup; something wearisomely familiar
cauldrife: chilly
caur: calves
causey, causie: street
cawandaris: (?)
cawkit: shat
chaft: cheek, jaw
chaft-blaid: jawbone
chaip: escape
Chairlwane: the Plough
chap: knock, stroke
chan(n)er: fret, grumble
channoun: canon of a cathedral
charne: shit
chaumer: chamber, room
cheatrie: deceitful; deception
cheer: chair
cheis: choose
chenyeis: chains
chevalouris: mounted knights
chevist: acquired
chiel: chap, fellow
chirtit: squeezed
chitterrit: shivering
choikis: quinsy; jaws, neck
choppin: half-pint
chuckie-stanes: pebble-stones
chuf: churl
chunty: chamber-pot
chymys: mansion
clag: stick to
claith: cloth
clanjamfries: crowds together
clarat-cunnaris: claret-connoisseurs
clarschocht: clarsach (Gaelic harp)
clart: dirt, mud, rubbish
claspis: mouth disease in horses
clatteraris: babblers
claucht: caught, clutched
clavers: chat
clayis: clothes
cled: clad
cleedin(g), cleething: clothes
cleek, cleik: crook, hook, clasp, lead
cleikis: cramp in horse's legs
cleuch, cleugh: steep slope
clever: clover
clew: thread
clinks: money, change
clinty: flinty
clog-fit: club-foot
clok: beetle
Clootie, Cloots: (cloven-footed) Devil
clour: batter
clouts: clothes
cluik: claw
clyter: cacophony; mess, muddle
coattis: portion of goods of deceased person paid for confirmation of his testament
coch(e): cough
cockernony: snood
cockle een: cock-eyes, squint
cockle up: improve (in health)
cod: pillow
coft: bought
cogue: feed
co(i)g: wooden dish, trough, pail
coirds: muscular neck disease in horses
Cokelbeis gryce: 'Colkelbie Sow', a farcical anonymous fifteenth-century popular poem
colt-evill: disease in young horses
condie: conduit, drain

connached: wasted
connoch(e): murrain
consuetude: custom
coonter-loupers: shop-assistants
coorse: coarse
cooser: stallion
cootie: tub
core: company
corning: (meet your c.) get your due punishment
corrie: hollow in mountainside
cosh: neat, snug
cot(-hous(e)): cottage
cottar: farm tenant
cotts: petticoats
cought: could
co(w)p: cup
coup: upset, upend
cout: colt
cowit: clipped, cropped
crabbet, crabit: grumpy, displeased
craig: rock; throat
craikaris: importunate whiners
crakraip: gallows-bird
cramasie: crimson
cran: crane
cranreuch: hoarfrost
crap: crop
crap an(d) keep: have more than plenty
cratur (the): whisky
craudoune: coward
creel, creil(l): basket
creesh, cri(e)sh: grease
Creilian crafts: fishing-boats from Crail in Fife
cro: sty
croodit: crowded
croose: self-assured, cocky
croslet: corslet
croudle: coo
crousie: oil lamp
crowdy: oatmeal and water, eaten raw
crowl: crawl
crozie: wheedling
crynd: withered, shrunken
cuddie: donkey
cude: baptismal cloth
cudnae: couldn't
culum: arse
Cumha na Cloinne: 'Lament for the Children' (Gael.), a pipe tune
cummer: woman, old wife, gossip, witch; trouble, encumbrance
cund: gave
cundy: conduit, drain
cunyouris: coiners
cunzied: known
curche: kerchief
cure: dominion
curis: offices, functions
cury: concoction
cushat, cuschet: pigeon
cutty spoon: short-handled spoon
cutty-stoup: small drinking-vessel
cyaurd: tinker

Dae: do
daffer: jester
daffin: fooling about
daiblet: little devil
daich: dough
daill: dealings
da(i)ne: aloof
daintiths: dainties
damys: pisses
dander: temper
dang: struck
dangerus: coy
dask: desk
da(u)d: strike; blow
daur: dare
daurk: day's work
daut, dawt: fondle, caress
dautit, dawtit: spoiled, darling
daw: dawn
daynte: favour, affection, delight
deaf-nits: 'chicken-feed', something to be scoffed at

deal: board
deave, deeve: deafen, stun
decore: decorate, adorn
dee: die
deef: insensitive
deese: seat
deid: dead; death
deid-chack: sound made by woodworm
deid dune: exhausted
deil-haet: nothing
deimit: gave judgement
dell: delve
dern(e): hidden, secret; secret place
devall: cease
devil's pictur'd beuks: playing-cards
devoir: duty
dew: dawned
dicht: wipe
din: dull, dingy, grey
ding: smash, hammer, overthrow, defeat; worthy
dink: neatly, finely
dinna: don't
dirk: dark
dirkin: lurk
disjaskit: worn out
disjune: breakfast
dispitous: malicious
displasit: driven out
dizzen: dozen cuts of yarn, a day's spinning
docht, dought: could
dod: God (expletive)
dog-days: July and early August
dogonis: worthless fellows
do(i)tit, doited: stupid, crazy, silly
dollin: buried
dolly: unhappy
donah: sweetheart
donkit: moistened
doss: neat, trim
dother: daughter
dotterel: idiot
douce, douse: sedate, good-living
doup: bottom
dour: hard, expressionless
dowie: gloomy
dowis: doves
dowk: dip, wash, plunge
downa: won't, wouldn't
doyt: idiocy
draff: brewer's grain
draiglit: bedraggled
draunt: drawl, drone
drawkit: drenched
dre(e): endure
dreich: dreary
dreid: (for) fear
droddum: backside
drouth: drunkard
drucken: drunken
drug: drag
drumlie: turbid
drup(e): feeble (person)
dryt: shit, dirty
dubbis: puddles
dublaris: large dishes
duddie: ragged
dud(di)s: rags, clothes
dude, duid: do it
duill: grief
dunk: dank
duris: doors
durk: dirk, dagger
dwaiblan: shambling
dwaum, dwaam: dream, daze, daydream, fainting-fit
dwynand: languishing
dynnit: made a noise
dysmell: melancholy
dyvo(u)r: bankrupt

Ear: early
e(e)(n): eye(s)
e'en: evening
eesed: used
effeiris: looks, bearing, approach; is proper
eik: increase

eild: (old) age; within perfit e.—
before coming of age
eistacks: dainties
eith: easily
elbuck: elbow
eldnyng: jealousy
eldritch: weird, uncanny
elwand: ell-measure
Embro: Edinburgh
empery: dominion
enchessoun: objection
eneuch: enough
engranyt: dyed
engyne: imagination, ingenuity
enoo: just now
etten: eaten
ettle: intend, try
Evan: a psalm tune
ev'n down: sheer
excep: accept
exeme: examine
eydent: eager

Fa(a): fall, befall, fall heir to
fae: from; foe
faem: foam
fain: fond
falling-evill: epilepsy
fan: when
fan(d): found
fang: get, take
fankles: gets confused
fannoun: maniple, band over
priest's arm during celebration
of mass
fant: weak
farl: oatcake
farne: fared
fash: bother, worry
fashous: troublesome
fat: what
fatna: what sort of a
fatt'rels: ribbon-ends
fauldan: folding
faur: where
fausont: presentable
fauters: offenders
fecht: fight
fe(c)k: majority, plenty
fed(d)rem(e): covering of feathers
feeder: fattened beast
feel: fool
feg: fig
fegs: faith (exclamation)
feid: enmity
feill: many
fe(i)nyeit: feigned
fe(i)rsie: farcy, glanders (horse-
disease)
fell: very
fell't: slaughtered
felt: stone (disease)
fensum: offensive
fenyeouris: tricksters
fepillis: pouts
fer: far
ferilie: nimbly
ferlie: wonder(ful)
ferrier: farrier, vet
fetrit: fastened
fiche: fish
fidder: measure
fidged: itched
fient (a, the): absolutely no
fier, feir: friend, comrade
fike: freak, nonsense, trouble,fuss;
vex oneself
fikey: troublesome
fir: for
fit: foot
fi(t)ch: fetch
flaff(er): flutter
flaik: hurdle
flainen: flannel
flair: floor
flame: (?) fever
flane: arrow
flead: flayed
flee: fly
fleean: extrovertly drunk

fleg: frighten
fleichouris: fawners
flewme: phlegm
flichter: flap (wings)
flichtmaflethers: fripperies
flingaris: (?)dancers
flower(e): adorn
fluikis: diarrhoea
flyp(e): turn outside-in
flyrand: fleering
flyrit: leered
flyt(e): scold, argue, vituperate
flyting: scolding, arguing; ritualized poetic contest
fone: dote
foo: how
foothing: (?) foot-halt, disease in sheep
forby(e): in addition, besides
for'd: for it
forfarne: forlorn
forfeuchan: exhausted
forky: vigorous, lusty
forleit: abandon(ed), forsake(n)
forlo: unlucky
forloppin: fugitive
for quhy: because
forthink: repent
forty-twa: Black Watch (42nd Highland Regiment of Foot)
foster: foster-child
fou: drunk; a fill, a tipple
four-nuickit: four-cornered
fowk: folk
fowmart: polecat
fowth: abundance
fozie-fousome: slobbery and disgusting
foziest: thickest, stupidest
frack: bold
fra(e): from; from the time that
fraiky: wheedling
fre(a)m(m)it: strange, alien, uncongenial
freik, freke: man, fellow
freir: friar
frenesie: delirium
frien, freen: friend
frore: frozen
fruster: useless
fu: fully
fud: arse
fudder: large number
fuggage: rank grass
fule: foolish
fulsome, fowsum: rank, disgusting
fulyeit: exhausted
fumyng: (?)raging, foaming at the mouth
fundin: found
fure: person; went
furlet: corn measure
furme: bench
furs: furrows
furthgangan: travelling
fussle: whistle
fust: roasted
fute-braid sawin: corn enough to sow a foot-breadth
fykis: anal itch
fyle: defile
fyles: now and again
fylt: soiled, defiled
fyre-flauch(t): lightning
fyre of St Antane: erysipelas

Gade: went
ga(e): go
gailies: well enough
gait, gate: way; goat(s)
gaithert: gathered
gall-hauld: gall disease
gallus: jauntily careless
gane: gone; suit
ganest: most suitable
gang: go
gangrel: vagrant, tramp
gan(n)oid: covered with smooth bony plates
gantan: gaping

gar: make
gardevyance: trunk
gardyloo: warning cry about slops thrown from windows on to streets
gart, gert: made
garth: garden
gash: shrewd, witty
gaun: going; go on
gaunt: yawn
gauntane: (?)stuttering
gawsie: ample, flourishing
gear: possessions, fare
geck: scoff
geet: child, bastard
geit: jet
gelling: shivery cold
gent: graceful, elegant
gentill: ladylike
genty: dainty
Geordie: guinea
gey(and): very
gib: tomcat
gie: give
gien: given
gie's: give us
gillot: mare
gilpy: rascal
gin: if
girdle: circular iron baking plate
girn: complain, fret; grin
girnal: granary
girsle: gristle
gizz: wig
gladderrit: smeared
glaid, gled: kite
gla(i)kit: silly
gla(u)r: mud
gled: kite
gledaris: (?)flatterers
gleg: quick; cleg
gleid: ember, red glow
glemys: glares
glengoir: syphilis
glent: gleam
gless: glass
glower: scowl
gloyd: old horse
godbarne gift: gift for a godchild
goif: gaze
golk: cuckoo
gollup't: gulped
goosie: young sow
goreis: scum
gorgeit: choked
gormaw: cormorant
gouk, gowk: fool
gowan: daisy
gowd: gold
gowk: stare
grain, grane: groan
graip: grope
graith: outfit, apparel, gear
graithing: equipment, furnishing
gramultion: common sense
grat: wept
grathit: clad, adorned
gree: prize, palm
green: yearn
greet, greit: weep
gress: grass
grett: wept
grieve: farm foreman
grips: pains
grome: man
groukaris: (?)pleaders
growsome: gruesome
grozet: gooseberry
grun(d): ground
gruntill: snout
grushie: lively, thriving
gryce, gryse: pig
gudeman, guidman: head of household, master
guff: stink
guid: good
gul(l)(z)ie: large knife
gulsoch(t): jaundice
gundy: voracious
gunnaris: gunners

gust: please the palate
gustit: flavoured
gut: gout
gutaris: gutters
gutsy: greedy
gwissorne: gizzard
gyan: giant
gyang: go
gyaun: going
gymp: slender

Ha(a): hall
hache: ache
hae: have
haet (fient haet o): not even one of
haffet, haffit: (hair on) temple
ha folk: servants
haill: draw, pull
hain: hoard
hair: hoary
haith: faith (exclamation)
haldin, haudden: held
hale: whole
halie: holy
hallion: rascal
halok: foolish
hals: throat, neck
hame(i)l: homely
hame-owre: homely
Hangie: (hangman) Devil
hank: fasten
hanlawhile: short time
hansell: reward, gift
hantit: accustomed
hanyt: sexually denied
hap: wrap
harb(e)rie: shelter
hard(e): heard
harin tedder: rope made of hair, for magic milking of cows
harl: drag (away)
harnis: brains
hartskaid: heartburn
ha(u)d: hold
haud their wheesht: keep quiet
haugh: flat ground beside river
hauld: habitation
ha(u)n(d): hand
haut: halt
hautand: proud
haverin: blethering
having: carrying (at a christening)
hawkie: cow with a white face
hawkit: streaked
hechar: higher
hecht, heght: promised
heels-owre-gowdy: head-over-heels
heese: lift
hegeit: hedged
heich: high
heildit: covered
hek: cattle-grid
heklis: rakes, scratches
helsome: wholesome
helter: halter, bridle
hely: highly
herle: heron
herried, herriet, herryit: plundered, harrowed (Hell)
herschaw: some kind of disease
het(t): hot
heuch, heugh: ravine, pit; crag, hill
he(y)nd(e): pleasant, welcoming, gentle (person)
hidderie-hetterie: hither-and-thither
h(i)e: high, main
hine: far
hing: hang
hinner lang wi: keep (someone) back
hint: clutch; took up
hippit: exhausted
hirplan: hobbling
hirsle: slide
hi(t)ch: hop, jerk along
hizzie: hussy
hobbill schone: clouted shoes
Hobble Jennie: a folk tune
hog: two-year-old sheep
hogeart: (?)twitcher

hoikis: acne, pitted skin disease
hoillis: holes
ho(i)st: cough
holyn: holly
hoo, hou: how
hoord: hoard, drift
horning: outlawry for non-payment of debt
hovand: rising
how(c)k: dig
howder: huddle
howe: hollow, valley
howff: pub, inn
howlat: owl
huff: scold
humphy(-backit): hunchback
hunkers: haunches
hunnle: handle
hurcheon(e): hedgehog
hurdies: haunches, buttocks
hurkland: cowering
husband: farmer
hussy: housewife
husyeskep: housewifery
hutit: derided
hydropasie: dropsy
hyow: hoe
hyre: reward
hyst, heist: lift
hytered: stumbled
hyves: skin eruption

Ilk(a), ilkie: each, every
ilkane: each one
ingan: onion
intermell: meddle
inthrang: pushed in
intill: into
intimmers: guts
invyit: maliciously regarded
irk: grow weary
Ise: I'll

Jak: coat of mail
jake: cheap drink such as 'reid-biddie', q.v.
jalouse: guess, suspect
jango: some kind of liquor
jaw: splash
jimpy: slim
jing-bang (the haill j.-b.): the whole lot
jist: just
jo(e): sweetheart
jolie: pretty
josit: enjoyed
jouk: dodge, jink
jow: toll; Jew, heathen
jowler: heavy-jawed dog
jumlit: shook
jyle: jail

Kaa: knock, drive
kail, kale: colewort
kail-ya(i)rd: kitchen-garden
kame: comb
kane: payment in kind
kayis: jackdaws
keek, keik: peer, peep
keelie: corner-boy
kelpie: horse-like water-demon
keming stock: stock for combs in wool-dressing and flax-breaking
kemmit: combed
ken: know; you know
kennin: understanding
kenrik: kingdom
kenspeckle: familiar
kent: knew
kerffis: carves
kich: shit
kill: kiln
killogy: kiln-hearth
kimmer: woman
Kinglis Ell: Orion's Belt
kinna: kind of
kintra: country
kip: brothel
kirk (mak a kirk or a mill o't): make what you can of it

kirn: churn; harvest festival
kirsp: fine linen
kist: chest, coffin
kitchie deem: kitchen maid
kite: belly
kittle: cunning
knaip: lad
knock: clock
knok: hull
know(e): knoll
kokenis: rascals
kuif: blow, cuff
ky(e): cows
kythis: reveals
kytrell: wretch

Laich: in a low position
laid-sadill: load-saddle
laif: rest, remainder
lair: family grave; learning
lait: seek
la(i)tis: manners, temperament, behaviour
lak: abuse, scold
Lallan: Lowland
lammer: amber
langit: belonged
lap: leapt
larbar: impotent
larbaris: impotent fellows
lat: let
lauch: laugh
laverok: lark
leaman: gleaming
lear, leir: learn; learning
ledder: leather
leddy: lady
lee-lang: livelong
le(i)d, leyd: person; language; learning
leif(e): live
leifer: rather
leill: faithful, loyal
leis me: I like
leit: (?)leave alone
leuch, leugh: laughed
libbit: castrated
lichtlyit: despised
lidder: slow, sluggish
lift: sky
lig: lie
limmer, lymmer: mistress; rogue
link: skip
lippen: trust
lipper: leper
lispane: lisping
list: enlist; wishes
lithargie: lethargy
lob: clumsy
lochan: small lake
loddin: swollen
loe: love
loff, loif: praise
loik: warm, luke-
lone: lane; paddock
loo: card game
loof: palm of hand
loon, lown: lad, bumpkin
loopy: crafty
loppin: leapt upon, covered (sexually)
losingeris: deceivers
loss(e): lose
lough: loch, lake
lounder: blow, buffet
loup: leap
lourd: heavy, lumpish
lous: discharge
louslie: lousy
lowan: fiery
lowe: flame, blaze
lowse(n): loosen
lowt: stoop
ludyeotis: (?)swaddling-bands
lug: ear
luk my heid: hope for the best
lum: chimney
lumbart: banker
lume: tool, penis
lum hat: 'chimney-pot' hat

Lunardi: balloon-shaped bonnet
lunscheocht: lung disease
lunt: smoke (a pipe)
lyand: building
lychour: lecher
lyk (as it was l.): according to its nature
lymphat: lameness
Lynkome-twyne: fine Lincoln cloth
lyre: body, skin
lyth: listen

Mae: more
Mahoun, Mahowne: Satan
maik: mate
maikles: matchless
mair: more; nightmare
maist: most
mak: make; making
makar: poet
makdome: fine appearance
mallange: some kind of disease
mangit: crazy
mant: stutter
mantane: stammering
mapamone: (map of the) world
mark: silver coin
marleyon: merlin
marrow: equal, mate, companion
mask: infuse (tea)
maskene-fat: tub for mashing malt
master: stale urine
mauch: maggot
ma(u)n, mon: must
mavis: thrush
maw: seagull
meikill: much
mell: mix, join; mallet
melt: (disease of) spleen
men: (?) way of life
mense: discretion
menseless: ill-bred
mensk: manliness
menskit: honoured
menye: household, multitude of things
menys: pity
merrens: annoyance
mes: mass
messan: cur
messillis: measles
milk-syth: milk-strainer
mim: affectedly modest
mirk: dark
mishanter: misfortune
miskennyt: deceived
mister(is), mystirs: business, needs
mither: mother
mittan, myttane: hen-harrier (hawk)
mizzer: survey
modewurk, mowdywart: mole
molet: bridle bit
monie: many
mools: grave-soil
moss: peat-bog
mot: may
mou, mow: mouth
moupit: downcast, sick-looking
mow: joke
mowaris on the moyne: bayers at the moon
mowe: fuck
mowing: moving
moy: mild
muckle: big; much
mudgeounes: scowls, grimaces
muillis: chilblains
muir: moor
mull: threshing mill
multiplie: transmute metals alchemically
mureill: cattle disease
murgeo(u)nis: capers, grimaces
mute: mutter
myance: resource
myngit: mixed
mytour: mitre

Na (=nor): than

nabbit: seized
na(e): no
nappie: ale
naukit: naked
Neander: a psalm tune
neb: nose, beak
nebstrous: nostrils
neist, niest: next
neive, nieve, neiff: fist
neuk, newk: nook
nice: choosy
Nikniven: Queen of the Witches
nipschot: backwards
nirlend: puny creature
nirrilis: skin eruption
nit: nut
no: not
noit: watchful
nok: notch
nor: than
norlan(d): northern
nowt(e), nolt: cattle
noy: annoyance
nune: nun
nurische: nurse

Ocht: anything
o-hone-a-ree: alas
onie: any
oniewey: anyway
or: before
orra: odd, occasional
oughtlins: at all
oulk: week
out-by: outside
outland: strange, uncouth
outwaled: chosen
owre, our: over; too
owrehailan: overflowing
owsen: oxen
owsprang: sprang out
oxteris: armpits

Pack: intimate, familiar
padill: pedlar's bag
painch: belly
pako: peacock
pallatt: head
pang: cram
papingay: parrot
park: take to the field
parlasie: palsy
parritch: porridge
party-match: card-contest
Pasche: Easter
pat: pot
pat him on: promoted him
pawkie: shrewd and sly
pawmies: strokes on the palm
pa(y)nsches: tripe
pease-clods: coarse rolls of peasemeal
pech, pegh: pant
pedder: pedlar
peer-hoose: poor-house
peerie: small
peghan: stomach
peild-pellet: bald-pate
peild-pollart: bald-head (Polwart)
peitpot: hole from digging peat
pek: measure, sixteenth of boll
pelody: some kind of disease
pene: pen(is)
pennis: feathers
pent: paint
Pentlands: hills near Edinburgh
perfurneis: accomplish
peronall: girl
perqueir: by heart
pertlyar: more vivaciously
phirasie: farcy, glanders
phtiseik: lung disease
pickle: a little, a few
pig: pot, crock, jar
pin: temper, humour
pit: put
pitten: put (p.p.)
plack: small coin
plane: (?)complaint
playfair: plaything

plet: plaited
pl(e)uch: plough
ploy: sport, game, frolic
pluckevill: (?)sheep-rot
pluirasie: pleurisy
plumb: £100,000, a fortune
plytered: dabbled
poikis: pustules, pox
poin(d): distrain
poistrume: some kind of disease
poke, polk: bag
pollis: poles
poortith: poverty
poplasie: apoplexy
pose: store of money
potingaris: apothecaries
pottingry: pharmacy
pou(t)ch: pocket
pow: head
poyd: toad
preve: secret
prie: taste, try out
prig: plead
proclame: denounce
proppit: primed
prunya: preen
pryme: early morning
puckle: a little, a few
puddock: frog
puirshous leir: poor-house learning
put: jab, thrust
pykis: thorns
pyot: magpie

Quake: heifer
quegh: two-handled drinking-cup
quhair: where
quhairfoir: why
quhairon: whereon
quhat: what
quhattrack: what (does it) matter
quhen: when
quhilk(is): which
quhill: till, as long as
quhittill: knife
quhryn: squeal
quhyllumis: at times
quhyt: white
quyt(e) quit

Rack: care
racked: exorbitant
rad: afraid
raep, rape: rope
ragment: tale, rigmarole
ragweed: ragwort
raid: (sexual) enterprise, ride; rode
rakit: reckoned; went
rakles: rash, risky
rale: real
ralis: jokes
ralyeit: joked
rame: clamour
rameist: crazy
rammie: disturbance, free-for-all
ramsh: rank, fiery
rane (in a): continuously
rang: reigned
rant: make merry
rash-buss: clump of rushes
raucht: reached
rave: steal
raveld the reillis: got the reels (dances) in a tangle
raw: row
rawchtir: rafter
rax: stretch, reach
ream: cream, froth
red(d): tidy, put in order
reek: smoke
reesle: clatter
reestet: restive
regent: professor
reid: red
reid-biddie: cheap wine and methylated spirit
r(e)id-wood: stark mad
reif: theft; (?)
reik: grant
reivand: raving

remeid: remedy, help
remord: cause to repent
repenting-stool: stool in church, for fornicators
repet: noisy disturbance
rerd: tumult, outcry
rest: sprain
revaris: thieves
revin: torn
revinis: ravens
rew: regret
rift: belch
rig-bane: backbone
rin: run
ringbane: disease of pastern-bones of horse
rise: brushwood
rive, ryve: tug, tear, burst
riz: rose
roch: rough
rock: distaff
rone-ruit(e): rowan-root
roose, ruse: praise, boast
rouk: fog, mist
roun: whisper
roup: hoarseness, croup
roust: rust
rousty: feeble, useless
rowe: roll, bring in
rowll: rule
rowt: bellow, low
rowth: plenty
rozet: resin
ruck: rick, stack
rug(e): tug
ruikis: rooks
run-deil: right devil
rung: cudgel
runkled: wrinkled, creased
ryp(e): ransack
ryte: custom, habit

Sabot: (?)God (Sabaoth)
sa(e): so
St Andrew's House: government office in Edinburgh
sair: serve; sore, heavy; strongly, much
sairt: tired; glutted
sakles: blameless
samyn: same
sanative: refreshing
Sanct Cloun: St Cluanus, sixth-century Irish abbot
Sanct Martynis fowle: martin
sane: bless
sanyne: blessing
sarie, sary: sorry, feeble
sark, serk: shirt
saul: soul
saut(he): salt
saw: sow; utterance, voice
sawin: sowing
saxpenny planet: worthless stuff
say: try
scaffaris: beggars
scald: scold
scamleris: spongers
scart: scratch
scate-rumples: hinder parts of skate
scaud: light; heat; scald
sca(u)r: afraid
scawl: scolding woman
schaiffyne: shaved
schalk: fellow, lout
schanker: gonorrhoea
schaw: thicket, wood
sched: separate, part
scheippisch: gonorrhoea
schene: beautiful
schevill: twisted
schevilland: contorting
schewit: sewn
schewre: tore off
scho: she
schore: threat
schowaris: shovers
schrew: rascal
schrift: confession
schrowd: gown

schuif: shaved
schulderaris: shoulderers
schule: shovel
schupe: aimed
schyre: bright, clear
sclent, sklent: flash, dart, glance, suggest
sclim: climb
Scotch-collops: stewed beef dish
scoup: scope
scranned: collected carefully
scrievit: written
scrunt: stunted person
scull: bucket
scunner: disgust; feel disgust; give disgust
scutarde: shitter
scutter: mess
scutter wi: dodge
sea-maw: seagull
secutit: followed
seen: soon
sege: talk
seggs: rushes
seill: happiness
sek: sack
sely: simple
sen: since
seraphine: musical instrument like American organ
sessio(u)n: elders of Presbyterian church; Court of Session
settin: for hatching
sew: sue
seyth: boil
shair: sure
shalt: pony
shanna: shan't
shargar, sharger: puny; weakling
sharn: cow dung
sheckle: wrist
sheen: shoes
sheuch, sheugh: dig, plant; trench, ditch
shog: jog
shool-the-board: shovel-board (game)
shorin: cutting
sib: related
sic(k)(can): such
sicker: secure, sure
siller: silver, money
simmer: summer; spend the summer
sing: sign
singit: singed; shrivelled
skait-birdis: skuas
skaith: injury, expense, trouble
skalrag: shabby, tramplike
skare: share
skarth: 'cormorant', monster
skeich: skittish
skellat: hand-bell
skelp: beat, thrash, slap; stroke, blow
sker: scared
skimmeran: shimmering
skink: portion
skinkle: sparkle
sklater: slater
skrippit: mocked
skryke: shriek
slae: sloe
slaur: muck
slee: sly
sma(a): small
smake: feebly ingratiating
smeddum: fine powder used as insecticide
smiddie: smithy
smirr: fine rain
smolet: (?)grimace
smo(o)rit, smorde: smothered
smoutie: smutty
smy: wretch
smytrie: crowd, host
snash: abusive insolence
sneck, snick: latch, catch
sneeshin-mill: snuff-box
snib: lock, shut

snod: neat, snug
snoir: stopped nose, head cold
snowck: snuff, sniff
snuf: snuffles, stopped nose
snytting: nasal catarrh
soddin: cooked by boiling
soipit: soaked
sok: ploughshare
sonsie: good-natured
sook, sowk: suck
soot(t)er, souter: cobbler
soss: mess
s(o)ugh: rushing sound of wind
soukaris: yes-men
sowther: solder
spail, spale: splinteı
spairge: splash, bespatter
spang-new: brand-new
spauld: shoulder
Spaw: Spa, in Belgium
speak: speech, talk
speal: holiday
speidder: spider
speil: climb
speir, speer: ask
speit: spit
spend: come (sexually)
spenyie: Spanish
splore: frolic, uproar
spounge: purse
spout: pump
sprattle: scramble
sprauchle: sprawl
spreckle: speckle
spunk-box: tinder-box
spunkie: will-o-the-wisp
spurtill: wooden rod for stirring porridge
spynist: blooming
spyre: projection from a wall
squatter: flutter in water
squattle: squat
squeel: school
staiffis: rams, thrusts
staig: stallion
stair: pause, block, dilemma
stanchell: kestrel
stang: sting
stan't: have stood
stap: step; stop
starnis, sternis: stars
stauchert: staggered
sta(y)ne: stone
steek: shut, clench; stitch
steer, steir: stir, trouble; disturbance
steerach: mismanage
stegh: stuff
steid: place
steive: firm, stiff
stellit: placed, set
stent: impost, duty; allowance of pasturage
stenye: (?)stain
sterk: stark, strong
stew: rush
stey: steep, stiff
stiddie, study: anvil
Stikis: Styx
stirrah: fellow
stobbed: stabbed
stock: old fellow
stookie: stucco
stoor: harsh
stoppell: stopper
stot: steer, bullock
stound: blow, shock, pain
stoup: jug
stour: run, rush
stouteran: stumbling
stouth: robbery
stown: stolen
strae: straw
straid: strode
stramash: hubbub, tumult
straucht: straight (line)
stravaig: wander
streel: urine
streen (the s.): last night
streikit: stretched

strene: bind tight
strene (the s., this s.): last night
stroan't: pissed
strunt: move confidently
stug: pricked, stabbed
stumpy: small and neat
sturdie: brain disease in sheep and cattle
sturrit: stirred up
sturt: vexation
sud: should
sugeorne: sojourn, delay
sumph: fool
sunkots: something
swalme: swelling
swame: (?)tumour
swaming: dizziness
swank: vigorous
swapit: quaffed
swaw: wave
sweel: whirl
sweillit: swaddled
sw(e)ir: reluctant, lazy; unwillingly
sweit: sweat
swelt: feverish exhaustion, suffocation
swentyouris: villains
swerf: faint
swevyng: dream
swippert: nimble
swith: away, quickly (interjection)
swither: hesitate; hesitation
sworlan: swirling
swyr: valley, glade
sybo: young onion
syde: extravagantly
syes the so'ens: strains the gruel
syiss: times
syle: hide
syne: then, next, since, ago
syphyr: cipher, non-performer
syse: judgement, doom

Tae: toe
taed, taid: toad
taen: taken
taidrell: wretched creature
taigilt: harassed
tak tent: take heed
tane: one
tansy: ragwort
tap: top
tarrow: hesitate
tarsall: peregrine falcon
tauld: told
ta(u)nty-ra(u)nty: fornication
taurds: tawse, strap
tawse: strap
tawtied: shaggy
taz: tawse, belt, whip
tedder: tether
tee: too
teemed: emptied
teind: tithe
tenty: careful
term: contracted time
terne: fierce
teuch: tough
te(y)ne: anger
thae, they: those
thaim, thame: them
the: thee
theekit: thatched
thewis: habits
thieveless: powerless
thig: beg
thir: these
thocht: though
thof: though
thole: put up with
tholit: bore, suffered
thon: yon, that
thow(e): thaw
thra: boldly
thrang: crowded, busy
thrapple: gullet
thrapple's-pap: Adam's-apple
thratch: throe
thraw: twist, wrench
thrawcruk: implement for

twisting straw-ropes
thrawn: obstinate, perverse
threepit: sung tediously
threip: reiterate
thrimlaris: jostlers
thristaris: thrusters
thristle: thistle
throu han: under discussion
til: to
timmer: timber
tine: lose
tint, tined: lost
tirl: strip; rattle at a door
tirrillis: (?)St Vitus dance
tither: other, another
tittest: soonest
tittis: spasm disease in horse's legs
tittlin: whispering
tocher-gud: marriage dowry
tod: fox
toom, tume: empty; clean
toon: farm
toozie, towzie: rough
tosh: neat
totteris: staggers (disease of sheep)
tottl'd: boiled
to(u)ne: tune
toush: short gown
tow: flax, hemp
towsilt: roughed up
toy: cap
traist: discreet, trustworthy
tratling: prattling
trauchled: burdened, fatigued
trauchlit: struggled
trawe: trick
tred: trade
trene: wooden
trig: neat
trip: flock
troch: trough
tron(e): weighing machine
truff: steal
trumpouris: magicians, deceivers
truncher, truncheour: platter
tryackill: medicine
tuche: tough
tuichandly: touchingly
tulzie: fight, brawl
turner: copper coin
turtor: turtle-dove
twal, twel: twelve
twin(e): sever; twist
twithyaik: toothache
tyauve: struggle
tyke: cur, mongrel
tyrit: tired out
tyt: soon

Ugsome: horrible
uly-pig: oil-jar
umbeset: besieged
unbeist: monster
uncame: some kind of disease
unco: uncommonly
uncunnandly: involuntarily
undeemous: extraordinary
undoche: wretched creature
unkennan: ignorant, unrecognizing
unkent: unknown
unsell: wretch; accursed
untrowit: unbelieved
up-alland: inland
upwith: upward thrust
usquebaugh: whisky

Vacandis: free, on holiday
vardour: verdure
verfluch: damn, dammit!
vild, vyld: worthless, vile, filthy
vincust: overcome
vogie: vain
vrang: wrong
vricht: joiner

Wab: web
wa(e): woe
waesuck: alas
waff: wave, flap, flutter
wainis: (?)

wair: spend
wairdless: ill-fated
waistie: broken
wait: know; hunt, stalk
waithman: outlaw
waitskaith: lying in wait to do harm
wa(l)d: would
wale, waill: choose; choice
walkand: awake
wallidrag: weakling, slouch
wallis: waves
wame: stomach
wandevill: (?) disease of penis
wanis: homes
wannert: confused
wanschaippin: misshapen
wantane: lacking
wanthre(i)vin: stunted
wanwordy: worthless
warbillis: tumours on backs of cattle
wariand: cursing
warit: conceived; poured out
wark: work
warklum: tool, penis
warlock: wizard
warpit: uttered
warslit: struggled
waryit: cursed
wast: west
waste: remnants of broken thread and fabric, in weaving
waucht: quaff
wa(u)r, wer: worse
wean: child
wecht: weight; winnowing-tray
wede awa: faded away, vanished
weet: wet, rain
weir: war
weird: fate
weis: (?) ulcerous discharge
wer: wire
wersh: tasteless
whartil: whereto
whaup: curlew
wha(u)r: where
wheeple: whistle plaintively
wheesht: hush
whigmaleerie: whimsical fancy or ornament
while: until
whiles: occasionally
whilk: which
whim-wham: fancy, fad
whinge: whine
whipper-in: huntsman who keeps hounds in pack
whuddran: rushing
whummle: tumble
whun stane: whinstone
wicht: strong
widdinek: gallows-bird
widdy: gallows-rope
wifie: woman
wildfyre: erysipelas
willawins: alas
wind-flaiffis: (?)flatulence
winna: won't
winnockie: gaping, full of holes
wirdersones: counter-sunwise
wirriand: complaining; growling angrily
wirsome: pus
wispin: bundling
wizen: throat
wlonkes: beauties, splendid women
woddit: married
wolroun: boar
womeit: vomit
wonner: wonder, creature
wood, woid, wud, woude: mad, raging, wild
wosp: stopper of straw
wo(w)bat: caterpillar
wo worth: evil befall
wraittis: warts
wrakit: tormented
wrinks: tricks
wrocht: worked, made
wrokin: avenged
wuff: whiff
wuid: wood

wulfire: wildfire
wurdie: worthy
wurn: whine and complain
wycelike: sensible
wylecoat: flannel vest
wyme: belly
wyte: blame

Yafa: awful
yaip: eager
yardies: gardens, back-yards
yawmeris: yells
Yeel: Yule
yeid: went
yeild: reward
ye(il)l(d): barren, sterile
yeis: you'll
yence: once
yenoo: just now
yerd: yard, penis
yestreen: last night
yet(t): gate
yill: ale
yin: one
ying: young
yirm: whine, complain
yoldin: flaccid
youplin: (?)howling
yout, yowt: yell
yuistae: used to
yuke: itch
yyrne: curdle